To
Bring the
WORLD
His Truth

To Bring the WORLD His Truth

Preparing to Be the Lord's Missionary

Matthew B. Christiansen

Covenant Communications, Inc.

Cover image: *Antique Globe of Europe* © RichVintage, courtesy iStockphoto.com.

Cover design copyright © 2012 by Covenant Communications, Inc.

Published by Covenant Communications, Inc.
American Fork, Utah

Printed in the United States of America
First Printing: April 2012

18 17 16 15 14 13 12   10 9 8 7 6 5 4 3 2 1

ISBN-13: 978-1-60861-230-7

To faithful parents, who were the greatest missionaries a son could have,
to President and Sister Jarvis, my ultimate mission heroes,
to Sorella Lemon, the cutest returned missionary I ever married,
and to Roman, Cami, and Kira, my favorite investigators ever.

Acknowledgments

While I alone am responsible for the content of this book, there wouldn't be a book to be responsible for without the help and assistance of dozens of people. First and foremost, to the wonderful people at Covenant Communications: thanks for believing in me and for granting a wish I've secretly harbored for years. I appreciate my editor, Samantha Van Walraven, who patiently and skillfully guided me through the adventure that is publication. And finally, I owe a special thanks to any and all who gave of their time to read chapters and offer feedback. This book is substantially better because of each of your efforts.

Table of Contents

Introduction

FROM THE DAY YOU ENTER the MTC you are on the clock. The hourglass is turned over, and the sands of your mission time are steadily slipping away. A mission is not a soccer game: there will be no overage; there will be no extra time. You don't get two years from the time you figure out how much you love being a missionary. You don't get two years from the time you catch the vision of what this work is all about and how important it truly is. You get two years or eighteen months from the day you enter the MTC. Period.

The purpose of this book is to help you prepare for and maximize this once-in-a-lifetime opportunity. Even though I may not know you personally, you have been on my mind as I've written each page. I've tried to picture your face, your life, your strengths, your struggles, your concerns, your questions, and—most of all—your incredible potential to become a powerful instrument in the hands of the Lord. I hope by the end of this book that you'll think of me as a friend—a friend who, like you, loves the Savior, loves this Church, and loves our fellow brothers and sisters scattered throughout the world.

A book such as this can have the unintended effect of glorifying the author. Please keep in mind that as a missionary, I was far from perfect. At times I struggled with homesickness, fear, discouragement, immaturity, laziness, and pride. But one thing I never struggled with was an unequaled love of being a missionary. I wept like a baby the day I left Romania and have thought about the people and experiences of my mission every day since. I believe it is this love that qualifies me to write such a book.

So my welcoming words of introduction are these: "Lift up your heart and rejoice, for the hour of your mission is come" (D&C 31:3)!

SECTION ONE
M&Ms

Chapter 1

The First M: Finding the Right Motivation

"As your understanding of the Atonement of Jesus Christ grows, your desire to share the gospel will increase." —Preach My Gospel, 2

I had officially been a missionary for seven hours. There I was in the MTC, crammed into a tiny classroom, the classroom where—according to my newly received planner—I would spend the majority of my time for the next two months. Mercifully, this was the final meeting of a very long, emotionally draining day.

The title of this meeting was "Orientation with Branch Presidency," and there sat three distinguished looking men before us. We began with a hymn and opened with prayer; then President Graves stood up, was silent for a moment, and asked us a single introductory question: "Why have you decided to go on a mission?" He gave us a moment to think about it then invited us one by one to share our response. When it was my turn, I mumbled some answer about being grateful for the gospel and wanting to share it with others. Apparently it was acceptable because President Graves moved on to the next missionary and the meeting ended shortly after.

Yet on my way back to the dorm, and while struggling to fall asleep that first night, I couldn't shake that question from my mind. Why was I there? And more importantly, would the answer I had given hold up under the challenges, pressure, and opposition that most certainly loomed over the course of the next two years?

So what about you? If you're reading this book, a mission is at least a possibility. Mentally travel back with me to that MTC room and think what your answer to President Graves's question would be. Maybe you haven't given it much thought, but the time to do so is now. In fact, your success and happiness as a missionary will largely depend upon your answer to this key question. Before addressing possible answers, let's analyze the actual question for a moment.

Why do you want to go on a mission? What is this question really asking. Clearly, the heart of the matter is *motivation*. Rephrased, the question could be, *What's motivating you in the prime of your life to leave behind your home, family, friends, job, college, and comfort zone to devote two years to the Lord?*

You might wonder why it even matters what your motivation is; after all, doesn't it only matter that you go? The answer to this is simple: not all reasons for serving the Lord are created equal. Having been around missionaries or prospective missionaries for the last decade, I have witnessed firsthand both the variety and disparity of reasons for which missionaries serve. They range from being selfish and shallow to selfless and noble. Consider the following examples drawn from my interaction with hundreds of young men and young women:

"My dad promised to buy me a new car and pay for college if I'd go on a mission."

"My girlfriend won't marry me unless I'm an R.M."

"All my friends are going, so I didn't want to be the only one left behind."

"Everyone would be disappointed if I didn't go."

"My older brother went and loved his mission. I just want to follow his example."

"It's a commandment, so I want to be obedient."

"Every time I serve others, it makes me feel good; I want that feeling for two years."

"I've been really blessed in my life. Going on a mission is the least I can do."

"I've gained a testimony of the truthfulness of the gospel; now I want to help others do the same."

"I believe there are people prepared for me that I am meant to find. How could I let them down?"

A quick glance at these missionary motivators illustrates the point. If I were grading them, I'd give them all A's. Some are Awesome, others Acceptable, and a handful simply Awful. We could spend time evaluating each reason, praising those that are good, passing on those that aren't, but such an evaluation would completely miss the point. You see, my experience has led me to believe that it is not enough for missionaries to be motivated by a *good* reason; they have to be motivated by the *right* reason.

So what is the *right* reason for sharing the gospel? I'm talking about the kind of motivation that will really enable someone to serve with power and conviction—the kind of motivation that will hold up under any circumstances, facing any challenge, going up against any level of opposition.

As a newly called missionary in the MTC, this was the question I desperately needed to figure out. Sensing that the answer could be found in the scriptures, I devoted my now abundant study time to this critical task. Naturally my study gravitated toward my scriptural heroes (especially the Hall of Fame missionaries), to see what motivated them in their efforts. In so doing, the scriptures clearly unveiled the right motivation for serving the Lord, and I believe every missionary should know it.

Let's begin with the story of Enos. I have always felt an affinity with Enos because he's a Book of Mormon character that I can relate to. He's not a bad guy by any means; but when it comes to the gospel, he just hasn't quite figured it out yet. You'll remember that his grandpa was Lehi, his dad was Jacob, and his uncle was Nephi. If that's not an intimidating family to be in then I don't know what is.

But family pedigree notwithstanding, adolescent Enos appears to have been pretty lukewarm about the Church and his testimony. Uncle Nephi he is not! I imagine Enos probably had his head down during a few Nephite sacrament meetings, sat in the back row in seminary, and may have even ditched Sunday School once or twice to grab a Slurpie with his buddies. And while Enos probably cringed the day his mom pasted an *RULDS2?* sticker on their cart, he never completely closed off his mind and heart to the Spirit, as evidenced by the events described in his personal account.

You know the story: On a solo hunting trip, something clicks, causing Enos to think deeply about the words he's often heard his father speak concerning eternal life. As he ponders his father's words, his soul begins to hunger for true nourishment and joy (see Enos 1:3–4). Accompanying these soul cravings is the unmistakable sense that he must first make things right with the Lord. This begins a repentance process that Enos aptly describes as a wrestle (see v. 2). Remember, wrestling involves an immense amount of focus and effort and can sometimes be painful.

After praying all day and all night, Enos hears the voice of the Lord speak peace to his soul, with the assurance and promise that his spiritual slate has been wiped clean.

He marvels at God's love and mercy and asks, "Lord, how is it done?" (Enos 1:7), to which the Lord responds, "Because of thy faith in Christ, whom thou hast never before heard nor seen" (Enos 1:8).

Now at this point it's important to keep in mind Enos's primary objective: his soul hungered and needed deep nourishment. He has now heard the voice of the Lord and received complete forgiveness for his sins. One might assume that his objective has been met and he can now move on.

But this is not the case.

After repenting of his sins and experiencing the miracle of forgiveness, a deep realization begins to take root within Enos's mind and heart. If God cares about him enough to forgive all his sins and sweep away his guilt, surely He must also care about Enos's neighbor down the street and his cousin and the guys on his football team. Now the assurance and promise he had previously attained for *his own soul* is not nearly enough. He suddenly wants to do all he can to help those around him share in the unmatchable joy of this divine gift.

Praying entirely on behalf of his fellow brethren, Enos hears the voice of the Lord bring yet another blessed assurance. If the Nephites would demonstrate the same broken heart and contrite spirit, the gift of grace and mercy would be theirs as well (see Enos 1:9–10).

What an amazing promise! Certainly Enos must be content with that. Not only has *he* been forgiven, but he has also petitioned the Lord successfully for *his entire people.* They will have the same opportunity to embrace God's love and gospel that Enos has. Surely now his soul is not just nourished but stuffed. Yet amazingly, Enos is still not done. Even now, with all he's accomplished, he still yearns to labor on behalf of one final group: the Lamanites.

The realization accompanying his initial forgiveness has taken full root; Enos now perceives that the love of God is not limited to himself or his brethren, the Nephites. No, Enos now comprehends that this infinitely loving Father must possess the same feelings of care and concern for all His children, *even* for those who have strayed. In spite of the unabashed hatred of the Lamanites toward the Nephites, Enos is now able to receive a portion of God's love for them.

With perhaps a measure of trepidation, though emboldened by his previous success, Enos pleads with the Lord to spare the Lamanites and bring them again to a knowledge of the truth. For a third time, the voice of the Lord comes, granting his fervent request. Yes, the Lord would, in His own due time, prepare the way for the Lamanites to return to the fold (see vv. 13–16). Only after Enos receives this all-encompassing assurance does he finally exclaim, "Wherefore my soul did rest" (v. 17).

The book of Enos clearly illustrates the right answer to President Graves's question. It's as if I could visualize Elder Enos sitting right next to me in that little MTC room. When it was his turn to respond, I could hear him say, *"I have felt the power of the Atonement of Jesus Christ. I've felt my guilt and pain and filthiness swept away by His infinite love and mercy; and ever since that moment all I've wanted to do is help everyone else feel it as well."*

The story of Enos shows that the Atonement of Jesus Christ is the ultimate motivation in serving the Lord. From Enos we see the power of the Atonement to both change our own hearts and then expand our desires outward toward the spiritual welfare of all around us. This was the answer I desperately needed, and the more I studied the more convinced I became that it was true.

The sons of King Mosiah are perhaps the most famous missionaries in Mormondom. Their miraculous story provides additional evidence for the motivating power of the Atonement. You'll recall that these missionary heroes were once described as the "vilest of sinners" (Mosiah 28:4) and together, with their friend Alma the Younger, sought to destroy the Church. One day, while en route to another antifaith rally, they have an angel appear to them with a divine warning: repent or be destroyed (see Mosiah 27:10–18). After heeding the angelic message, these young men made the unlikely transformation from destroyers to declarers, traveling from city to city, seeking to repair the damage they had previously done.

After diligently laboring for several years, these sons were summoned home by their aging father so he could anoint his successor. While one would be chosen as king, we can assume that the others would be appointed to positions of leadership and counsel in the land. Aaron, being the eldest, was given the honor but (audible gasp) refused. To the astonishment of King Mosiah, the rest of Aaron's brothers did likewise. How could this be? What could possibly be more important than governing the affairs of the kingdom in a peaceful and honorable manner?

Hesitating for a moment, the king's sons informed him of yet another mission call. This news must have confused him; how could they be planning another mission? He had deliberately and patiently waited until they had completed a full circuit throughout all the land. There was nowhere else to go!

Imagine the shock and bewilderment this father experienced upon learning that the planned destination of his sons' next mission was the land of Nephi, aka "Homeland of the Lamanites." As we've already discussed from the story of Enos, the Lamanites were the sworn enemies of the

Nephites and delighted in the plunder and murder of those who were once their brethren.

In order to fully grasp the predicament of King Mosiah, allow me to offer a modern-day equivalent. Imagine an LDS youth who had rebelled during his teenage years but then turned his life around and served an honorable full-time mission. Arriving home, the young man is joyously welcomed by his family, and his father soon expresses the desire that he take over the family business. The son hesitates for a moment and then informs his parents that he has other plans. "What other plans?" they inquire.

Reluctantly he confesses that he loved his mission so much that he has decided to travel to the mountainous region along the Afghanistan/Pakistan border where he will seek to share the gospel message with members of the Taliban and Al-Qaeda. Naturally his parents would experience a great deal of frustration and anxiety at the seemingly rash and unwise life plan of their son. They would do everything in their power to talk him out of his decision.

Obviously this fabricated scenario is both extreme and implausible, but the dynamics are strikingly similar to that of these sons of Mosiah. What could possibly have been the motivation of such remarkable and courageous young men? You guessed it: "Now they were desirous that salvation should be declared to every creature, for they could not bear that any human soul should perish; yea, even the very thoughts that any soul should endure endless torment did cause them to quake and tremble. And thus did the Spirit of the Lord work upon them, for they were the very vilest of sinners. And the Lord saw fit in his infinite mercy to spare them" (Mosiah 28:3–4).

What motivated Ammon to enter a hostile land and assume the role of humble shepherd? What motivated Aaron to endure imprisonment and starvation rather than take his rightful place as heir to the Nephite throne? What kept them going until they were finally blessed to reap an unimaginable harvest?

They had felt the saving power of the Atonement. They had been the recipients of undeserved mercy. And now they simply couldn't bear the thought that *any* human soul should be lost, even if it meant putting their lives at risk by embarking on a mission fraught with peril and uncertainty.

Simultaneous with the foreign missions of the sons of Mosiah, their friend Alma was laboring to build and strengthen the Church back at home. Of his overwhelming drive to impart the gospel message, he writes: "But behold, my limbs did receive their strength again, and I stood upon my feet, and did manifest unto the people that I had been born of God. Yea, and from that time even until now, I have labored without ceasing, that I might bring souls unto repentance; that I might bring them to taste of the exceeding joy of which I did taste; that they might also be born of God, and be filled with the Holy Ghost" (Alma 36:23–24).

Alma the Younger shared the same motivation as his friends: the Atonement of Jesus Christ. This motivation culminated in a life filled with dutiful service. In his later years, Alma apparently came to a point where he felt it necessary to scale back his own involvement with the day-to-day leadership and missionary efforts of the Church. He entrusted these responsibilities to his adult sons and settled in for a twilight of well-deserved rest. Yet as his sons went forth to carry on in his mighty footsteps, the scriptures note: "And now it came to pass that the sons of Alma did go forth among the people, to declare the word unto them. *And Alma, also, himself, could not rest, and he also went forth*" (Alma 43:1, emphasis added). Whether you are nineteen or ninety, whether you've never knocked on a single door or knocked on thousands of them, the motivating power of the Atonement remains the same: infinite and limitless.

While the point has hopefully been made, the Bible is not silent on this matter and deserves to be included. From the great record of the Old World we learn of a man who was tireless in his desire to bring people to Christ. The apostle Paul may arguably be the greatest missionary in the history of Christianity. Neglecting to include his ministry as a case study would be a huge oversight.

The story of Paul is markedly similar to that of Alma and the sons of Mosiah. Paul was a nasty persecutor of the early Church who, through divine intervention, was transformed into a powerful proclaimer. While Paul was traveling on the road to Damascus to further harass and inflict terror upon the Saints of that region, the Lord Himself appeared to this "chosen vessel" (Acts 9:15), setting him on a new path of discipleship. What do the scriptures say of this unlikely new convert? "And straightway [immediately] he preached Christ in the synagogues, that he is the Son of God" (Acts 9:20).

This initial burst of evangelism would eventually become Paul's life work—life spent traveling, exhorting, preaching, testifying, warning, writing, and eventually giving his very life for the cause of Christ. What a miraculous change of heart! To think that this was the same man who consented to and witnessed the martyrdom of the disciple Stephen; the same man who made havoc of the Church, "breathing out threatenings and slaughter" against the

Saints (Acts 9:1); the same man who enjoyed great power and status as a henchman of the Pharisees. Yet the infinite power of the Atonement settled deep in his soul, leading him to trade his life of privilege and prosperity for a life of duty and devotion to an unpopular cause—the cause that would cost him his life.

Is it any wonder that this same Paul elucidates so beautifully the doctrine of charity? To the Saints at Corinth he wrote, "Though I have the gift of prophecy, and understand all mysteries, and all knowledge; and though I have all faith, so that I could remove mountains, and have not charity, I am nothing. And though I bestow all my goods to feed the poor, and though I give my body to be burned, and have not charity, it profiteth me nothing. Charity suffereth long, and is kind; charity envieth not; charity vaunteth not itself, is not puffed up. . . . Charity never faileth" (1 Corinthians 13:2–4, 8).

What was Paul trying to teach about the doctrine of charity? First, he asserts that those who lack charity—though abundantly blessed with other spiritual gifts—are nothing. Talk about the ultimate attention-getter. He may as well be saying, "Wake up, people! Pay attention to what I'm about to explain." He then proceeds to draw a clear distinction between alms, or charitable giving, with the actual doctrine of charity. Finally, he concludes with the ultimate endorsement: "charity never faileth."

Clearly Paul esteemed this doctrine as being essential in the life of a Christian, yet the Bible is somewhat vague as to what charity actually is. Fortunately the Book of Mormon restores such plain and precious truths. In this additional witness of Christ we find clarifying insight into Paul's discourse.

During the later, lonely years of his life, the prophet Moroni began abridging the Jaredite plates as his father, Mormon, had previously done with those of the Nephites. This abridgment is known today as the book of Ether. In the middle of this book, Moroni gives some priceless insights on the doctrine of charity. He writes: "And again, I remember that thou hast said that thou hast loved the world, *even unto the laying down of thy life for the world*, that thou mightest take it again to prepare a place for the children of men. *And now I know that this love which thou hast had for the children of men is charity*; wherefore, except men shall have charity they cannot inherit that place which thou hast prepared in the mansions of thy Father" (Ether 12:33–34, emphasis added).

In the history of the world there was an exact moment when charity, or the pure love of Christ, was manifest in a way beyond comprehension to the mortal mind. This moment came as the Son of God voluntarily laid down His life in order to give life to the world. Moroni's prophetic commentary leaves no doubt that the doctrine of charity is completely centered on the Atonement. This understanding gives new meaning and vitality to Paul's message to the Corinthians.

Take, for instance, Paul's seemingly exaggerated statement that if we do not have charity, we are nothing. Understanding that charity is synonymous with the Atonement instantly vindicates this declaration. Paul knew that despite our works, whether they be good or evil, if we have not made the Atonement a fundamental, even daily, part of our lives, we will not fulfill our potential in the plan of salvation. In essence, we are nothing.

But even more striking are the implications for missionary work. Here, Paul the proselytizer emphatically states that "charity never faileth" (1 Corinthians 13:8). In other words, anyone who taps into the Atonement as their primary source of motivation has tapped into a reservoir of love, power, courage, faith, and energy that will never run dry. Their motivation will never fail. Any other motivation (even the good ones) could, under the most distressing circumstances, fail.

Perhaps an example will help illustrate this point. Let's look at a companionship of elders serving 12,000 miles away in the Siberian city of Novosibirsk, Russia. It's February, it's freezing, and at 5:00 p.m. it is already pitch dark. They've been in and out of apartment buildings all day—a day which has brought little success and lots of rejection. They have no appointments set up for the evening—just four more long, daunting hours on the street. They're cold, tired, hungry, and discouraged.

Attempting to stop a passing man, they are rejected and sworn at, causing one of the elders to reach his breaking point. He turns to his companion and begs to call it a day. After all, they've given an honest effort, yet nothing seems to be working. "Let's just go home, get a warm meal, make some phone calls, and gear up for a fresh start tomorrow."

Only one who has experienced these or similar circumstances knows the magnitude of the physical, emotional, and spiritual exhaustion weighing down on these young missionaries. In this extremely trying moment, only the power of the Atonement can provide enough strength to press forward. Why? Because the Atonement never fails! Just as Jesus Christ never gives up on any of us, the Atonement-motivated missionary will never give up when somebody out there might need his message.

Although every instinct in his body screams at him to acquiesce to his companion's plea, something deep inside will propel him on, giving him the strength to turn to his companion and say in an encouraging manner, "Just one more house, Elder. Just one more stop. Maybe it's the next house that's been praying for us to come; maybe the next guy will listen. We've been rejected three hundred straight times today, maybe the three hundred and first will finally say yes."

This missionary scenario is not hypothetical. In fact, I experienced it many times and have played the part of both companions. It reminds me of a motto we adopted in the Romania Bucharest Mission. Romania is a former Soviet bloc country that suffered greatly during the long decades of tyranny and oppression. Sadly, the toll of Communism is still visible today in the architecture. Before World War II, Bucharest was known as "Little Paris," being home to hundreds of classical European museums, churches, and places of culture. Under the new regime, however, many of these architectural treasures were demolished and replaced with drab, uniform, concrete apartment buildings called "blocks." These buildings were constructed one right next to the other, with an unvarying blueprint of ten floors, each floor housing eight apartment units.

As "block knocking" (or tracting) was a common practice in our mission, a favorite motto became "last floor, last door." The message of the motto was simple: We don't quit! Indifferent of the treatment received at the previous seventy-nine doors, the "last floor, last door" missionary approaches the eightieth with the same optimism and faith as he did the first. Quite simply, a "last floor, last door" missionary was one who had tapped into the motivating power of the Atonement.

When a visiting area authority learned of our motto, he stood at the pulpit and, overcome by emotion, offered his endorsement of the phrase. He proceeded to tell his own story of finding the gospel. After the birth of their second child, he and his wife began discussing more seriously the topic of religion and the church in which they would raise their young family. During this period, two young men knocked on their door sharing a message they asserted came from God. This young couple quickly embraced the message of the restored gospel and went on to rear a righteous family in the Church. They had served in many positions of leadership and were now having grandchildren born within the covenant. The epilogue to the story came as he concluded, "By the way, my wife and I happened to live on the last floor, and *we were* the last door."

In addition to numerous scriptural examples, modern witnesses have also attested to the power of the Atonement to motivate and give life to the missionary. One of these comes from the book *In the Eye of the Storm* by Elder John H. Groberg. In vivid detail he describes the culture shock he experienced during the beginning phase of his mission to Tonga. Living in a thatched hut, sleeping on the ground, eating strange food, and struggling to speak an indecipherable language—all combined to create overwhelming feelings of homesickness, discouragement, and frustration. Sensing the need for divine aid and instruction, the young Elder Groberg devoted a number of days to fasting, prayer, and scripture study. The message received during this period of spiritual communion not only changed the course of his mission, but ultimately his entire life. In serene and insightful prose he describes what was learned:

> From that moment I tried to never look back. I realized that any small place or any small number of people was more complex than I could comprehend and contained more potential than I could possibly realize. The infinite cost of the Savior's suffering and dying for all of us makes even one soul anywhere of infinite worth and deserving of all the energy, effort, sacrifice, and love our whole lives are capable of giving. . . . True love, God's love, is the answer to all concerns. It fills the universe and should fill our lives and our thoughts and our actions. To know that He suffered and died for others as well as for us is the greatest single force in the universe to give us the desire and power to help others. We all fall short in many ways. We all love much less than we should. But the Savior did not fall short, nor love one whit less than He should. Literally, the universe is filled with His love, and we should be filled with love because of Him. Oh, how we should try with all our hearts to become part of this infinite love! I was determined to do so. (Salt Lake City: Bookcraft, 1993, 40)

Elder Groberg beautifully sums up what the right motivation must be. Truly, as he declares, the Atonement of Jesus Christ is deserving of "all our energy, effort, and sacrifice" and is "the greatest single force in the universe to give us the desire and power to help others." Joseph Smith taught the same principle when he declared, "A man filled with the love of God, is not content with blessing his family alone, but ranges through the whole world, anxious to bless the whole human race" (*History of the Church of Jesus Christ of Latter-day Saints*, ed. B.H. Roberts [Salt Lake City: Deseret Book Company, 1978], 4:227).

Sometime in the near future it will be you sitting in that tiny MTC room. On that night you'll probably be feeling a little lonely, overwhelmed, and maybe even afraid. But when your branch president stands up and asks, "Elder or Sister _____, why have you decided to go on a mission?" you will know what your answer must be. It will be ingrained into your head, but more importantly it will be engraved upon your heart. The Atonement of Jesus Christ is the infinite and limitless power source that is rightfully yours. As you go forth to serve, this motivation will give you the confidence and capacity to "press forward . . . having a perfect brightness of hope, and a love of God and of all men" (2 Nephi 31:20).

Up until this point our discussion has focused on establishing *what* should be the missionary's motivation. Hoping this has been accomplished, we will now turn our attention to exactly *how* that motivation can be attained. Let me offer two suggestions:

1. To see the need for an atonement, we must first understand that "all mankind [are] in a lost and in a fallen state" (1 Nephi 10:6). This understanding is centered on the Fall of Adam and its associated consequences. After the Fall, mankind became "carnal, sensual, and devilish" (Moses 5:13). Such a stark assessment should not be depressing but instead should propel us in our quest to shed the natural man and become "a saint through the atonement of Christ" (Mosiah 3:19).

How does this happen? An event detailed in the Book of Mormon provides an illustration. In his final sermon, King Benjamin candidly outlined the effects of the Fall and then bore testimony of the future Atonement that would rebalance the scales between justice and mercy. At the conclusion of their king's message, the people were so moved that they fell to their knees and prostrated themselves upon the earth. They cried, "O have mercy, and apply the atoning blood of Christ that we may receive forgiveness of our sins, and our hearts may be purified" (Mosiah 4:2). Only in this moment of complete humility and submission were they able to receive the sweet assurance Elder Groberg, Paul, Alma, the sons of Mosiah, and Enos received that His "grace is sufficient for all men" (Ether 12:27). That as Jesus Christ was lifted up on the cross, so too can

He lift each and every one of us out of our lost and fallen state (see Mosiah 4:1–4).

In the scriptures this transformation is often referred to as spiritual rebirth. Spiritual rebirth begins with faith in Jesus Christ and manifests itself in sincere repentance. The repentance process is solidified through covenants and followed by the reception of the Holy Ghost. Through the sanctifying power of the Holy Ghost, each of us receives the promise that we can become new creatures in Christ (see 2 Corinthians 5:17).

Has this process occurred in your life? If you're like me as a teenager, you're probably wondering, *How can I even know?* Thankfully, the Book of Mormon prophet Alma provided us with a type of "spiritual rebirth" quiz in Alma 5. To the members of the Church in Zarahemla he asked a series of questions that, when answered truthfully, are designed to assess one's status in the process of spiritual rebirth. Consider a sample of his questions, with modern-day equivalents provided in italics:

> "Have ye spiritually been born of God?" (v. 14) *Have you settled it in your mind and heart to follow Christ, allowing Him to be the Father of your spiritual rebirth?*
>
> "Have ye received his image in your countenances?" (v. 14) *Are you seeking to develop Christlike attributes? Do you reflect these attributes in your daily interaction with others? When people see you, are they able to see Him?* (For an in-depth study on this topic, please see *Preach My Gospel*, chapter 6.)
>
> "Have ye experienced this mighty change in your hearts?" (v. 14) *Do you notice yourself changing the things you talk about, the things you do, even your thoughts? Is the combined effect of these changes leading you to become a new person in Christ?*
>
> "Do you look forward with an eye of faith?" (v. 15) *Do you feel confident about your spiritual standing before God? Are you optimistic about the future?*
>
> "Can ye look up to God at that day with a pure heart and clean hands?" (v. 19) *Are you trying your best to keep your life clean? Are you choosing friends and media that help you keep your thoughts, language, and actions pure?*

"If ye have felt to sing the song of redeeming love, . . . can ye feel so now?" (v. 26) *Have you felt the boundless joy that comes through repentance and the miracle of forgiveness? Is there anything in your life that needs to be taken care of today?*

"Are ye stripped of pride?" (v. 28) *Do you fall into the trap of comparing yourself with those around you? Do you think you're better than others?*

"Is there one among you who is not stripped of envy?" (v. 29) *Where is your focus? Is it a focus of gratitude for the blessings you do have? Or is it a focus of envy and jealousy for the things you do not have?*

"Is there one among you that doth make a mock of his brother?" (v. 30) *How do you treat those around you? Do you treat* everyone *with kindness, respect, and love?*

While taking this quiz and pondering where you are on the path of spiritual rebirth, remember that this process happens in a variety of ways. For some, spiritual rebirth may be a dramatic 180-degree turnaround, but more often the change comes in subtle and gradual ways, with the power of the Atonement steadily deepening and refining a spiritually sensitive soul. Regardless of how it happens, each missionary must have confidence that they have indeed been, and are continuing to be, spiritually reborn. In this way, the Atonement will become an inexhaustible source of strength, courage, and motivation in bringing the good news of the gospel to the world.

2. Though often overlooked and underutilized, the sacrament provides another opportunity to tap into the Atonement. Previously we noted that repentance is an essential component in the process of spiritual rebirth: simply put, repentance is the key that unlocks the power of the Atonement in our lives. For this purpose, the Lord instituted the sacrament as a weekly ordinance that provides us with regular, quality practice with the repentance process. Of course, we do not intentionally sin to provide additional practice opportunities, but naturally, we all fall short of perfection and need the Savior's help. Long before he or she enters full-time missionary service, a prospective elder or sister needs to make the sacrament the spiritual highlight of each week. Each second of the sacrament needs to be carefully spent reflecting, pondering, praying, evaluating, expressing gratitude, setting goals for the upcoming week, and so on.

As a seminary teacher, I am often invited to attend the sacrament meetings of departing missionaries whom I have taught. When it doesn't conflict with my own church meetings or place undue strain on my family, I try to attend and support my former students as often as I can. As many know, these meetings can quickly become a "must be seen" social gathering for the local teenage population. Usually I will recognize dozens of former and current students among the congregation and am curious to observe how these teenagers approach the sacrament when surrounded by peers and absent from parents.

In most instances I have been extremely impressed with what I see. The spiritual maturity of these youth is evident in their level of respect and reverence for this sacred ordinance. But occasionally I have also seen behavior that was disappointing. Talking, texting, laughing, flirting, sleeping, getting impatient and restless—they are wasting the priceless opportunity to deeply internalize the greatest act in human history. Your weekly experience with the sacrament can be viewed as a type of spiritual rebirth barometer. When you reach the point where the ten minutes of the sacrament do not seem nearly long enough, you're getting closer to where you need to be.

In conclusion, I believe that understanding the power of the Atonement to motivate and then tapping into this motivation are the first keys to becoming a successful missionary. Near the end of my stay at the MTC, Elder Jeffrey R. Holland came and spoke at our weekly devotional. His entire talk centered on the essential role of the Atonement in missionary work. Without mincing words, he described the real challenges missionaries face but then bore powerful testimony of the Savior's ability to carry a missionary through any difficulty or struggle ("Missionary Work and the Atonement," *Ensign*, March 2001, 8–15).

I sat there in awe. For me his words seemed to put an apostolic seal of approval on the conclusions I had drawn from my personal, two-month study. Along with ancient prophets, a living apostle had now confirmed what my motivation must be.

Throughout this chapter I've shared my experience of finding the right motivation. Now it's up to you. The Savior has performed the Atonement so that you can repent and help others to do so as well. He needs and is counting on you to spread the salvation of this divine gift. The scriptures teach, "How great is his joy in the soul that repenteth! *Wherefore, you are called to cry repentance unto this people*" (D&C 18:13–14, emphasis added). It is my prayer and challenge that you answer this call.

Chapter 2
The Second M: What Is Your Message?

"No matter where you serve or whom you teach, center your teaching on the Restoration of the gospel of Jesus Christ." —Preach My Gospel, 6

ONCE A MISSIONARY HAS TAPPED into the right motivation, a strong foundation is laid for success in preaching the gospel. This leads to the next logical question: *So what is your message?* When you stop a man on the street, when you knock on an apartment door, when you meet a member referral, *what is the message you are called to bring to the world?*

There are many good messages that a missionary can share. These include, but aren't limited to, the nature of God and our relationship to Him, the answers the plan of salvation provides to life's great questions, the doctrine of eternal families, standards of morality that anchor us in a drifting world, etc. All of these are extremely powerful messages that in certain situations may be highlighted. But in most cases all of these topics are subsidiary to the central message of the missionary: the Restoration of the gospel through the Prophet Joseph Smith.

Why is it so important that your message be focused on the Restoration? Because this is what makes us unique and sets us apart from anything else being offered in the world. It's simply a reality that among the thousands of Christian denominations, there are other churches that profess to know the attributes and nature of God, there are other churches that promote moral chastity and a regimented health code, and there are other churches that emphasize the need to focus on and strengthen the family. But The Church of Jesus Christ of Latter-day Saints stands alone in its declaration that a complete restoration of Christ's ancient Church has occurred, with the necessary authority, doctrines, ordinances, and organization that had been lost from the world for centuries.

If indeed the Restoration should be our central message, then surely the Prophet Joseph Smith, the great restorer, would have emphasized it. From the following account by Parley P. Pratt, we can clearly decipher Joseph's stance on the subject:

> While visiting with Brother Joseph in Philadelphia, a very large church was opened for him to preach in, and about three thousand people assembled to hear him. Brother Rigdon spoke first, and dwelt on the Gospel, illustrating his doctrine by the Bible. When he was through, Brother Joseph arose like a lion about to roar; and being full of the Holy Ghost, spoke in great power, bearing testimony of the visions he had seen, the ministering of angels which he had enjoyed, and how he had found the plates of the Book of Mormon, and translated them by the gift and power of God. He commenced by saying: "If nobody else had the courage to testify of so glorious a message from Heaven, and of the finding of so glorious a record, he felt to do it in justice to the people and leave the event with God." (*The Autobiography of Parley P. Pratt,* comp. and ed. Scot Facer Proctor and Maurine Jensen Proctor [Salt Lake City: Deseret Book Company, 2000], 362)

In a nutshell, there you have the two different approaches to the message. Notice how Sidney Rigdon based his discourse solely from the Bible, illuminating many passages of scripture but largely failing to showcase the distinct aspects of their message. Joseph, on the other hand, got quickly to the point by declaring that the gospel had been restored, the heavens had been opened, and a new religious age of light and glory had commenced. Note the effect Joseph's message had upon this large group of people: "The entire congregation were astounded; electrified, as it were, and overwhelmed with the sense of truth and power by which he spoke, and the wonders which he related. A lasting impression was made; many souls were gathered into the fold. And I bear witness, that he, by his faithful and powerful testimony, cleared his garments of their blood" (*Autobiography of Parley P. Pratt,* 362).

What a fascinating event to analyze. Here we have Sidney Rigdon—the lifelong preacher, the skilled orator—who is polished, eloquent, and intelligent stacked side by side with Joseph, a backwoods farm boy with little education and no formal religious training. If one were to predict which of the two speakers would draw rave reviews from this crowd of learned city dwellers, the obvious favorite would be Sidney. So what do we learn? (And this is important.) Where conversion is concerned, *the message* is much more important than *the messenger.*

Doesn't knowing this give you hope? Before my mission I felt inadequate, intimidated, and overwhelmed at the prospect of sharing the gospel. I imagine to some degree you probably feel the same. But I quickly learned that it wasn't about me, and you can take comfort in the fact that it won't be about you. If you will focus on the right message and declare that message by the Spirit, you too can have a Joseph-type impact on those you are called to teach.

The importance of focusing on the right message is further illustrated in the following story. Amasa Potter was a very young missionary in the early days of the Church. Before he departed, Heber C. Kimball took him aside and prophesied that the time would come when he would be at a loss for words, not knowing what to say before a large congregation. He then gave Amasa the following counsel: "'At that time . . . if you will commence to declare the divine mission of Joseph Smith in this our day, and the divine authenticity of the Book of Mormon, the Lord will loosen your tongue and you shall say the very things that are needful to be said to the people'" (*Best-Loved Stories of the LDS People,* 3 vols., ed. Parry, Lyon, Gundry [Salt Lake City: Deseret Book Company, 2000], 3:220–221).

As foretold, the young elder soon found himself behind a pulpit for the first time facing a numerous audience. Trembling, he began a sermon based on a biblical text but quickly became dumb and could not speak. He stood frozen for nearly two minutes until the words of Brother Kimball came searing back into his mind. He writes: "When this came to my mind I commenced declaring [the message of the Restoration] to the congregation. I had spoken but a few minutes when I thought I saw several lines of large letters printed on the walls of the house, and I commenced to read them and spoke about one hour. When the letters faded from my sight I then stopped speaking. I could not tell all that I had said; but my companion told me it was an excellent discourse" (*Best-Loved Stories of the LDS People,* 221).

If the Prophet Joseph and men such as Heber C. Kimball felt it imperative at the outset of this dispensation to focus on the message of the

Restoration, how much greater is the urgency to do so now! More recently, Elder Bruce R. McConkie offered a modern witness of the importance of presenting the right message. Part of his opinion was shaped by an experience he had at the world's fair in Osaka, Japan. He writes:

> I went to the United States Pavilion and I went to the Russian pavilion. The United States pavilion was marvelous in some very minor respects. They had the capsule that the astronauts went to the moon in and this sort of thing, and people were tremendously interested. They may have had just volumes and rooms full of modernistic art and all sorts of things that supposedly show our culture, but didn't really project any image of the United States. Not one word about the Constitution. And then I went into the Russian pavilion. Now it's godless communism. . . . Floor after floor and room after room it was just pure propaganda for Russia, and there were quotations from Lenin and all the rest. And I thought, "These people know how to get their message over." Now their message is false, and it is not good and it is unrighteous, but the fact is they knew how to launch a message to the world, and as far as I was concerned, the United States pavilion was just a failure.
>
> Well, I didn't believe a thing, propaganda-wise, that I got out of the Russian pavilion, but I went out of there knowing that they thought they had the message for the world, and at least I was impressed with that much.
>
> Now I'm not too impressed with the fact that we try to be very soft and gentle in all the visitors centers and in missionary work and in everything else, just trying to leave people feeling good. I think we've got a message and it ought to be delivered. It's a worldwide message, and our centering should be on Joseph Smith. Here is Joseph Smith and he revealed Christ, and here is Christ, and here is salvation through this system. That kind of approach will have the effect of dividing people on the one hand or on the other, but so you divide them. You divide them— you get some people who are interested. You don't make friends with everyone.

[President J. Reuben Clark said:] "You can't tell the Joseph Smith story without offending people. . . . We don't need to be so anxiously concerned about not offending the world." (*The Bruce R. McConkie Story* [Salt Lake City: Deseret Book Company, 2003], 302–304)

Let's consider for a moment Elder McConkie's experience at the world's fair. The United States actually possessed a powerful message (liberty, equality, opportunity, justice, etc.), but this message was not presented, and the result was a diminished and diluted experience. The Soviets had a flawed and corrupt message but made a strong impression by presenting it with force and vigor. Now think of the position we are in as Latter-day Saints. We have been entrusted with the most powerful message in the world. It is a message of truth, knowledge, peace, and joy. If only we can launch this message with commensurate power and conviction, the potential harvest is beyond imagination.

In order to effectively "launch" the message of the Restoration, we must teach it in proper context. This means that certain prerequisite doctrines must first be explained and understood. The following is an example of a five-minute lesson and is, in content and structure, much like the lessons found in the great missionary handbook *Preach My Gospel*:

There is a God. He is our Father and has prepared a plan of happiness and progression for each of us. Jesus Christ is the Son of God, our Savior, and the central figure in this plan. God reveals His plan through prophets. He gives prophets the authority to act in His name and commands them to teach and warn others. Adam, Noah, Moses, Elijah, and John the Baptist were all prophets. Sadly, the scriptures show that in many instances the prophets were ignored, rejected, or even killed. When the world rejected and killed the prophets, apostasy occurred. Apostasy means a period of time when the people fell away from the truth.

In the ultimate act of love, God sent His Son, Jesus Christ, into the world. Christ called disciples and organized His Church, but even He was rejected and crucified. After His death the Church continued for a while, but eventually the apostles whom Jesus had chosen were persecuted and killed. The authority to act in Christ's name was lost, along with many of the truths of His gospel. Centuries passed in darkness and confusion, until the year 1820 when God again reached out to the world by calling a young boy named Joseph Smith to be a prophet.

With a proper context in place, the missionaries can now proceed to teach the message of the Restoration with a strong emphasis on the

Joseph Smith story. Encompassed in this story would be the young boy's confusion about the many different churches, his study of the Bible and discovery of the beautiful promise in James 1:5, and most importantly his prayer and accompanying vision.

I believe that Satan trembles when he sees a missionary introducing an investigator to the Joseph Smith story, especially when it gets to the grove. Oh, how Satan must have loved those centuries of the Great Apostasy, filling the world with darkness, misery, and confusion. But the grove signified the end to his unchecked era of dominion. Accompanied by His Father, the King of Kings had now returned to restore His kingdom, to bring order and light back into a troubled world. For the adversary, Joseph humbly praying in that grove of trees must have been a horrific sight. Is it any wonder that Satan personally attacked the young boy before the light finally broke through? While he wasn't able to stop Joseph, it doesn't mean he won't try to interfere with others gaining the same knowledge that Joseph did—the knowledge that God knows them personally, the heavens are open, and the kingdom of God has been restored on the earth today. An experience I had as a missionary confirms this belief. While street contacting in the Carpathian city of Sibiu we met a very prominent doctor. He was well known in the community and well respected in his profession. He was open to new ideas and extremely curious about two Romanian-speaking Americans. We asked if he wanted to learn more, and he readily agreed to an appointment. A few days later we went to his home and began sharing the message of the Restoration. When we reached the Joseph Smith story and described the young boy's overwhelming confusion, this man sighed deeply and said, "I've felt that exact same way all my life."

We continued to teach until a loud noise suddenly interrupted our lesson. The man's wife (who refused to join us) had begun to vacuum in the adjoining room. He apologized, excused himself, and hurried off to address the problem. Soon he returned, begged our pardon, and we continued. After only a minute, we were sidetracked by yet another jarring noise. His wife was now watching a big-screen TV with the volume maxed out. Chagrined, he again left to remedy the situation and came back pleading for us to resume.

By this point we had detailed Joseph's study of the Bible and his discovery of the promise in James 1:5. We then explained how Joseph decided to ask God in prayer which of all the churches was true and how he went into a grove of trees for this purpose.

The Spirit was already palpable in the room as I began to recite Joseph's account of the First Vision. But before I could complete a single line, the loudest phone I've ever heard (certainly from the Communist era) screamed from the neighboring desk. Our investigator sprang to his feet, picked up the phone, didn't even ask who was calling, but simply stated, "I can't talk right now!" and hung up. He sat back down, and I started again from the beginning. As if on cue, the cell phone attached to his belt began its little jingle. Visibly annoyed, he flipped the phone open and repeated the same hasty plea to the new caller. The very instant the cell phone call ended, his desk phone was again emitting its shrill ring. He ran over, disconnected the phone by pulling the wire from the wall, and rushed back to his chair.

Exhausted, he plopped down, composed himself, and then motioned for me to speak. My companion and I were looking at one another in amazement, and I proceeded for a third time to recite the opening line: "I saw a pillar of light . . . " Halfway through this attempt we were halted yet again by his cell phone. This time he turned it off, but the vibration persisted as I finished quoting Joseph's account. Upon my completing the last line, his wife appeared and beckoned him from the doorway, making it nearly a dozen interruptions and distractions over the span of a few short minutes.

When we left this appointment my companion and I were drained. We both had sweat running down our faces and walked in stunned silence. Finally, Elder Sechcrest turned to me and said, "Elder Christiansen, it felt like we were fighting against a real, physical force in there." I couldn't have agreed more. While this story may seem dramatic, it certainly isn't unique. Most returned missionaries I've spoken with have experienced something similar. It's simply a fact that the adversary hates the story of the First Vision and will do anything in his power to prevent the honest in heart from receiving it. For this reason we must not only match, but exceed his vigor in sharing it to all who will listen. Yes, we will shout it from the very housetops if necessary.

As you focus on the message of the Restoration, it's helpful to understand that certain doctrines of the gospel complement each other. I call these "sister" doctrines, or "peanut butter and jelly" doctrines. As we have previously seen in chapter 1, an appreciation for the Atonement is predicated upon an understanding of the Fall. These are sister doctrines. The message of the Restoration is also tied to a sister doctrine. Those we teach will never understand the need for a *restoration* if they do not understand and accept the reality of a universal *apostasy*. Consequently, an essential part of a missionary's preparation is a thorough study of the Apostasy from the scriptures and *Preach My Gospel*.

When introduced to the concept of an apostasy, many investigators I taught as a missionary frequently asked an excellent question phrased something like this: "If a universal apostasy was going to take place that would last for over 1700 years, wouldn't the Bible have something to say about it?" Of course the answer is yes! The real question, however, is whether you, the missionary, can effectively use the scriptures to show it. *Preach My Gospel* contains an extensive list of apostasy references; this list would be a great place to start (see *Preach My Gospel*, 35; for the ultramotivated, a classic treatise on the subject is the book *The Great Apostasy* by James E. Talmage). In the hopes of sparking an interest within you for this important topic, allow me to share a few of my favorite "apostasy" passages. The latter half of the Old Testament is both fascinating and frustrating. God continues to send prophets to idolatrous Israel, but the covenant people largely persist in their wicked and worldly ways. Being rejected by the people of their day, many of these ancient prophets turned their prophetic focus and attention to the latter days. Examples of such are Isaiah, Daniel, Ezekiel, Jeremiah, and Amos. The prophet Amos gives perhaps the most vivid prophecy of a great and utter apostasy. He foretells of a time when there will be a famine in the land, "not a famine of bread, nor a thirst for water, but of hearing the words of the LORD: And they shall wander from sea to sea, and from the north even to the east, they shall run to and fro to seek the word of the Lord, and shall not find it" (Amos 8:11–12).

Not only does this passage illustrate the universal scope of the prophesied falling away, but it also conjures up images of a later assessment offered in modern revelation some two thousand years later: "For there are many yet on the earth among all sects, parties, and denominations, who are blinded by the subtle craftiness of men, whereby they lie in wait to deceive, *and who are only kept from the truth because they know not where to find it*" (D&C 123:12, emphasis added). Of course the Savior Himself warned His disciples of the impending apostasy. In the masterfully crafted parable of the wicked husbandmen (see Mark 12), Christ paints the picture of a beautiful vineyard which is lent out to certain husbandmen (or caretakers). At the appointed time, the Master of the vineyard sends one of His servants to receive an accounting from these caretakers. But instead of welcoming the Proprietor's servant with respect and deference, they treat him with contempt and violence. The Master of the vineyard continues to send servants, but all are rejected and sent away "shamefully handled" (v. 4).

Finally, in exasperation the Master of the vineyard declares that He will send His own Son; surely they will reverence His flesh and blood. However, as the wicked husbandmen spy the approaching Son, greed sows murder within their hearts, and they exclaim, "Let us kill him, and the inheritance shall be ours" (v. 7).

The symbols of the parable are clear: The Master is our Heavenly Father, the vineyard is the world, the servants are the prophets of various dispensations (such as Noah, Abraham, Moses, Elijah), and the husbandmen are the idolatrous and prideful groups that have corrupted God's kingdom, cutting it off from His direction. The Son of the Master is the Lord Jesus Christ.

The next verse vividly portrays God's frustration with the wickedness and spiritual blindness of His children and also points to a future falling away. "What shall therefore the lord of the vineyard do? he will come and destroy the husbandmen, and will give the vineyard unto others" (v. 9).

While allusions to the Apostasy are scattered throughout the standard works, the real gold mine for apostasy references is found in the latter half of the New Testament. During this period the beleaguered Church faced dire circumstances. Jerusalem remained a hotbed of persecution; apostolic leadership dwindled as the Twelve were targeted and eliminated one by one; and the once-zealous branches of the gentile nations were collapsing under the weight of cultural contamination. Studying the New Testament epistles is akin to watching a sailor plug up a major leak in his vessel only to have two more spring up simultaneously. While the apostles are devotedly laboring to "plug up the leaks" within the Church, their efforts become inconsequential as the waves of apostasy increase in size and frequency.

Take, for instance, Paul's second epistle to his faithful companion Timothy. This epistle was written near the end of Paul's life as he awaited execution in Rome. While Paul encourages his beloved friend the best he can, the tone of nearly the entire letter is ominous. He writes: "For the time will come when they [the congregations of the Church] will not endure sound doctrine; but after their own lusts shall they heap to themselves teachers, having itching ears; And they shall turn away their ears from the truth, and shall be turned unto fables" (2 Timothy 4:3–4).

The contents of this letter give indication of serious trouble. The apostasy alarm is definitely being sounded. Consider Paul's warning regarding the gospel teachers. He foresaw that in the near future teachers who imparted gospel truths would be replaced by those who teach "smooth things" (Isaiah 30:10). Let's face it; the gospel requires discipline, effort, sacrifice, and change. When teachers or leaders tell the people what they *want* to hear instead of what they *need* to hear, they are practicing priestcraft and stand condemned before the Lord. Furthermore, the practice of priestcraft creates a religious climate of "itching ears": the congregations itching to hear words of approval and justification for whatever they deem to be right and the teachers itching to hear words of praise—and perhaps monetary pledges—for their labors.

Paul also warns that the changing nature of *the messengers* will be compounded by the changing nature of *the message*. Doctrines of the gospel, eternal truths essential for our salvation, will be replaced by fables—fictional stories.

Could this really happen? Sadly, I witnessed it every day as a missionary in Eastern Europe. The people were vaguely familiar with the doctrines of faith, repentance, and prayer, but they *knew* their fables and centered much of their religious convictions upon them. Over the course of my mission I heard hundreds of expressions of belief based solely on such fables. Surely the adversary must have personally directed the substitution from prayer, scripture study, weekly worship, covenants, and guidance from the Spirit to fables—further stamping out the gospel light and deepening the darkness he had designed for the world.

While an investigator must understand the Apostasy in order to fully embrace the Restoration, it is important to note that we should never belittle or look down on other churches and their beliefs. Rarely as a missionary will you find a person who is instantly willing to cast aside their belief system or church to embrace the gospel message. Occasionally it does happen, but it's the exception, not the norm. In most cases, teaching investigators about the Apostasy must be done with extreme tact and sensitivity. That doesn't mean we soften the message of the Restoration or apologize for the truths we possess. But our knowledge of the Apostasy never gives us license to be condescending to or critical of other religions. Perhaps a missionary scenario will be helpful:

You've just taught an investigator family about the Apostasy and notice the father and mother both seem troubled and deep in thought.

In your introduction to this family they made it very clear that they were members of another prominent church. Now the implications of what you've taught are obviously sinking in. Finally the mother speaks up and timidly says, "So . . . you're saying that our church is wrong?"

Do you see why the Savior admonished his servants to be *"wise as serpents, and harmless as doves"* (Matthew 10:16, emphasis added)? Critical junctures such as this occur frequently in missionary work and, when encountered, must be navigated with care and caution. There are two very opposite errors in judgment that could be made in this situation.

On the side of tactlessness, an overbearing missionary could matter-of-factly respond to the mother's question by saying, "Yes. We believe that not only your church is wrong, but all others except ours are wrong," which comment is the spiritual equivalent of making moose horns with your hands and shouting, "Neener, neener, neener!" Such a response would be extremely unwise. It's obvious that this couple possesses deep feelings about their own church. It's also likely that their religious beliefs are intertwined with a cultural identity and family heritage. Do you see why this mother's sincere question cannot be handled in such a callous manner? Imagine for a moment what would have happened had Ammon been this arrogant and uncouth with King Lamoni. You'll recall that as the teaching process began, Ammon asked Lamoni if he believed in God. Confused by the question, Lamoni answered that he believed in a Great Spirit but was unsure if the Great Spirit was Ammon's God (Alma 18:24–28).

Think how damaging it would have been had Ammon taken a hard-line doctrinal stance on Lamoni, correcting him in the following manner: "Uh, that's actually wrong, Your Majesty. God is not the Great *Spirit*; He's an exalted personage who has a body of flesh and bone. Wow, you're the king, and you don't know these things? You Lamanites really have been duped by those false traditions; I can't wait to tell this story at my homecoming in Zarahemla. The Nephites are all going to die laughing when they hear how dazed and confused you guys are. It'll be hilarious. *Ooohhh, a spooky Great Spiiiriiittt.* Give me a break!"

Of course, Ammon handled this delicate situation perfectly. He momentarily settled on a position of common ground but quickly proceeded to take Lamoni to higher ground. It's no coincidence that the scriptures describe Ammon as being "wise, yet harmless" (Alma 18:22).

While an overbearing and tactless missionary will experience little success—and can actually cause much harm—there is an equally ineffective approach that lies on the opposite end of the spectrum. Wanting to remain on friendly terms and fearing to hurt the investigators' feelings, a timid missionary might respond in a way that greatly softens the truth, diluting the inspired nature of the message. It might sound something like this: "Oh, no, that's not what we're saying at all. We know and admire many members of your church."

Sadly, in this instance, the desire to tread lightly comes at the very cost and purpose for which you are there. After demonstrating such little faith by backpedaling in order not to give offense, the missionary is in no position at all to proceed with the message of the Restoration because his investigators will not see the need for it.

Clearly the proper approach lies somewhere in the middle of these two extremes. To me, it's the approach taught so simply by President Gordon B. Hinckley. Repeatedly throughout his presidency, President Hinckley issued the following invitation to members of all faiths, religions, and creeds: "We simply say to the people of other churches, bring all the good that you have and let us see if we can add to it" (*Discourses of Gordon B. Hinckley, Volume 1, 1995–99* [Salt Lake City: Shadow Mountain, 2004], 498).

It is in this spirit of tenderness and truth that a missionary must maneuver in our hypothetical situation. Silently pleading for the Spirit to guide his words and soften the investigators' hearts, the missionary could respond with something like this: "We realize that you have deeply rooted feelings about your own church. It's obvious that your church has made you the good and honest people that you are. We have not come to replace your faith but are here to add plain and precious truths that will bring you greater knowledge, peace, and joy.

"As we have taught, we believe that the true Church which Christ established was lost from the earth. Our message is that a merciful and loving Heavenly Father has again restored His Church upon the earth. More importantly, we testify that you can find out for yourself if what we have taught is true. God is the source of all truth and will let you know by the power of the Holy Ghost."

The message of the Restoration is the most powerful message on earth. It is a message of prophets, priesthood, the plan of salvation, and the very word of God. The Book of Mormon gives insight into the power of the word: "And now, as the preaching of the word had a great tendency to lead the people to do that which was just—yea, it had had more powerful effect upon the minds of the people than the sword, or anything else, which had happened unto them—therefore Alma thought it was expedient that they should try the virtue of the word of God" (Alma 31:5).

As Alma of old, we must trust in the power of the message we are called to bear. If we demonstrate this trust, the message of the Restoration will penetrate the minds and hearts of the elect. It will bring them to a testimony of the Prophet Joseph Smith, not as a final destination but as a key landmark in their search to draw closer to our Savior, Jesus Christ, and our Eternal Father. As they embrace the message of the restored gospel they will find in it a well of salvation, springing forth pure waters of peace, joy, knowledge, and truth. This is what we desire for the world. And this is why you must know what your message is for the world.

Chapter 3
The Third M: The Means

"The Book of Mormon, combined with the Spirit, is your most powerful resource in conversion." —Preach My Gospel, 104

I LIKE BASEBALL. BASEBALL IS a game of skill and strategy, the strategy largely revolving around team signs. Every player on the team has to know the signs, especially when up to bat. Depending on various situations, the coach may need the batter to bunt, to execute a hit and run, or to "take" (or not swing at) a pitch. For each of these plays there is an associated sign. Similarly, in this, the dispensation of the fullness of times, the Lord has promised and provided a sign, or *means*, whereby the motivated missionary can declare the message of the Restoration with increased power and credibility. During His visit to the Nephites, Christ prophesied regarding the Restoration of the gospel and the accompanying sign:

> And verily I say unto you, I give unto you a sign, that ye may know the time when these things shall be about to take place—that I shall gather in, from their long dispersion, my people, O house of Israel, and shall establish again among them my Zion;
> And behold, this is the thing which I will give unto you for a sign—for verily I say unto you that when these things which I declare unto you, and which I shall declare unto you hereafter . . . shall be made known unto the Gentiles . . .
> . . . it shall be a sign unto them, that they may know that the work of the Father hath already commenced unto the fulfilling of the covenant which he hath made unto the people who are of the house of Israel. (3 Nephi 21:1–2, 7)

What is the sign or means whereby the gospel will be proclaimed? It is none other than the book described by Isaiah as a voice from the dust (see Isaiah 29:4). The great sign is the coming forth of the Book of Mormon.

For more than 175 years, the Book of Mormon has been seen by first hundreds, then thousands, and now millions as a heavenly sign that led them to embrace the fullness of the gospel. Many of these instances provide powerful evidence of the ability of this sign to do what was foretold in prophecy—that is, serve as the primary tool in gathering the house of Israel. Let's consider a few of these examples.

In the early nineteenth century, a frontiersman named Parley P. Pratt was restless about the religious movements of his day. Like many, he longed for the divine manifestations which had accompanied the Master and His apostles in biblical times. Had the heavens truly closed as many asserted? Had God abandoned His children leaving them to make do with the divine wisdom of ages past? Surely, thought Parley, these things could not be so. In fact, he could feel the Spirit of the Lord brooding over the region, the intensity of this feeling leading him to sell his home and farm in search of additional light and truth. Traveling by boat to Albany, New York, he felt impressed to debark near Rochester. In this region he soon met a man who, upon discovering that Parley was a preacher, spoke of a strange book—purportedly delivered by an angel and written on gold plates. In his autobiography, Parley describes the peculiar curiosity he felt toward the book and his first encounter with it:

> I opened it with eagerness, and read its title page. I then read the testimony of the several witnesses in relation to the manner of its being found and translated. After this I commenced its contents by course. I read all day; eating was a burden, I had no desire for food; sleep was a burden when the night came, for I preferred reading to sleep.
>
> As I read, the spirit of the Lord was upon me, and I knew and comprehended that the book was true, as plainly and manifestly as a man comprehends and knows that he exists. My joy was now full, as it were, and I rejoiced sufficiently to more than pay me for all the sorrows, sacrifices and toils of my life. . . .
>
> I esteemed the Book, or the information contained in it, more than all the riches of the world. Yes; I verily

believe that I would not at that time have exchanged the knowledge I then possessed, for a legal title to all the beautiful farms, houses, villages, and property which passed in review before me, on my journey through one of the most flourishing settlements of western New York. (*Autobiography of Parley P. Pratt*, 31–33)

Parley P. Pratt's experience is not unique; when Dr. Willard Richards first obtained a copy of the Book of Mormon, he reportedly opened it to the middle, read for a moment, closed the book, and then exclaimed: "God or the devil has had a hand in [this] book, for man never wrote it" (Susan Easton Black, *Who's Who in the Doctrine and Covenants* [Salt Lake City: Deseret Book Co., 1997], 242). He spent the following weeks in deep study, reading the book from cover to cover twice, eventually coming to the undeniable conclusion that only God could be responsible for such a work. I find it noteworthy that Willard Richards remained a lifelong convert, ultimately accompanying the Prophet Joseph to Carthage.

Why Is the Book of Mormon the Ultimate Means/Tool in Conversion?

As the head of the Church, the Savior Himself has always directed the work of spreading the gospel. Most are familiar with the famous injunction, "Go ye therefore, and teach all nations, baptizing them in the name of the Father, and of the Son, and of the Holy Ghost" (Matthew 28:19). I have always preferred the less-quoted instruction: "Ye have not chosen me, but I have chosen you, and ordained you, that ye should go and bring forth fruit, and that your fruit should remain" (John 15:16). From this passage we learn that missionaries are chosen and ordained to do two related but distinct things:

They should go and bring forth fruit, and
Their fruit should remain.

Everyone is aware of the missionaries' responsibility to "bring forth fruit" (or to baptize), yet the second facet of the Savior's instruction deserves equal if not greater emphasis. He clearly teaches that it is not enough to bring forth fruit but that fruit must be brought forth in a manner such that it will remain. In other words, *lifelong conversion* is the true aim and purpose of missionary work.

Speaking on this topic, President Hinckley emphatically stated: "There is absolutely no point in doing missionary work unless we hold on to the fruits of that effort" (*Preach My Gospel*, 213). Most missionaries have had the disheartening experience of being assigned to a branch and seeing hundreds of names on the membership rolls, only to find out that the majority are less active. These names represent fruit that has been brought forth into the waters of baptism yet has not remained faithful to those sacred covenants.

Now, I'm not naive. I realize that the Church will never have a 100 percent activity rate. Agency, apathy, and opposition will inevitably cause a percentage of converts to lose the flame of testimony and revert to their former habits and lifestyles. But we must believe that where the Savior has given the commandment to bring forth lifelong converts, He will provide a way to do so. As Nephi of old testified, "The Lord giveth no commandments unto the children men, save he shall prepare a way for them that they may accomplish the thing which he commandeth them" (1 Nephi 3:7). In His infinite wisdom, the Lord *has* prepared the way, and it requires centering the conversion process squarely on the Book of Mormon.

If missionaries are to bring forth fruit and have their fruit remain, the Book of Mormon must be the primary catalyst for conversion. Joseph Smith taught that the Book of Mormon is the keystone of our religion (see *Preach My Gospel*, 104). What does this mean? A friend of mine who is a skilled brick mason explained that the keystone holds all other stones or bricks in place and actually supports the weight of the entire arch. In what way, then, does the Book of Mormon serve as the keystone? When explaining this concept to investigators as a missionary, we would utilize a visual aid fittingly called the "Triangle of Truth." We would start with the top vertex and label it "The Book of Mormon."

THE TRIANGLE OF TRUTH

The Book of Mormon

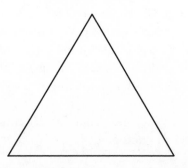

If someone will take Moroni's challenge and gain a witness of the Book of Mormon, they will not only gain a witness of *that* truth, but also of others which are inextricably connected to it. Because the Book of Mormon was translated by Joseph Smith, one cannot claim that the Book of Mormon is true yet deny Joseph's prophetic call. They are a package deal. Thus the Book of Mormon connects a line in the triangle to the Prophet Joseph Smith.

THE TRIANGLE OF TRUTH

The Book of Mormon

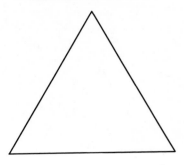

The Prophet Joseph Smith

Likewise, one cannot affirm that Joseph was a prophet without accepting the authority of the Church that was restored through him. This connects the final line to The Church of Jesus Christ of Latter-day Saints.

THE TRIANGLE OF TRUTH

The Book of Mormon

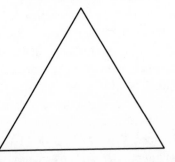

The Church of Jesus Christ
of Latter-day Saints

The Prophet Joseph Smith

While the Book of Mormon, the Prophet Joseph, and The Church of Jesus Christ of Latter-day Saints all serve as essential sources of truth, it must not be forgotten that the purpose of each is to bring people to Christ. The Book of Mormon is another testament of Jesus Christ. Joseph Smith is a prophet who bore witness of the reality and divinity of Christ, and the Church is His whose name it bears. Thus the triangle would be incomplete without Christ at its very center, for truly He was and is "the way, *the truth*, and the life" (John 14:6, emphasis added).

THE TRIANGLE OF TRUTH

The Book of Mormon:
Another Testament of Jesus Christ

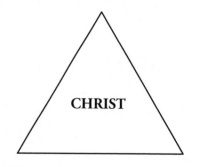

CHRIST

The Church of Jesus Christ   The Prophet Joseph Smith—a
of Latter-day Saints   special witness of Jesus Christ

The basic premise of the Triangle of Truth is simple: gaining a personal witness of the Book of Mormon sets you on a clear course toward securing a testimony of additional pillar truths. Understanding this premise will be a source of great spiritual strength and stability for those you teach.

As you diligently labor to bring fruit to the Savior, Lucifer will be working equally hard to spoil your efforts. Just count on him to send his torrents of opposition, his whirlwinds of confusion, yea, even his fiery darts of temptation (see 1 Nephi 15:24; Helaman 5:12).

One of the adversary's favorite tactics takes aim at the Prophet Joseph Smith. If the devil can demean and discredit Joseph, his goal of spoiling the fruit is greatly advanced. This can happen in a variety of ways. Perhaps a relative or friend will pepper an investigator or new member with questions and information gleaned from anti-Mormon literature. Maybe the investigator will stumble onto a website that twists the facts or even fabricates lies about Joseph. More commonly, an investigator simply may struggle to believe that a fourteen-year-old boy really saw God in vision and was called to be a modern-day prophet. In these vulnerable moments of doubt and confusion, those who are firmly grounded in their testimony of the Book of Mormon will be able to withstand these fiery darts of the adversary, while those who haven't built their foundation upon the Book of Mormon will likely fall.

How does this work? An analogy may be helpful. Imagine a rock climber ascending the face of a steep mountain at a considerable height. Using the proper equipment, the climber drives a metal hold into a crevice of rock and then fastens his harness to this hold using a strong rope. As he begins to climb higher, the metal hold fails: it wasn't strong enough to support his weight. In this perilous moment of free fall, our climber had better hope that he took the time to secure an emergency safeguard hold some ten feet below. If so, the fall will be brief, little or no injury will be incurred, and the journey toward the summit may continue with only a slight interruption. If not, the fall will be long, resulting in serious injury or perhaps even death.

The analogy is easy to decipher. The mountain represents mortality, and the climb toward the summit is our journey upward to eternal life. The climber is the person you are seeking to bring (or have already brought) to the Savior. The metal hold represents their testimony of the Prophet Joseph; the shallow crevice in which the hold was placed signifies any experience or false information that could shake their testimony of the Prophet. The emergency safeguard hold that became a crucial lifeline represents their testimony of the Book of Mormon. If an investigator has a strong testimony of the Book of Mormon, then Satan's deceptive attacks against the Prophet Joseph will do little harm. But if the investigator's testimony of the Book of Mormon is lacking or shallow, these attacks will be spiritually devastating—even fatal.

If Satan is unable to defame the Prophet Joseph, he will most likely shift his attention and cunning to the "only true and living church upon the face of the whole earth" (D&C 1:30). The Church of Jesus Christ of Latter-day Saints is filled with good but imperfect people who are largely trying their best to follow the Savior. Within the Church we learn to work and worship with other members who have different personalities, opinions, talents, backgrounds, and even cultures than our own.

Integrating an investigator or new member into this "life laboratory" can sometimes be a challenging process. They need to be fellowshipped, they need to feel involved, and they need their fledgling faith to be nurtured and strengthened. While the missionaries and members work together to help a new convert assimilate smoothly into a ward or branch, the adversary seeks to exploit and disrupt this process.

Many new members stray because they have taken offense. They may feel that some fellow ward member has been vicious or insensitive in word or deed. They may complain that they are no longer receiving the love and attention they previously enjoyed as investigators. They may observe the faults or weaknesses of other members and use this as an excuse for their own inactivity. In such moments, missionaries will try to help an offended member understand the adage that "the Church is true, but sometimes its members are not." However, this will not be easy unless the converts are rooted to something firm and immovable—something like the Book of Mormon.

If before baptism the missionaries have properly rooted potential converts' testimonies in the Book of Mormon, they will be in a much stronger position to help their precious fruit wade through the moments of spiritual crisis that will surely come. In meeting with a new member who is wavering, they can simply look them in the eye and ask if they know the Book of Mormon is true. Even though the offended individual may be irritated, a smile will probably creep onto their face as they answer, "Of course the book is true; *you know* that I know that." Then the implications of their own words will begin to sink in; you can almost see them visualizing the triangle of truth that you've ingrained into their head.

At this point I've had beloved converts who were struggling say, "I know, I know . . . the Church is true. I'm not going to quit. It's just hard right now; don't worry about me though." Moments such as this furnish missionaries with an excellent teaching opportunity. These infants in the gospel need to realize that Satan is furious with the changes they have made in their lives. He has lost them and is fighting to get them back. But no matter what happens in the branch or ward, no matter what happens with you the missionaries, no matter what happens at all—they will always have the beautiful blue beacon of light and truth. And if they will feast each and every day from its pages, they will never fall.

Whether it be opposition, whether it be offense, whether it be pressure or temptation to return to a former lifestyle, the fruit you bring into the gospel will need something to support the weight of their decision to join the

Church. They'll need something to hold their kindling faith and testimony intact. In sum, they'll need a personal keystone to provide stability along their new path of discipleship. The Book of Mormon has been divinely provided for just this reason. Missionaries who help investigators plant deeply rooted testimonies of the Book of Mormon are anchoring their fruit in the safe harbors and still waters of activity and progression in the Church.

Anchoring our fruit to the Book of Mormon requires a concerted and consistent effort. Sadly, many who are baptized lack the sturdy anchor and deep roots associated with a Book of Mormon–centered conversion. During the teaching process, many things can provide a *temporary* foundation for an investigator's faith and testimony. Some investigators join the Church because they love the missionaries who first brought them the gospel and shared with them sweet life-changing experiences. Others join primarily because of their friendship with the members of their ward or branch. Those who were referred by a member can base their conversion on the person who invited them to hear the gospel message. Still others are attracted to and converted by the wonderful programs of the Church (Primary, youth groups, quorums, Relief Society, etc.).

On the surface there is nothing wrong with any of these scenarios. Investigators should love and admire their missionaries. Investigators should develop an affinity and kinship with the members of their ward or branch. Member referrals are so effective because of the relationship of trust already in place. The programs and standards of the Church should be showcased and highlighted during the teaching process.

The problem comes when these temporary foundations become the *only* foundation for a person's testimony. Converts who seek to build an eternal house of faith upon a temporary foundation are setting themselves up for a tragic fall. A missionary who allows this to happen is not following the strict admonition of the Savior to bring forth fruit that will remain.

When we evaluate these temporary foundations, it quickly becomes apparent that none can support a convert's faith and testimony indefinitely. Missionaries get transferred and eventually return home, ward or branch boundaries may change or friendships may fizzle, the member who referred the investigator may stray and leave the Church, or certain programs may be altered or eliminated. Yet in the midst of all these possibilities for change, the Book of Mormon will remain the same permanent foundation it has been for nearly two hundred years. The divine tool is there: clearly the responsibility now rests upon us to use it more effectively in the Lord's work.

So What Do We Do?

So how do we use the Book of Mormon more effectively as the means of conversion? First, every missionary needs to have and display an infectious love and enthusiasm for the Book of Mormon. If you aren't passionate about the Book of Mormon, don't expect your investigators to be either. Such a love cannot be fake or "for show"; it should also not be distracting or over the top. Instead it should be genuine and inspiring to those around you.

When I teach this to young men and women in a mission prep class setting, I often ask if they've had their own "Parley P. Pratt" experience with the Book of Mormon—not just one good scripture study session or occasional spurts of reading but a prolonged period of time in which they really feasted from its pages. A period where they read not only for a few minutes a day, but for a few hours. A period when their desire to study from the Book of Mormon was equal to or greater than their desire to eat, drink, sleep, hang out with friends, play video games, hold hands with their girlfriend, etc. Have they become so immersed and entranced by what they were reading that they didn't want to stop?

After asking and explaining this first question, I always follow it up with a second question, which I'll put to you, the reader, now. If you haven't yet had your "Parley" experience with the Book of Mormon, *what are you waiting for?* The book is there, just waiting to bring greater light and truth into your life, just waiting to anchor you to Joseph and, more importantly, to Jesus. What are you waiting for?

Developing this authentic love for the Book of Mormon truly is half the battle. Those around you will observe its powerful influence on you and will feel a spark of interest and curiosity in turn. In a very real way your love and testimony of the Book of Mormon can become contagious to hundreds, even thousands, of people. Your example will compel the honest in heart to engage in a serious examination of the book. When this happens, the miracle of conversion rarely lags far behind.

This leads to my next point. A new missionary might wonder if there is a secret that separates and distinguishes successful missionaries. The following thought is not so much a secret, but I do believe it may be the key in bringing forth much fruit that remains true and faithful. Succinctly stated, successful missionaries know how to help investigators *make and keep commitments* (see *Preach My Gospel*, chapter 11).

The Savior emphasized this approach to discipleship when He declared, "If any man will do his will, he shall know of the doctrine, whether it be of God, or whether I speak of myself'" (John 7:17). The formula is not complicated. If gospel inquirers truly desire to *know* whether our message comes from God, there are certain things they must *do*. Consider the supplemental teaching of the apostle James that all must be "doers of the word, and not hearers only" (James 1:22). Further on He warns that any persons who expect to receive knowledge by simply hearing rather than acting are "deceiving your own selves" (James 1:22). Yes, it's a little humbling to the ego, but wise missionaries understand and embrace the reality that an investigator's greatest strides toward conversion occur when the missionaries *aren't* there, rather than when they *are*.

Of the many commitments a missionary will extend to an investigator, none may be of greater import than the practice of daily scripture study from the Book of Mormon. The first few appointments are the ideal time to sow the seeds of this lifelong habit, yet accomplishing this feat is not without challenges. For many people the scriptures are unfamiliar literature. Investigators may feel intimidated by the Book of Mormon and express doubt in their ability to comprehend what they are reading. For this reason missionaries should not hesitate to study alongside those they teach. Doing so will familiarize them with the format, language, and style of the book, helping ease the transition into their own personal study.

When reading the Book of Mormon with investigators, missionaries should model how to find, understand, and apply key principles and doctrines contained therein. Missionaries can also introduce the concept of marking scriptures and writing down insights, feelings, and questions in the margins or in a separate study journal. These joint studies will certainly fortify testimonies and yield sweet spiritual experiences; however, the focus and purpose must remain on preparing the investigators to have meaningful experiences *on their own* with the Book of Mormon. When used for this purpose, these study sessions will nicely complement the lessons from *Preach My Gospel*.

This leads us to our next point: the lessons outlined in *Preach My Gospel* are divinely inspired. When teaching these lessons, missionaries should appeal often to the Book of Mormon for scriptural support of the doctrines being taught. Doing so will illustrate how clearly this additional book of scripture unfolds the plain and precious truths of the gospel. It will also help investigators begin to see how central Christ is to the very purpose of the book.

After each lesson, invite your investigators to read specific Book of Mormon passages that reinforce and expound on what has been taught. Explain the context of these passages in order to facilitate a more meaningful experience.

Before leaving, ask if you can call or visit within a few days to discuss what they have read and answer any questions that may arise. When you return, ensure that the commitment has been fulfilled in a satisfactory manner. If it has not, be supportive and respectful, but do not accept excuses or halfhearted efforts. Instead, use the occasion right then and there to help the investigator fulfill the commitment. After this, extend another commitment and set up a return appointment.

Too many missionaries make the mistake of brushing off an unfulfilled commitment. (I've done it countless times.) By doing so you're sending a dangerous message that the commitment was unimportant in the first place. Nothing could be further from the truth. The commitment to read daily from the Book of Mormon lays the foundation for conversion. Maybe that's why Elder Holland said we should be devastated when learning that someone has failed to read the Book of Mormon (see *Preach My Gospel*, 8). Clearly Elder Holland esteems this commitment as a matter of spiritual life and death, as do all successful missionaries.

In addition to those previously discussed, there are many ways to use the Book of Mormon as the means of sharing the message of the restored gospel. The following suggestions may give you some ideas:

- Never let a visit with an investigator or new member go by without asking how their personal or family reading is going. If it is not going well, do not use guilt trips, manipulation, or be negative in any way. Instead be encouraging, show confidence, and focus on the positive of what *can* happen rather than what *hasn't* happened. Let them know that you'll be asking again, and, for that matter, that they can ask you the same question.
- In your visits with investigators and new members, frequently share things that you are learning from your own personal Book of Mormon study (preferably that morning). Set up a reading program for your investigator or new member, and do it alongside them. This provides a common goal and many opportunities to compare and discuss what you are studying.
- Teach investigators that the answers to life's problems are found within the Book of Mormon. This world is filled with challenges, choices, and trials. Investigators need to understand that the Book of Mormon is essentially a guidebook for life. They need to develop trust in the power of God's word. As a

missionary, you should never be too quick to rush in and solve an investigator's problem. Instead, ask, "Have you turned to the Book of Mormon for help?" and then direct them to its pages for guidance.

- Encourage and invite members of your ward or branch to join you in teaching investigators and new members. When they are present, give them opportunities to share their feelings and testimony of the Book of Mormon. Have them discuss the process by which they gained a testimony of the book and the blessings that have followed. Wise missionaries quickly learn that their investigators relate better to local ward or branch members, especially if the missionary is serving in a foreign country.

- When teaching families with young children, get them involved by using the great Book of Mormon reader for kids. Take it one step further by selecting powerful stories from the Book of Mormon and teaching them in creative and fun ways. One of my favorite mission memories was teaching a family with four kids under the age of eight. My companion and I had so much fun coming up with ways to get those kids excited and involved in our lessons and Book of Mormon reads. We even built little paper boats and tested their seaworthiness in the family's bathtub to help introduce the story of Nephi building the boat. What a blast!

- Never recommend a candidate for baptism if their testimony of the Book of Mormon is shallow and underdeveloped. An investigator's testimony of the Book of Mormon is often an accurate barometer of their preparation for baptism. This doesn't mean that an investigator needs to have memorized Jacob 5 or read the entire book from cover to cover. But they should demonstrate a practice of daily study and be very firm in their knowledge of its truth.

As a missionary, you must honestly evaluate an investigator's progress in obtaining a testimony of the Book of Mormon. Since this testimony is central to conversion, it will have a profound impact on investigators' desire and ability to keep their baptismal covenants. The sacred promises made at baptism entail serious obligations in this life and the next, and missionaries will be held accountable if they knowingly allow someone to be baptized when they are unprepared or unworthy. Now, this shouldn't give you a complex or an anxiety attack. Just focus on deepening your own conversion to the Book of Mormon so you can help others do the same.

These are just a few ways to more fully utilize the Book of Mormon in the teaching process; invariably you will think of others. As a missionary you should do everything in your power to make this book come alive for those you teach. Doing so is worthy of your best efforts.

In conclusion, Joseph Smith declared that "the Book of Mormon [is] the most correct of any book on earth . . . and a man would get nearer to God by abiding by its precepts, than by any other book" (Introduction to the Book of Mormon). Isn't that what we desire for our brothers and sisters scattered throughout the world? For surely the decision to draw closer to God is a decision to enjoy His abundant blessings. Drawing closer to God helps people become better husbands and wives, better parents, better employees, better neighbors. If only every missionary could grasp the potential impact of "flooding" the earth with this book of incomparable value (see Moses 7:62; Ezra Taft Benson, "Flooding the Earth with the Book of Mormon," *Ensign*, Nov. 1988).

It makes me want to write a script for one of those MasterCard commercials. The first scene would be at the Church's production facility and would show hundreds of copies of the Book of Mormon being printed. The voiceover for this scene would be the following: "Cost of printing: two dollars." The next scene would show the books being boxed up and loaded onto trucks, airplanes, boats, trains, scooters, rickshaws, camels, whatever. The voiceover of this scene would be, "Shipping throughout the world, twenty-five dollars." The final scene would show a man on the street receiving a copy of the Book of Mormon from two missionaries and then immediately sitting down on a nearby bench to check it out. The voiceover for this final scene would be, "Value in the hands of a seeker of truth? Priceless!" And so it is: priceless.

The Book of Mormon truly is one of the greatest gifts entrusted to man by a wise and loving Father in Heaven. Its importance in both spreading the message of the restored gospel and aiding the missionary in acquiring the right motivation cannot be overstated. I too can bear testimony of the power of this great sign. I've been an awed witness as it transformed the life of a depressed teenage girl who was atheist and suicidal. From this girl's mouth I heard the miraculous words, "Elder Christiansen, the Book of Mormon saved me!" I've seen modern-day Parley P. Pratts who immediately recognized the Book of Mormon as the missing piece in their puzzle of faith. But even more importantly, I continue to see the power of this book as it anchors me and now my family to Christ and His Church. So why don't you go right now and open it up yourself.

What are you waiting for?

There you have the M&Ms of missionary work. Let's quickly review:

Motivation—*The ultimate motivation in missionary work is the Atonement of Jesus Christ.* Phrased simply it would be, "I've felt the power of the Atonement in my own life, and now I want to help others to feel it as well."

Message—*Our message is that the gospel of Jesus Christ has been restored through the Prophet Joseph Smith.* This message is what makes us distinct and unique from all other churches in the world.

Means—*The means whereby the message of the Restoration should be taught is the Book of Mormon.* Centering the conversion process on the Book of Mormon will help you bring forth fruit and ensure that your fruit will remain steadfast.

SECTION TWO
An Instrument in the Hands of God

Chapter 4

"Be Ye Clean That Bear the Vessels of the Lord"

"Virtuous people are clean and pure spiritually. . . . They obey God's command-ments and follow the counsel of Church leaders. They pray for the strength to resist temptation and do what is right." —Preach My Gospel, 119

Disclaimer: *No chapter in this book will challenge you more than this. If you are comfortable in your current state of righteousness, you might want to skip it. But if you want to become a powerful instrument in the hands of the Lord, there's no getting around what I have to say. Just know that I believe in you, but a million times more importantly, God believes in you. Good luck.*

POWER AND PURITY GO HAND in hand. As a missionary, you personally represent the Lord Jesus Christ. I will never forget that moment when I first put on my name badge and saw my name and the Savior's name so closely aligned. With such a sacred privilege and responsibility pending, now is the time to purge your life of any evil or impure influences. The purpose of this chapter is to help you become aware of these influences and make choices that will enable you to access greater spiritual power.

Music

Whether we recognize it or not, music is an incredibly powerful influence in our lives. Music has the power to invite or offend the Spirit. For this reason music can either be a blessing or a curse in your life. But before we start discussing the *quality* of different music and its influence on you, let's take a moment to discuss the *quantity* of music you listen to.

Today's teenagers have been plugged in from the time they could walk. If you constantly need to be surrounded by noise, it would be wise to remember that you are about to go cold turkey from iPods, MP3 players,

Facebooking with friends, texting, and all other nifty gadgets. Your life is about to produce its *Unplugged* album, and you want it to be good. The Lord instructed His servants in revelation to "be still, and know that I am God" (D&C 101:16). As a prospective missionary, you need to ask yourself, *Am I comfortable in silence? Do I take time to simply ponder and reflect?*

Depending on your answers to these questions, you may need to set aside more time each week for quiet prayer and meditation. By regulating the quantity of music and technology, you can cut through the distractions and noise that so easily drown out the Spirit.

Now let's turn our attention to the *quality* of your music. As a measuring stick we'll use Elder Oaks's brilliant concept of "good, better, and best" ("Good, Better, Best," *Ensign*, Nov. 2007, 104–108).

Good

Good music adds richness and enjoyment to our lives like very few things can. Listening to a good song can instantly improve your mood, put a smile on your face, and make you feel happy and optimistic. Good music does not contain *any* profanity, vulgarity, or suggestive and inappropriate content. It does not dull the senses by its tempo, volume, or style. Good music will never leave you feeling agitated, depressed, tainted, guilty, or out of control.

According to the above criteria, I believe that good music can be found in any genre be it pop, hip-hop, techno, alternative, rock, country, oldies, classical, and maybe even rap. Today I challenge you to scan your iPod or MP3 player and hold each of your songs to the standards above. Yes, you will most likely have to delete some songs—maybe lots of songs. Discipleship starts with discipline and will always require sacrifice and change. If it seems hard, ask yourself, *Do I really value this song more than the companionship of the Holy Ghost, more than the holy priesthood I bear, more than my love for the Savior?* The answer is clear. Please do it!

Better

Better music serves a higher purpose than merely enjoying some tunes. Better music helps you relax when you feel stressed, brings calm when you feel troubled, and replaces pessimism and negativity with optimistic thoughts and feelings. Better music not only entertains, it inspires. While scanning your iPod or MP3 player for songs that don't belong, make sure there's some *better* music sprinkled in among the *good.*

Best

The best music calls down the powers and feelings of heaven to surround us here on earth. The Lord declared, "The song of the righteous is a prayer unto me" (D&C 25:12). The best music brings peace, joy, and comfort. It makes you want to repent, improve, serve others, and fulfill your divine purpose. The best music invites the Spirit and focuses your thoughts and feelings on the Savior. Any iPod or MP3 player devoid of the best music is like a meal with no seasonings or a dinner without dessert. Here's a piece of practical advice. Now that you have all that room on your iPod or MP3 player (from the songs you deleted), why not fill that space with the best music? In fact, for every one song you delete I challenge you to add two songs that should have been there.

TV

In my short lifetime, television has changed from a basically harmless time-waster to a dangerous outlet for worldly images, philosophies, and behaviors: immodesty, sensuality, immorality, cruelty, violence, vulgarity, crudeness, light-mindedness, materialism, vanity, selfishness. Most of the shows on TV are little more than elaborate advertisements for sin.

While I've stated my position very clearly on the sad state of television, I hardly expect you to yank the family's new flat screen off the wall and throw it out the window. Let me offer five simple guidelines that can help you in your television choices:

Never sit down to watch TV if you don't know exactly what you're going to watch (in other words, don't channel surf). Doing so is like playing Russian roulette with your standards. If you want to watch the game, watch the game—but don't loiter around on the tube.

There are certain channels you should just give up entirely. (I don't need to spell them out for you; you know which ones they are.) There is nothing on these channels that is "virtuous, lovely, or of good report or praiseworthy" (Article of Faith 13).

Don't watch TV late at night. It's not a coincidence that networks program their most edgy, crude shows during the hours when viewers' sensibilities are dulled and impaired by exhaustion. Establish a set time when the TV is off limits—the earlier the better.

Just because it's funny doesn't make it acceptable. Sadly, the crudest and most offensive shows are also the funniest and most popular with teenagers.

These shows are extremely casual with the Lord's name and treat lightly many things which are sacred. Watching them will tempt you to adopt the same or similar attitudes. The world needs missionaries who are courageous and clean, not cowardly and compromising.

While doing an inventory of your music library, you should include your TV watching as well. If any of your favorite shows include any of the inappropriate content listed in the first paragraph of this section, now is the time to bid them adieu. Believe me, they're just not worth it.

So when it comes to TV, feel free to watch general conference, *Sesame Street*, the occasional game, clean shows that you could watch with your mom, and any amount of C-Span that you want. But beyond that, you're better off without it.

Movies

Knowing what I said about TV, what do you expect me to say about movies? For the most part, Hollywood today is the Babylon of yesterday. I find it ironic that the older I get the more kids' movies I see. Not just because I have kids, but because they're about the only ones I feel comfortable watching. Everything else is too violent, too vulgar, or too casual with the name of God and the Savior.

What a scam Satan is running with today's cinema! You trade the companionship of the Holy Ghost, priesthood power, peace of conscience, and virtue for a couple of cheap laughs, entertaining action scenes, or a surprise plot twist. Oh, and you pay him $8.50 up front to do so. As a prospective missionary, it's time to wake up. The filth we allow into our minds does not take kindly to eviction notices. While on your mission you will certainly want to "evict" such things but may find it harder than you imagined to do so. I distinctly recall several missionaries expressing regret about their premission media choices. Don't let this be you.

The Savior often warned His disciples of the unholy influences in their lives. He said, "Let them alone: they be blind leaders of the blind. And if the blind lead the blind, both shall fall into the ditch" (Matthew 15:14). Hollywood is the blindest of the blind guides. And, sadly, it's leading many LDS youth and adults right off the edge of a steep cliff.

Internet Usage

Ditto everything I said about TV and movies, but consider the warning even stronger. The adversary would love nothing more than to derail your future mission using the lure of Internet pornography. If you have a computer with the Internet in your room, put this book down, go grab the monitor and throw it out your window (but be careful not to hit anyone below). Nothing makes Satan's job easier than a private computer with unfiltered access to the world's filth. Make it a practice to only use the family computer and avoid being on late at night. Do not surf the Web. It wastes time and opens you up to temptation. The funny YouTube video or Facebook friend isn't worth exposing yourself to surrounding smut. The adage "better safe than sorry" should always guide your Internet and computer use.

Gaming

It's been said that you can tell a lot about a man by the way he uses his free time. If that's true, the gaming trend of the past decade is a telling indicator that the bar has not fully been raised by many of our missionaries.

Maybe today's youth and parents justify excessive gaming because "there are a lot worse things we/they could be doing." But, c'mon, is that really the standard we should be applying to this most valiant generation of spirits? Shouldn't we replace that terrestrial standard with "What better things should we/they be doing?" Think about the greatest missionaries this world has ever known. Can you really imagine Ammon and his brothers staying up all night playing Halo the week before they headed out to teach the Lamanites?

I'll admit it; I don't get this one at all. I don't see how anyone could justify or feel comfortable wasting so much time in a dark basement playing a game that has absolutely no significance or meaning in real life. The scriptures warn that the devil will seek to cheat men's souls (see 2 Nephi 28:21). Surely an obsession with video or computer games is one of Satan's most successful ways to cheat a young man's soul.

The excessive amount of time spent playing would make these games bad enough, but the content of the games makes this issue something far more serious. Think about it. Most of the video games popular with teenage boys are graphically violent. You are not only watching life being taken, you are participating in the act. Exposing yourself to this type of entertainment desensitizes you to things that are clearly wrong. Never forget that murder is the most serious of all sins. The blatant disregard for life depicted in many video games is extremely offensive to the Spirit. When you choose to play these violent games, you do so at the expense of the companionship of the Holy Ghost.

Video games are also addictive. Similar to pornography, these games produce a powerful chemical stimulus in the brain that is difficult to overcome. They are specifically designed to keep you playing for long stretches of time and to keep you coming back for more. I know I've already said it, but the amount of time some of our Aaronic Priesthood holders spend "gaming" is ridiculous. They become out of touch with the real world and preoccupied and obsessed with the virtual gaming world.

So here Satan has a powerful tool that deprives you of the Spirit, is addictive, and wastes countless hours of time diverting you from far more important things that you should be doing. Are you still failing to see the problem here?

Now, I know what you're thinking: you're terrified I'm going to ask you to give up your precious video games cold turkey. Sorry to be so predictable, but if a game is violent or contains any content that is offensive to the Spirit, I strongly suggest you give it up.

However, I realize there are lots of fun, appropriate games out there too. With these games, I propose the simple rule: time for time. Every second spent on the PlayStation 2, Xbox, Wii, or computer needs to be matched by time spent in the scriptures or *Preach My Gospel.* Isn't that the least the Lord deserves?

Relationships

I saved perhaps the hardest one for last. Preparing for missionary work means preparing for missionary rules. As a missionary you are *never* to be alone with a member of the opposite gender for any reason other than a baptismal interview (and even then your companion is waiting vigilantly right outside the door). I repeat, preparing for missionary work means preparing for missionary rules. There is absolutely no reason for you to be alone in a romantic situation with a girl before your mission. Period. If you can't double or group date, don't go. I see far too many prospective missionaries getting way too comfortable in these types of relationships when they should be focusing on other things.

I know there are a lot of you reading this who think I'm going overboard. You're rolling your eyes and shrugging off my advice. In your mind, you think you and your girlfriend are both righteous and you're obviously going on a mission, so nothing inappropriate could ever happen. There's just one problem: it does happen, and it happens every day. Satan brought down mighty King David because he got a little too confident in his own righteousness and a little too lax in his obedience. The same goes for you: The moment you begin to think you're the exception to rules and standards is the moment you are primed for a major fall.

I know I'm extreme, but blame the adversary. He's the one who knows you're on the verge of entering the Lord's ranks. He sees all the people you will help bring into the Church. He hates you for your virtue, for your priesthood, and most of all for your desire to bring souls to his enemy—the Lord Jesus Christ. Do you naively think Satan's going to let you coast your way into the MTC without multiple last-ditch efforts to knock you off track?

Wake up! Like a wounded animal, the adversary's going to come at you with everything he's got. Having a steady girlfriend is like handing Satan a powerful piece of ammunition right before he launches a major assault. Not wise. In fact, pretty dang stupid. So if a certain young lady is the type of girl you should be dating, she'll not only understand your new standards, but she'll also agree with you one million percent. So let me review: unless she's a sister, cousin, or cousin twice removed, don't be alone together.

At an early conference of the Church the Lord instructed his elders to "go ye out from among the wicked. Save yourselves. Be ye clean that bear the vessels of the Lord" (D&C 38:42). In order to be a powerful instrument in the hands of the Lord you must be clean. The "vessels" entrusted to you are the hearts, minds, and souls of men. God is trusting you to be a literal representative of His Son Jesus Christ. Please decide right now to live worthy of this trust.

If anything in this chapter has bothered you, it's time to turn to the Lord and ask what He would have you do. Please don't wait. The greatest items you can bring to the MTC are clean hands, a pure heart, and a clear conscience.

Chapter 5
Faith and the Missionary

"Faith is a principle of power. God works by power, but His power is usually exercised in response to faith. . . . Doubt and fear are opposed to faith."
—Preach My Gospel, 116

LONG BEFORE SERVING AS THE fourth president of the Church, Wilford Woodruff was one of the first missionaries called to labor in the British Isles. Arriving at Liverpool, he received the assignment to preach in the Staffordshire potteries region of central England and was soon enjoying great success. The people responded favorably to the message of the restored gospel, and many were baptized.

One evening, while conducting a meeting with a large congregation, Wilford heard a voice. He records the following in his journal: "While singing the first hymn the spirit of the Lord rested upon me and the voice of God said to me, 'This is the last meeting that you will hold with this people for many days'" (Matthias F. Cowley, *Wilford Woodruff: His Life and Labors* [Salt Lake City: Deseret Book Company, 1909], 116). This must have been a confusing prompting for Wilford. The work was prospering among the people of Staffordshire; why would God ask him to leave?

Praying to receive further direction, Wilford felt impressed to travel south to the little town of Herefordshire. Upon arrival, he met a prominent resident named John Benbow, who had organized a community of people seeking greater light and truth from God. Without delay, Elder Woodruff asked permission to preach to these people, and a cottage meeting was quickly assembled. He spent the remainder of that day and night imparting the sweet truths of the restored gospel. But even more telling is what he did next. He writes, "I spent most of the following day in clearing out a pool of water and preparing it for baptizing, as I saw that many would receive that ordinance" (*Wilford Woodruff*, 117).

Wilford Woodruff understood that faith is a principle of action. By toiling the following day to prepare a location suitable for baptism, he demonstrated great faith in the message he was called to bear. As the residents of this community observed his labor and perhaps inquired what he was doing, they came to know that Wilford truly believed they would accept the fullness of the gospel. Furthermore, his actions became a token between him and God that he was serious in his desire to administer the ordinances of salvation. The result of Wilford's faith is one of the greatest stories in Church history. He writes, "I afterwards baptized six hundred persons in that pool of water" *(Wilford Woodruff,* 117). Is it any wonder that God had reserved such a bountiful harvest for this faithful servant?

Nearly everything a missionary does requires great faith. Leaving your home for two years, getting on the plane when you can't speak the language, knocking on your first door, approaching a family in the park, speaking to a man on a silent bus, visiting an inactive member—and on and on it goes. Faith to the spirit of a missionary is like blood to the body. Just as a sufficient supply of healthy blood brings life to the body, so it is spiritually with faith. Thus, anyone who would seek to become an instrument in the Lord's hands must be filled with faith. With this in mind, there are certain things that enhance faith and certain things that diminish it. Let's look at a few of them.

Prayer

Our first faith enhancer is obvious: frequent and sincere prayer. In one of his Psalms, King David noted that "the eyes of the Lord are upon the righteous, *and his ears are open unto their cry*" (Psalm 34:15; emphasis added). Prayer is the means whereby man and woman communicate with an all-powerful Father in Heaven. This divine communication allows missionaries to gain confidence in God's ability to magnify their own efforts. Prayer will confirm that this is His work, that He is in control, and that He will help you. Through prayer you will come to know that the God you serve *is* a God of miracles and that *nothing* is impossible to Him.

On my mission I had a unique experience that provided a valuable lesson on prayer. I'd been in the country for only a few months and was looking forward to an upcoming combined zone conference. The conference was held at our chapel in Bucharest with three zones (approximately fifty missionaries) in attendance. This conference was especially exciting because our Area President, Elder D. Lee Tobler, had traveled from Germany and would be presiding.

Before coming, Elder Tobler had issued an interesting request. He wanted the three zone leaders and ten district leaders to prepare brief presentations detailing the statistical performance of their missionaries. As the first zone leader stood up and began his presentation, Elder Tobler arose from his seat, descended from the stand, leaned up against the doorway, and then listened intently to the elder's report. When the missionary concluded, Elder Tobler gazed at him for a long moment and then said, "Elder, the Spirit is telling me to tell you that your zone would be greatly blessed *if* you'd begin obeying the mission rules with exactness." He continued to reprimand this elder and then admonished him to accept the counsel that had been given. He concluded with a word of encouragement and expressed confidence in his ability to lead.

The chapel was silent. We were all stunned by what we had just seen. Elder Tobler called for the next presentation to begin, and, trembling, another missionary stood up and began to give his accounting. When he finished, Elder Tobler again paused for a moment, staring directly at this missionary, then said, "Elder, the Spirit is telling me to tell you that you and your fellow laborers are serving as true representatives of the Lord Jesus Christ and that the Lord Himself is aware of your efforts and pleased with your devotion."

On and on it went for nearly an hour, with some missionaries receiving approval and others reproof. But each time the opening statement was the same: "Elder, the Spirit is telling me to tell you . . . " or "Elder, I feel impressed to tell you . . . " Needless to say I had never seen anything like this man. It was amazing how completely in tune he was with the Holy Ghost. During this conference he spoke to us twice, and both talks were powerful and inspiring.

Finally, in the late afternoon, he concluded with a soul-stirring testimony of the divinity of God's work and the importance of magnifying our callings. He sat down and immediately began whispering something urgent to our mission president. President Jarvis hastily scribbled down notes on the program then stood up and made the following announcement: "Elders and sisters, we have been greatly blessed today by the instruction we've received from Elder Tobler. We appreciate him traveling from Germany to be with us. Elder Tobler has now expressed the desire to conduct personal interviews with a select few of you. He will be interviewing the following missionaries . . ."

Now before I continue with the story, let me interject for a moment. As soon as President Jarvis announced that Elder Tobler was going to be interviewing missionaries the entire chapel seemed to fill with anxiety and dread. Yes, he was a spiritual giant, but he was also very intimidating. No one wanted to be chosen. It was almost as if you could hear the silent prayers: *Please don't be me! Please don't be me!*

While I shared the foreboding sentiment of those around me, I was also realistic and figured that my chances of being chosen were slim to none. There were over fifty missionaries in the room, and I had only been in the country for a few months. I was unknown to basically everyone and was certain that Elder Tobler would want to interview the more important missionaries. In other words, I considered myself safe.

Back to the story and my mission president at the pulpit.

"Before I read the names of the four missionaries, Elder Tobler asked that I mention these missionaries were selected through inspiration. Elder _____ [a zone leader], Elder _____ [the other zone leader; *see, my prediction was right*], Elder _____ [a missionary who was departing for home the following week], and finally . . . Elder Christiansen. That will be all. Will those four missionaries please wait outside the branch president's office where they will have their interviews with Elder Tobler? Thank you."

As soon as my name was called, my companion gasped, turned to me, and said accusingly, "What did you do?" I sat in shock. Certainly I had misunderstood. Surely he had not said my name. Quickly I scanned all fifty missionaries hoping to find an Elder Christensen or Christopherson— someone with a name similar to mine whom he intended to interview but was not me.

No luck. It was me.

The other forty-six missionaries breathed a collective sigh of relief and were now casually socializing with each other. Occasionally someone would pass by me or one of the other "interview" missionaries and offer their condolences at our fate. One missionary expressed sympathy and then with a tinge of fear said, "I wouldn't want any piece of that guy."

Elder Tobler eventually got off the stand and walked past us to the branch president's office; we followed behind in single file. I felt like I was going to the firing squad. As we walked he informed us that he would conduct the interviews in the order announced at the pulpit, which meant I would be last. Each interview took about fifteen minutes, so I had nearly an hour to sit and wait with my thoughts.

This was not helpful.

Every sin I had ever committed, every evil thought I'd ever had, every character flaw I possessed—all resurfaced with a vengeance to the forefront of my mind.

With only moments to go before I was up, my head finally started to clear and I began to reassess the situation. Maybe it wouldn't be so bad. In fact, maybe I was looking at this all wrong and I should be excited that I had been chosen. I was going to have the privilege of speaking one-on-one with a General Authority. No, I wasn't perfect, but I hadn't committed any grievous sins. This would be a once-in-a-lifetime opportunity!

Just as these optimistic thoughts began filling me with hope, the door opened and the missionary who had just been interviewed stepped out. His eyes were red and his face stained with tears. Not happy, joyful, woman-on-her-wedding-day tears but stereotypical I-just-left-the-bishop's-office-and-won't-be taking-the-sacrament-till-I'm-ninety kind of tears. Instantly my optimism faded, leaving only one thought behind: *Who am I kidding? This guy is going to eat me alive.*

I warily entered the small office and sat in the seat across from Elder Tobler. The interview began. All I can say is that the interview was nothing like I imagined it would be. Elder Tobler had such an amazing ability to put me at ease and show genuine love and concern. The twenty minutes we spent together were almost like receiving another patriarchal blessing. He seemed to know so much about my past and even began describing things that would occur in my near and distant future. It was amazing!

As the interview was winding down and pleasantries were being exchanged, I stood up to leave when he stopped me. "Elder Christiansen, I actually do have one more question for you." By this point I had become so comfortable that I didn't think anything of it.

"Sure," I said.

He looked at me for a second and then said, "Elder Christiansen, tell me about your prayers."

Inwardly I cringed. Recently my personal prayers had become extremely casual and insincere. Our companionship prayers were even worse and bordered on light-mindedness most of the time. Of all the questions, why did he have to ask this one? Our interview had gone so well, and now I was going to spoil it and leave a bitter taste in his mouth.

As I reluctantly confessed to Elder Tobler the pathetic state of my prayers, I'll never forget his response. He looked down for a moment, a long moment that felt like an eternity. I braced myself for a severe verbal lashing, but when he finally looked up I was stunned. He was not angry or even upset; instead his eyes were moist with tears and filled with sadness. He paused for a moment to regain his composure and then, in a quiet tone, said something I'll never forget: "Elder Christiansen, you've got to guard your prayers; you've got to guard them." He smiled kindly at me, gave me a warm embrace, and the interview was over.

Exiting the office I felt like I'd matured several years. I had a burning desire to find my journal so I could write down the feelings and details of this powerful experience. At the end of that journal entry I recorded two lessons that I learned about prayer:

Lesson #1: I had only been personally acquainted with Elder Tobler for the span of minutes, yet the impression his pained response left upon me was unforgettable. If you're like me then you'd rather that those you care about be angry rather than disappointed with you. In that moment Elder Tobler was not only disappointed, he was also deeply hurt; and seeing this genuine expression of sorrow and pain cut me to the very center. In an instant I realized that his reaction was only a glimpse into how my Heavenly Father must be feeling. Thankfully, Elder Tobler was inspired enough to not only give me such a vivid lesson, but also a piece of counsel that could guide me in my desire to change and improve. This leads us to lesson number two.

Lesson #2: I will never forget the instruction I received that day to *guard my prayers.* Sensing that it was important, I began thinking a lot about that phrase to see what deeper meanings it might carry. The first thing I realized is that people only guard objects they consider to be of great worth. My current approach and attitude toward prayer were clearly sending the wrong message that prayer was of little value to me. I instantly saw the gravity of this mistake. What could be of greater value to a missionary than direct communication with God?

My focus then shifted to the question of *how* people guard things of great value. Brainstorming, I realized that people given the charge to guard and protect things of great value must be alert and focused, vigilant and serious. Moreover, they should devote their full attention to the task at hand, allowing no distractions or diversions to set them off course. These were the changes I knew I had to make in my personal and companionship prayers. As I did so, my faith was dramatically strengthened, bringing me greater power in serving the Lord.

Scripture Study

In addition to prayer, immersing yourself in the scriptures is another powerful way to develop and strengthen faith. In a letter to the Saints in Rome, the apostle Paul taught, "So then faith cometh by hearing, and hearing by the word of God" (Romans 10:17). How exactly does this work? To begin with, daily scripture study is one of the most effective ways to invite the Spirit into your life. The constant companionship of the Holy Ghost may be the single greatest enhancer of faith.

Beyond that, the scriptures contain a wealth of stories in which men and women had to exercise great faith. Enoch was young, slow of speech, and hated by the people, but he believed in God's ability to compensate for his weaknesses and through faith founded the city of Zion. Abraham's very heart must have broken at the thought of sacrificing his son, yet the faith he exercised on Mount Moriah further cemented the mighty covenant he had made with God. The mother of Moses nudged the basket containing her infant son into the murky waters of the Nile; surely this was a noble woman who possessed great faith in the God of Israel. The examples are seemingly numberless: from David and Goliath to Daniel in the lions' den, from Peter walking on water to Nephi building a boat.

Each of these stories detail courageous men and women who exhibited faith in the face of trying circumstances. Daily exposure to these stories is like receiving a daily injection of faith. Furthermore, the stories found in the scriptures can serve as "case studies" designed for close study and inspection. Analyzing such stories, you can see the faith-testing circumstances confronting the scriptural character, the way they respond, and the result. Time and time again, students of the scriptures will observe that those who put their faith in God see His hand manifest in mighty ways.

One of my favorite faith stories comes from the Book of Mormon. Alma the Younger had many instances in his life that required great faith, but perhaps none was greater than his confrontation with Korihor in Alma 30. You'll recall that Korihor was an anti-Christ preaching with great success among the Nephites. His message was simple: There was no God, there would be no Christ, and life should be enjoyed without the cumbersome restriction of commandments and standards. He viciously attacked the Church and its leaders, claiming they taught and clung to such false traditions solely to maintain power and control over the people (see Alma 30:27).

Korihor's confrontation with Alma came via Korihor's attempt to preach among the people of Ammon and then to the righteous inhabitants of Gideon. Though Korihor had misled many Nephites in other areas, these good Saints knew a skunk when they smelled one and took decisive action. The people of Ammon bound Korihor, carried him to the outskirts of town, and kindly sent him on his way. The people of Gideon took it a step further. They arrested Korihor and brought him before the chief judge, who in turn delivered him to Alma. Alma knew there were no legal grounds in detaining Korihor but saw this as an opportunity to reach out to this blinded and confused soul. Korihor's intentions were far less noble. He knew that Alma was revered as a prophet among the people. If he could somehow discredit their prophet, his efforts at destroying the Church would be greatly advanced. Thus this encounter quickly escalated into an epic showdown of good versus evil.

To fully appreciate Alma's faith, you have to put yourself in the story as if the drama were unfolding before your eyes. Let's imagine we are Alma's guards watching it all take place. The pivotal moment of the exchange comes as Korihor demands a sign. He claims that if Alma will show him a sign, he'll believe. Alma counters, "I have all things as a testimony that these things are true; and ye also have all things as a testimony unto you that they are true" (Alma 30:41) but adds that such signs go unnoticed and unheeded by the spiritually blind and hardhearted. Yet again Korihor blasphemes by denying the existence of God, and Alma has heard enough.

Seeing that Korihor is spiritually comatose and desires to prey upon the testimonies of others, Alma warns that if Korihor denies once more, he will be struck dumb. Korihor immediately responds with the taunting reply: "I do not deny the existence of a God, but I do not believe that there is a God; and I say also, that ye do not know that there is a God; and except ye show me a sign, I will not believe" (Alma 30:48).

Here is the moment of truth for Alma. Korihor has mocked God and is clearly baiting him into following through on his previous warning. Obviously Korihor doesn't believe in miracles and thus shows no fear or concern that Alma can or will strike him dumb. As for Alma, the stakes are incredibly high. This man Korihor represents the single biggest threat to the peace and stability of the Church. If in this instant his faith wavers, if for some reason he utters the decree for Korihor to be struck dumb and nothing happens, the results will be disastrous. In his mind's eye, he had to see the scene that would unfold: He knew Korihor would immediately leave the judgment hall, run out into the city square, and clamor for all of the people of Zarahemla to gather together. Once a sizable multitude had assembled, he would begin his smug little show:

"My dear fellow citizens, you are familiar with me and my unceasing efforts to bring greater enlightenment and wisdom to you. Though many of you have resisted my message, new developments have recently occurred that may change your minds.

"Just moments ago, I had the chance to converse with your so-called prophet, Alma. Of course, I took the opportunity to try to enlighten him as I have so many of you. I told him there was no God and that his belief was the effect of a frenzied mind. I told him that life is to be enjoyed, not wasted in keeping concocted and pointless commandments. And most importantly, I told him that his days of deceiving you, the people, were quickly coming to an end.

"Do you know what he said to me?

"He said that if I continued sharing my message of true freedom and enlightenment and if I denied the existence of his fantasy God one more time, he would strike me dumb. Knowing there is no God, I fearlessly repeated my previous assertions, upon which he invoked the name and power of his God and commanded me to be struck dumb."

(At this point, Korihor would pause for dramatic effect, and a sinister smile would spread across his face.)

"Well, do I look struck dumb to you? I don't think so. C'mon, people, take the blinders off; can't you see it's a sham? If there were a God, don't you think He would support His supposed prophet? The only other alternative is the one I've been teaching. There is no God! There is no Christ! There is no sin! *There should be no church!*"

I have a feeling that in a split second, Alma is able to see all of this unfold in his mind: the jubilant Korihor, a confused people, the resulting crisis of faith. Yet with the stakes astronomically high and the prospect of a spiritual catastrophe looming, Alma doesn't hedge; he doesn't waver. He shows absolute faith and confidence, and the result is one of the most powerful miracles in the entire Book of Mormon: "Now Alma said unto him: This will I give unto thee for a sign, that thou shalt be struck dumb, according to my words; and I say, that in the name of God, ye shall be struck dumb, that ye shall no more have utterance. Now when Alma had said these words, Korihor was struck dumb, that he could not have utterance, according to the words of Alma" (Alma 30:49–50).

Because of Alma's unshakable faith, Korihor's destructive influence ceased and order and harmony were restored to the Church.

Do you see how studying a story like that could benefit a missionary during the morning hours? Soon that same missionary will be leaving his apartment to begin proselytizing for the day. While working he will most likely encounter resistance and opposition of his own. When this adversity comes, how powerful would it be to have the story of Alma confronting Korihor still burning in his mind and heart? To know that God does support His servants—especially in extreme moments of difficulty? Take advantage of every precious second you have to feast upon the words contained in the standard works. Doing so will provide a rich source of much-needed faith.

Obedience

Obedience to mission rules is another prerequisite to strong faith. The Prophet Joseph Smith revealed that "when we obtain any blessing from God, it is by obedience to that law upon which it is predicated" (D&C 130:21). Thus exact obedience to mission rules enables God to bless His servants with an abundance of faith. Conversely, elders and sisters who show disregard for mission rules will not have the faith necessary to preach the gospel with power and conviction. Simply put, disobedience kills faith.

Sadly, I can attest to the truth of this principle. One morning my companion and I left our apartment several hours late. Breakfast had stretched too long, some phone calls had turned from mission business to social chitchatting, and we were just sluggish getting out. When we finally left the apartment we knew full well that we could not honestly ask God to bless us with His Spirit. We had not held companionship study, and our personal studies had been distracted and ineffective. As we descended the three flights of stairs down to the entrance of our apartment building, I remember hoping that we wouldn't have an opportunity to share the gospel that morning. Can you imagine that! Do you see the toll of disobedience?

Opening the door, we walked down our main porch and immediately intersected with the most beautiful family. My heart sank. Should we stop them even though we weren't prepared? We really didn't even have the option because we basically ran right into them. Solely out of duty, I asked if they would be interested in a religious message, and they enthusiastically replied, "Yes!"

I began to speak, but words would not come. The message was disjointed; there was no power. Seeing my struggles, my companion jumped in and tried his best to clarify what I had said, but he only muddled things further. When we extended the invitation to hear more of the message the father politely declined and abruptly ushered his family away.

Watching this family walk away, I experienced a wave of guilt, embarrassment, and reproof that pierced me to the very core. It was obvious that they would have responded to the message of the restored gospel had we been able to share it with faith and conviction. It was obvious that they were honorable, successful, stable people—just the type of family our struggling little branch needed. Even more, it was painfully obvious that their appearance at the exact moment when we had just exited our apartment was not a coincidence. Both my companion and I realized that this family had been sent to teach us a very difficult and painful lesson. If we were to continue in our lazy and sloppy ways, the consequence would be a withdrawal of power. We wholeheartedly pledged a renewed commitment to morning obedience and, as a result, received again the blessings we so heavily depended upon.

From the moment you enter the MTC to the moment you board the plane to come home, you must be filled with faith. Situations often arise unexpectedly that require a missionary to exercise great faith. Just as Alma didn't have his confrontation with Korihor scheduled on his daily planner, neither will you have the luxury of forewarning for many of your faith-testing situations. The following story illustrates this point.

On a winter afternoon a missionary companionship left their apartment to contact people on the street. Street contacting was a staple in their mission, so this was something they had done literally hundreds of times. They soon saw an approaching gentleman, stopped him, and began to introduce the message of the restored gospel. While speaking, they noticed that the man was wearing medical scrubs underneath his coat. There was a hospital nearby so they asked if he happened to work there. He shook his head then timidly confessed that he was actually a patient at that hospital.

He proceeded to tell the missionaries that he had recently been very ill and was diagnosed with a rare disease. The doctors had admitted him to a wing of the hospital for cases such as his, together with others who suffered from incurable ailments. Once a week he was permitted to leave the hospital grounds to pick up a prescription from a nearby pharmacy, and he felt it extremely fortunate to have met the missionaries on his brief excursion out.

The elders didn't quite know what to do and were actually looking for a tactful way to end the conversation and move along to other prospects. They went to wish him the best but were caught off guard by what happened next. The man expressed sincere interest and asked if they'd be willing to share their message with him and all his fellow patients in the quarantined wing. Unnerved at the thought of entering such a place, yet not knowing how to politely decline, the missionaries soon found themselves accompanying this man toward the hospital complex. Arriving at the gates, they navigated the hospital's outer perimeter and followed him to a building that was isolated and tucked away on a far corner of the property.

When they entered, they found an enormous room that was open in the middle, with beds jutting out from each of the four walls. Gazing into the faces of the surprised patients, the missionaries tried hard to suppress the feelings of uneasiness and anxiety that were rapidly growing. From a simple glance it was obvious that these people were in bad shape. Many of them had been diagnosed with terminal illnesses. Some were badly disfigured, with others suffering from severe skin diseases. The man led them to the center of the room, stood on a chair, and announced in a loud voice that he had brought some missionaries from America who were now going to share a message with the entire group. He promptly got down, returned to his own bed, and then waited with all the other patients for the visitors to speak.

Having no other options, one of the elders shakily stood up on the chair and began to share the first lesson. After teaching a few principles, he got down, and his companion picked up from where he left off. On and on they continued in this manner until they arrived at the end of the lesson. Despite the unusual teaching environment, these missionaries were surprised to note the Spirit enter powerfully as they taught. When they had completed the lesson, both missionaries closed with their testimonies, and then the senior companion volunteered to offer a prayer as a signal that they had reached their conclusion.

After the prayer the missionaries thanked the group for their time and attention and then went to make a graceful exit. Yet as the elders were gathering up their backpacks to leave, they noticed the man whom they had originally met going from bed to bed, whispering to his fellow patients. After consulting nearly everyone, he intercepted the missionaries at the door and asked if they could stay for just a moment longer. Confused, they nodded their heads and made their way back to the center of the room.

What followed next was a missionary moment that completely stunned these elders. In front of everyone the man said, "We have all felt the power of your message and believe that it truly comes from God. As you began, we couldn't help but notice that you introduced yourselves as personal representatives of the Lord Jesus Christ. We are a Christian people who believe in Christ and are familiar with His life's work. Throughout His ministry Jesus healed those who were sick and afflicted. He even had power to raise the dead. I have discussed it with my fellow patients, and we would like you to heal us."

These missionaries were absolutely floored. They could not believe the situation they were in. *What were they supposed to do?* Only an hour earlier they had set out from their apartment to do one of the most mundane and routine missionary activities. Now they were in a quarantined section of a hospital, facing a room full of gravely ill persons who expected to be healed. Both missionaries offered silent prayers, but no direction seemed to come.

Not knowing what to do, the senior companion finally broke the heavy silence and spoke: "The message that we shared with you does come from God, and we are true representatives of Jesus Christ . . . but . . . we just don't have the faith to heal you at this time." A sense of disappointment and shattered expectation quickly spread throughout the room. The man then ushered them to the door, politely thanked them, turned, and was gone.

The missionaries wandered aimlessly for a period of time, shaken by the experience they had just had. Soon they found themselves at the exact spot where they had first stopped the man. Only a few hours had elapsed, but they felt so different.

This was a true story that happened to a close missionary colleague of mine. I first heard him recount this experience while we were teaching together at the MTC. I never once saw him share the story without becoming extremely emotional. This friend of mine was an extremely obedient, diligent, and successful missionary; but it was evident that he was still haunted by the events of that day.

Now, I do not include this story to scrutinize or criticize this elder and his companion. I can't imagine how difficult that moment must have been, and I know that if this particular missionary felt inadequate, I would have felt doubly so. My purpose in sharing the story is to illustrate a much broader point: *As a missionary you never know when you will be called upon to tap into your storage of faith.* For this reason a missionary must constantly be doing those things that nurture and strengthen faith.

When new missionaries would arrive in Romania, my companion and I wouldn't ask them how their language skills were or how well they had learned the missionary lessons. Instead we would ask a single question: "How's your faith?" If a missionary will utilize the power of prayer, search the scriptures, and obey mission rules with exactness, their faith will be like that of the ancients: sufficient to meet any trials, challenges, or opposition.

Chapter 6
"The Spirit Giveth Life"

"You need to seek and receive personal revelation through the Holy Ghost as you help people become baptized and confirmed. Have faith that you will receive personal revelation to guide you day to day. The Holy Ghost will help you in every aspect of your work." —Preach My Gospel, 90

IMAGINE THE SCENE WHEN FATHER Lehi gathered his sons and informed them that they needed to make a return trip to Jerusalem. The Lord had spoken and issued the command to get the brass plates from Laban.

We learn from the scriptural account that Laman and Lemuel were not happy. Why hadn't their dad remembered to do this before they left? How were they supposed to get these plates, and why did they need them anyway? In contrast, Nephi responded by giving the now famous reply: "I will go and do the things which the Lord hath commanded, for I know that the Lord giveth no commandments unto the children of men, save he shall prepare a way for them that they may accomplish the thing which he commandeth them" (1 Nephi 3:7).

Despite Nephi's optimism, actually obtaining the plates proved much more formidable. The little band of brothers made two attempts, first relying on pure chance and then banking on the allure of worldly riches. However, both of these attempts derailed badly, and Lehi's sons barely escaped Laban's palace with their lives.

Taking refuge within a cave outside the city walls, Laman and Lemuel turned nasty. They began beating Nephi with a rod until an angel came to intercede on his behalf. The angel stiffly rebuked the two elder brothers for their rebellion and announced that the Lord would deliver Laban into their hands. Seconds after the angel's departure, we find Laman and Lemuel murmuring, but Nephi had received the message loud and clear: God would provide the way (see 1 Nephi 3:28–31).

That moment must have been crucial in Nephi's divine tutoring. In spite of his youth, he had thus far demonstrated an impressive desire to become acquainted with and obey the commandments of God. Now he needed to learn what it meant to follow the Spirit. Doing so under such circumstances would require a tremendous amount of faith, trust, and courage.

It is important to note that the angel did not give Nephi a detailed explanation of *how* Laban would be delivered into his hands. He didn't say, "Look, Nephi, we've already made all the arrangements. Laban's had a little too much to drink tonight, so he'll be completely out of commission. This is where you'll find him; this is what you'll need to do . . ." Nephi knew none of this as he entered the city under the cover of darkness. He had absolutely no idea how things were going to unfold; and perhaps this was the very lesson the Lord had intended for his spiritual development.

The scriptures describe what followed: "I, Nephi, crept into the city and went forth towards the house of Laban. *And I was led by the Spirit, not knowing beforehand the things which I should do*"(1 Nephi 4:5–6; emphasis added). That is a valuable passage for missionaries to consider. As previously discussed, Nephi didn't know exactly how everything was going to work out. He had to put trust in the Spirit. Nephi's determination to do so is illustrated in the brief but powerful line that follows: "Nevertheless I went forth" (1 Nephi 4:7).

As a missionary you'll receive many promptings. Many will make logical sense, but some will not. There will be promptings that seem irrational or unreasonable. You may even doubt whether they come from God at all. Like with Nephi on the dark streets of Jerusalem, these are the promptings that will really test your faith to follow.

I received such a prompting as a missionary. The Romania Bucharest Mission also includes the beautiful country of Moldova. Moldova lies northeast of Romania, and the border between these two countries is heavily monitored and extremely secure. During the last portion of my mission I traveled around the country with my mission president and would enter Moldova on a monthly basis. At the time, the Church's status was extremely tenuous in this country. Suspicion of all foreign churches was high, and in spite of our persistent efforts, the Church had not been granted official recognition. Instead, the Church operated under the legal title of an association and trod very carefully to maintain positive relations and standing with the Moldovan government.

Due to these circumstances, we approached each trip through the border with extreme caution. We were careful to remove from sight any paraphernalia associating us with the Church (i.e., name badges, copies of the Book of Mormon, pamphlets, etc.) and would occasionally change into civilian clothes so as not to attract undue attention to ourselves. Our code of conduct at the border was simple: blend into the scenery, be as inconspicuous as possible, and avoid doing anything stupid!

No matter how careful we were in our border etiquette, a border crossing was never uneventful. A review of my passport shows that I crossed back and forth between the Romanian/Moldovan border sixteen times, and not once do I remember it going smoothly. It was always nerve-racking; it was always tense. Invariably complications, glitches, or run-ins of some fashion would occur. Still to this day the Moldovan/Romanian border ranks as one of my least favorite places on earth.

As vivid as these border crossings remain in my mind, one day stands out in particular. The previous night we had held a conference in Chişinău (the capital city of Moldova) and woke up early the next morning to head back into Romania. Arriving at the border we saw a line of about twenty cars, which from previous experience meant about a two-hour wait. Border waits were just another element of this dreadful place that I absolutely loathed. The average wait was over an hour, but on one occasion we sat there for nearly six. Time at the border seemed to stand still, and with no radio or music to enjoy, boredom set in very quickly.

So there we were, stuck in an unmoving line. I was driving the mission van, and President Jarvis was in the front passenger seat, with his wife and my companion seated behind us. My companion soon took off his suit coat, rolled it up into a pillow, and settled in for a nice border's nap. Shortly afterward my mission president's wife was also asleep. But President Jarvis never slept in the car, and so he and I just sat there, frustrated. After a while he started telling historical stories about World War II, and my mind started to wander. I began thinking about my boyhood dreams of what a mission would be like and then compared those dreams to my current situation. Here I was, sitting at a border in the middle of nowhere with my name badge removed, prohibited from sharing the gospel and listening to my mission president talk about the superiority of the German tanks. Nope, in all my imaginative wonderings I had never pictured anything remotely similar to this.

At that point we had been waiting for nearly thirty minutes. Looking up, I noticed that the car ahead had given up hope that the line would actually move. The driver had put his car in park and had exited to take a cigarette break. Watching him I suddenly had a distinct feeling: *Elder Christiansen, you need to go talk to that man.*

Inwardly I scoffed at such a crazy idea: *we were at the border; we didn't contact people at the border.* I quickly attributed the prompting to my own brain and my dissatisfaction with my present conditions. Yet as I tried to refocus on my mission president's story, the prompting returned with increased force and clarity: *Elder Christiansen, you really need to go talk to that man.* This time I mentally debated the prompting: *Look, if I go talk to that man, it could raise suspicion. A border patrol agent could come over and ask us what we're talking about. I could deny it, but the man certainly would not. The very status of the Church in Moldova could be jeopardized. I'm not going to go talk to that man!*

Confident that I had settled the matter, I decided to engage in the conversation with my mission president, but doing so did not prevent the feeling from coming back again a third time. This time the impression was much stronger and harsher in the implications if I did not obey. There was no other course to take—I had to act.

As I opened the door to get out of the van, my mission president asked what I was doing. I told him I just needed to stretch my legs and get some air. He nodded his head, so I quickly got out and stretched my legs right on up to this man who was leaning against his car. As I approached, my mind was racing. *Why was I doing this? What would I say to him? What if I got into trouble?* Nothing about the situation made any sense to me. The man looked extremely confused when he saw me heading toward him. I said hello, and he responded with the same short greeting. An awkward silence ensued, and I squirmed, not knowing what to say or do.

Finally I decided to talk about the only thing I was passionate about at the moment. "Don't you hate crossing through this border?" I asked.

His face lightened, and he laughed. "Tell me about it!" he said. "I have to pass through this place two or three times a week!"

I had noticed that his license plates were Romanian issued and asked what he had been doing in Moldova. He responded that he owned several businesses in Chișinău that required his supervision. With the ice now broken, we settled in and began to chat.

As we spoke the most incredible phenomenon occurred. It is a phenomenon I have experienced only two other times in my entire life. In a flash of perfect and pure knowledge, the Spirit communicated to me that this man had a son living in the United States with an LDS family. As unlikely and improbable as that information seemed, I knew it as surely as I knew my own name.

Armed with this information, I steered the conversation toward family. I asked if he was a family man, and he replied that he was married and had two kids. I couldn't suppress the smile that crept onto my face as I asked if one of the children was a son. He nodded his head and said that his oldest was a thirteen-year-old boy. My smile only grew as I asked if this boy was living in America.

He was stunned! His face went white and confused; he asked how I knew that. I didn't know how to explain it to him so I deflected his question and instead asked how his son had ended up in the States. He explained how his county had held a lottery for all qualified middle school students to study abroad for one semester in America. Out of more than 30,000 students, his son's name had been drawn. He had been gone for nearly four months and was living with a family in Kansas.

Now came the big question: "This family your son's living with in Kansas," I began, "are they Mormon?"

The man's face went ashen, and he could hardly speak. "H-h-h . . . how did you know *that*? Are you with the FBI?"

I couldn't contain myself any longer. I informed him that, no, I was not with the FBI but that I was a missionary for the Mormon Church. He couldn't believe it; he was so excited. The fact that his son was living with a Mormon family had sparked a deep curiosity about the Church, but he didn't even know if there were any Mormons in Romania. He talked about how impressed he was with his son's host family, that in every e-mail his son mentioned how kind they were and how they made him feel like one of the family. The man then went on to tell how he had just received a letter the day before in which his son described a morning ritual of reading from a "Mormon's book."

Obviously I could infer that he was talking about the Book of Mormon, so I told him that we had a copy of the book in the van if he was interested. Again he was stunned. His son's letter had prompted him and his wife to wonder aloud about the unknown Mormon's book. They wanted to write their boy and ask for a copy but knew that he and the American family were reading the book in English. They doubted that the book had been translated into Romanian and didn't know what to do. I assured him that this was not the case and sprinted back to the van to retrieve a copy.

I opened the front passenger side door, and my mission president asked what was going on. He had been watching all of this unfold from the van and was extremely curious about what was happening. I promised an explanation then located a copy of the Book of Mormon in the glove box and took a moment to write my testimony in the front. Hurrying back to the man's car, I gave him the book, briefly explained what it was, and then invited him to read and pray about it. He thanked me profusely and marveled aloud at the coincidence of meeting a Mormon missionary at the Romanian/Moldovan border. Then we parted.

I returned to the van, where everyone was awake and demanding an explanation. As I related what had happened they were absolutely amazed. Recounting the experience took five minutes or so, and when I concluded, Sister Jarvis smiled and said, "Elder Christiansen, look!" I had been turned around telling the story, and she was pointing past my ear toward the windshield. As I faced forward I saw right away what she was directing me to look at. The man was seated in his car with the Book of Mormon propped open on his steering wheel. We sat behind him for nearly an hour longer, and the entire time, he turned page after page, devouring the book.

Sitting in line at the border that day, I had absolutely no idea that the man just one car ahead of us had a son living in America with a Mormon family and that just the day before this man and his wife had been talking about the Book of Mormon, wishing they could somehow get a copy. *I* didn't know any of this, but *God* did! How grateful I was that I had followed this unusual prompting! I will always treasure the memory of that little miracle. As a missionary, you must always remember that God's ways are higher than your ways and His thoughts higher than your thoughts (see Isaiah 55:8–9). Because of this, all promptings—no matter how irrational, illogical, or unreasonable—must be obeyed.

A moment in Church history provides a powerful example of this principle. In the fall of 1827, Joseph Smith finally received the golden plates from the angel Moroni. After experiencing a number of setbacks and delays, Joseph was at last able to begin the work of translation with Martin Harris serving as his scribe. Soon pressure began to mount upon Martin. He was spending a great deal of time and money on the project, and his wife was becoming suspicious. Fearing that her husband was wasting his time and being duped by Joseph, she demanded proof verifying the authenticity of the plates. If only she could examine the pages they had completed, her suspicion would be placated (see Joseph Fielding Smith, *Essentials in Church History* [Salt Lake City: Deseret Book Company, 1974], 55).

We all know how the story goes from here. Martin asks Joseph if he can take the pages to appease his wife; Joseph petitions the Lord and is promptly denied. This process is repeated three times until the Lord—knowing the stubbornness of both men—consents. In granting approval, Joseph places Martin under strict stipulations to guard the manuscript with utmost vigilance and show it only to the appointed persons. Martin disobeys, and the result is disastrous. The 116 pages, or the book of Lehi, are lost.

The repercussions of this event were colossal. Martin was immediately dismissed from his duties as scribe, Joseph had to relinquish the plates back into the protective custody of Moroni, and the Spirit was completely withdrawn from the Prophet's life for an agonizing period of time.

Chastened and humbled, Joseph eventually received a reinstatement of his former blessing and was desirous to commence again the work of translation (see D&C 10). It was then that the Lord dropped a bombshell on him: *Joseph would not be retranslating the lost portion.* Doing so would play right into a trap set by the adversary to discredit both Joseph and the new book of scripture.

Think how devastating this must have been for the young Prophet. He alone had read the faith-promoting events and powerful truths taught in the book of Lehi. Now, because of his disobedience, the priceless material of the book of Lehi would be forever lost to the world.

As heartbreaking as this moment must have been, the news the Lord delivered next must have been equally exhilarating. I picture the Lord smiling as He informed Joseph that, in fact, *none* of the vital stories, truths, and information were lost, that thousands of years earlier He had prepared for just this scenario.

It began in 569 BC when the Spirit prompted Nephi to forge a new set of plates and include a lengthy synopsis of all that had occurred until that point. This commandment must have been extremely confusing to Nephi. Why was this necessary? He had already copied large portions of his father's journal onto his first set of plates. Why would he have to spend so much time and effort duplicating something that had already been done? Despite his confusion, Nephi obeyed the prompting and made the additional record.

Nearly 1,000 years later, the prophet-historian Mormon had a similar experience. Upon completing his abridgment of the Nephite record, he felt impressed to include the small plates of Nephi along with his own work. This impression must have confused him. Certainly he had perused the contents of these plates and seen that the information was already contained in his own abridgment. Why did it need to be in there twice? Despite his confusion, Mormon obeyed.

Both of these scriptural accounts talk about the Lord's greater purpose: *"for a wise purpose in him, which purpose I know not"* (1 Nephi 9:5; see also Words of Mormon 1:6–7; emphasis added). What was the wise purpose? Centuries later, in Joseph's sickening moment of agony, the Lord was kindly able to inform him that He had prepared another set of plates in anticipation for this precise situation. These plates were located at the back of the record and contained the same basic information as the lost 116 pages. By translating these plates, all the vital truths that had been lost would be restored. God's purposes would not be frustrated: He was, is, and will always be in control of His work.

As a missionary you will have many such experiences with the Spirit. If you, like Nephi and Mormon, will place your trust in an infinitely wise Heavenly Father, you too can become a powerful instrument in His hands. Oh, how I wish I could have seen the moment when Joseph Smith had the chance to personally thank Nephi and Mormon for obeying those promptings they didn't fully understand! Now think of who may eventually thank you for having the courage to obey your own promptings.

While God's ways are higher than our ways and He is without question in charge of His work, not all promptings you receive as a missionary will result in miraculous stories. If that were the case then faith would be an unnecessary component in the equation. Promptings that don't work out exactly as we think they should are no less important or inspired than those that yield favorable results. A loving Heavenly Father may simply be using such promptings to further shape, mold, and refine you in your spiritual development. Remember what He said to the Prophet Joseph: "All these things shall give thee experience, and shall be for thy good" (D&C 122:7).

I've experienced this type of prompting as well. With only a month left on my mission, my companion and I set aside a week to work with the various missionaries in Bucharest. There was a zone leader in that city who was experiencing some challenges, so I focused my efforts on him and his zone. This elder was an awesome missionary and a good friend, so I desperately wanted to see him succeed in his leadership assignment.

On one of our evenings together we decided to go back to the basics and just pound the streets for a few hours. I'll never forget those hours of street contacting. For some reason it seemed like we both received an additional measure of power; it was our own little "Alma and Amulek" moment. The night flew by, and soon it was time to meet back up with our companions. We were running a little bit late, so we ducked into the subway to catch a train. The appointed meeting spot was toward the outskirts of the city, so our side of the platform was virtually deserted. The other side of the platform was packed with people heading toward the city center.

While talking and rejoicing with this elder, I glanced around to check my surroundings and happened to glimpse a father and son join the waiting crowd on the other side of the platform. Suddenly I had the feeling that I should go talk to them. I quickly brushed the feeling aside with the justification that I had just spent the last four hours talking to every person in sight. Wasn't that enough? Besides, I'd kind of shut things down for the night and gone into "off" mode.

I instantly tried to engage myself in a conversation with my companion, but the prompting returned. This time I had a more sophisticated argument. If I went over and talked to that man, our train might come and we'd miss it. Then we'd have to wait twenty more minutes for the next one. This would not only cause us to be late, but also our companions who were waiting for us. We would all be out past mission curfew in a blatant act of disobedience. *Nope!* I said to myself, convinced and satisfied. *It's not happenin'.*

A moment later, the prompting came again, and similar to my previous story at the Moldovan border, this time the feeling could not be ignored or rationalized away. Almost without knowing it, I found myself walking across the platform toward the huge gathering of people. Scanning the crowd, I located the father and son and headed their direction. About ten feet away I made eye contact with the man, raised my hand to say hello, but was stunned to hear him yell out, "If you think you're going to talk to me, just stop right there!" His tone was menacing, and he looked extremely angry.

He then proceeded to give me the most thorough, profanity-laced, verbal thrashing I have ever received in my entire life. The tirade was so nasty that I only recall bits and pieces. I remember him saying, "You come here from America and you think you can teach *us* about Christianity. I've got a message for you! We've been Christians for over 2,000 years. We don't need you here! We don't want you here! No one invited you here!"

Of course, all of this was peppered with colorful language. In my mind I can still hear the last thing he yelled at me, which in Romanian happens to be a deep insult. He pointed right at me and said, "You should be ashamed of yourself! You should be ashamed of yourself!" With that, he grabbed his son by the hand and stormed off.

There I stood, paralyzed in front of this huge group of people. They were all witnesses to what had just happened. As soon as the man left the whispers began: "Mormon, I think he's Mormon." "I've heard they're a strange cult." "Why are *they* here?" I had never felt more embarrassed and helpless in my entire life. There was nothing left to do but turn and walk back to the other side of the platform.

When I got back to my companion he was highly entertained. "Oh man! I saw the whole thing. That guy chewed you out worse than I've ever seen anyone get chewed out before. He was using swear words that I've never even heard of. What were you thinking trying to talk to him?"

Lucky for us our train came within the next minute, and we were on our way.

But sitting on that train I was fuming mad. Why in the world had I received that prompting? I didn't deserve that! Here I had just worked my tail off all day, and *that* was my reward. I didn't get it. We met up with our companions, and, of course, this elder had to tell everyone the story. This only aggravated me further. Soon I was home in my apartment, and it was time to go to sleep. Confused and angry, I skipped my nightly prayer and, lying in bed, continued to stew over the concluding event of the night. What had I done wrong? Why had that happened? How could I trust or follow any more promptings?

After an hour of stewing I realized that sleep was not going to come until I dealt with this problem. Going into our front room, I knelt beside a chair and let it all out. I tried not to be insubordinate to God, but I also couldn't lie and pretend like everything was okay. I think I may have crossed the line when I bitterly muttered, "I don't need promptings like *that*. I don't want promptings like *that*. There are enough people out here who hate our guts without You sending us to them."

It was at this point when I came to learn that God is patient—but not that patient. Like lightning, the beatitude "Blessed are all they who are persecuted for my name's sake," jolted across my mind (3 Nephi 12:10). These words penetrated me to the core and zapped away all pity, anger, and confusion. Now quieted and humbled for the first time since the incident, I felt the Spirit whisper very clearly to me: *Elder Christiansen, I need to know if I can trust you. I need to know that every time I send my Spirit you will obey. I need to know if I can trust you.*

Tears flowed down my face. What a lesson. In an instant my entire mission seemed to flash before my eyes, and unmistakably I realized how every blessing I had received, every miracle I had seen, every person I had touched—all had been the direct result of following promptings. Still on my knees, I renewed my pledge to follow any prompting that would come *and be grateful for them*, REGARDLESS of the outcome.

While this story was mine, I share it because the lesson is universal and applies to everyone. There are some promptings we receive that are given as a test. The test is twofold: (1) Will we be obedient under any circumstances? (2) How will we respond to the outcome? I came to understand even more deeply that all aspects of our relationship with Heavenly Father must be two-directional. Yes, we know that we can trust Him. He is our Father who "doeth not anything save it be for the benefit" of His children (2 Nephi 26:24). But the true question is not whether *we* can trust *God*, but whether *He* can trust *us*.

How grateful I am that faithful men and women throughout the ages of the world have followed the Spirit, acting on promptings that may have seemed foolish, irrational, or impossible to the human intellect. From my own experience I can add my testimony to theirs that truly "the spirit giveth life" (2 Corinthians 3:6).

Chapter 7
"A Teacher Come from God"

"Teaching is central to everything you do. You develop Christlike attributes, study the missionary lessons, improve your ability to speak in your mission language, and rely on the Spirit in order to teach with convincing power."
—Preach My Gospel, 175

JESUS CHRIST WAS THE MASTER Teacher. From the beginning of His ministry at the River Jordan to the end of His life at Calvary we find an unbroken chain of simple yet profound teachings. Whether speaking to a congregation of thousands or to a single individual, the Savior never passed up an opportunity to teach the eternal truths of the gospel. How fitting that one of the first stories from the life of Christ depicts Him as a twelve-year-old boy teaching the scribes and Pharisees at the temple. How appropriate that Nicodemus, a ruler of the Jews, respectfully addressed Jesus as "a teacher come from God" (John 3:2).

Missionaries are set apart and ordained as personal representatives of the Lord Jesus Christ. As such, their primary role is that of gospel teacher. It becomes critically important then that missionaries learn *how* to teach effectively. The purpose of this chapter is to assist you in this sacred responsibility.

It might be helpful to begin with a definition. Gospel teaching is the process whereby truth is transferred from one person to another. Effective teaching builds investigators' faith in Jesus Christ and results in an increased understanding of the gospel. It sounds silly, but nothing has been taught until something has been learned. Let me explain what I mean.

Recently I accompanied the full-time missionaries to an appointment with a part-member family in my neighborhood. We were there for nearly an hour, and the missionaries talked about the gospel the entire time.

After the lesson the missionaries appropriately excused themselves to fulfill another appointment, but I lingered behind to spend a few extra minutes with my neighbor friends. We all went to the porch to wave good-bye to the elders, and then we headed back inside. As soon as the door closed, this family turned to me and asked, "What the heck were those guys talking about?"

All my suspicions were confirmed; they had understood almost nothing the elders had said. The elders thought they had taught a meaningful lesson, but in reality they had taught nothing. I realize that sounds harsh, but it's the truth. Always remember this simple mantra contained in *Preach My Gospel*: Teach for understanding (see 182).

When someone *understands* the gospel they are then in a position to *live* the gospel. *The application of truth is the ultimate desired outcome of gospel teaching.* It is the only prescribed way to gain a testimony. In fact, we could think of these two outcomes as the formula for conversion:

Understanding + Application = Conversion

As one who will participate in this process of conversion, it's important to note that anyone can be a good teacher. You don't have to fit a specific personality type or adopt a particular teaching style. You don't need to be charismatic, eloquent, funny, persuasive, or brilliant. Whatever talents, strengths, and skills *you* possess can be utilized in producing effective gospel teaching. While there is not a specific mold for good teachers, there are certain inviolable principles to which all effective teachers adhere. Now that we've defined the process of effective *teaching*, let's evaluate some principles that make effective *teachers*.

Principle 1: "If ye receive not the Spirit ye shall not teach" (D&C 42:14).

The foremost characteristic of all effective gospel teachers is their ability to teach by the Spirit. In order to teach by the Spirit you must live in a righteous and honorable manner. Just as a musical instrument must be in tune to produce a beautiful sound or a medical instrument must be sterilized to be used in surgery, your high level of personal worthiness allows you to become a pure conduit for the Holy Ghost.

You must also be humble enough to desire and rely on the Spirit. Always remember that you alone can never convince or convert those you teach—that is not your role. As you gain more experience, the natural tendency will be to trust in your own abilities more and rely on the Lord less. Doing so will quickly quench the Spirit, leaving you helplessly and hopelessly on your own.

The Lord clearly revealed His stance on the matter when He asked, "Unto what were ye ordained? To preach my gospel by the Spirit, even the Comforter which was sent forth to teach the truth. . . . Verily I say unto you, he that is ordained of me and sent forth to preach the word of truth by the Comforter, in the Spirit of truth, doth he preach it by the Spirit of truth or some other way? And if it be by some other way it is not of God" (D&C 50:13–14, 17–18).

Please note the ominous "some other way" category which is "not of God." "Some other way" to me denotes a teacher who relies on his or her own knowledge, intellect, abilities, charisma, personality, experience, or anything besides the Spirit. Teaching by "some other way" will never result in the blessing described further on in the passage: "Wherefore, he that preacheth and he that receiveth, understand one another, and both are edified and rejoice together" (D&C 50:22).

If you want to be a powerful and effective teacher, live worthy of the Spirit, pray for the Spirit, and teach by the Spirit. As the Lord clearly instructs, there is no other way!

Principle 2: "Obtain my word" (D&C 11:21).

To be an effective teacher you have got to pay the price. Trying to teach something you don't know is like trying to tell someone about a place you've never been. As a prospective missionary, now is the time to amp up your study of the gospel. The ten minutes per day you studied for seminary will not be enough to gain the understanding that a full-time mission requires. When you're within a year of your mission I'd recommend studying a half hour to an hour per day. When you receive your mission call, increase your study time to an hour to two hours per day. Minimum. Keep a study log to hold yourself accountable, and ask someone you trust (a parent, priesthood leader, or friend) to regularly review your log and discuss your progress. Above all, be diligent in your study. Diligence to me means consistency combined with quality. Successfully "obtaining the word" is more than just studying daily; it's studying in a meaningful and intense way.

When you diligently pay the price, you will come to own the doctrine. A teacher owns the doctrine when he can explain it clearly and accurately to someone else. We've all had occasions where we really do understand a concept, but when we try to explain it to another person, it's a struggle. We resort to phrases like "Well, that's just the way it is," or "I don't know why. It just works," or "It's kind of hard to explain, but . . ." The gap between your brain and your mouth is wider than you think. Just because you've heard a thousand lessons on repentance doesn't necessarily mean you can teach someone else about repentance. You have to own the doctrine.

The sons of Mosiah are a great example of this principle. We all love the story of Ammon hacking off the robbers' arms and converting King Lamoni. We love seeing Aaron teaching and baptizing King Lamoni's father. Even more, we love watching the converts of these missionaries bury their weapons as a token of their commitment to repent.

With stories as dramatic and miraculous as these, it's easy to overlook the few short verses that describe how Ammon and his brethren prepared to serve. While simple, these verses unlock the secret to their incredible success. Look carefully at what these young men did before they ever dared cross into the territory of the Lamanites: "Yea, and they had waxed strong in the knowledge of the truth; for they were men of a sound understanding and they had searched the scriptures diligently, that they might know the word of God. But this is not all; they had given themselves to much prayer, and fasting; therefore they had the spirit of prophecy, and the spirit of revelation, and when they taught, they taught with power and authority of God" (Alma 17:2–3).

Ammon and his brethren had to pay the same price to obtain the word that you will. Or, phrased more appropriately, *you* will have to pay the same price to obtain the word that Ammon and his brethren did. They devoted themselves to prayer, fasting, and study, and you will have to do likewise. If you are faithful in your preparation, the blessings they received will be yours as well. You will have the spirit of prophecy, and when you teach, it will be with power and authority of God.

Throughout principle 2, we have used phrases such as "pay the price," "own the doctrine," and "search diligently." Implied in each of these expressions is the element of desire. At a Utah Valley North Area inservice meeting in 2009, S. Michael Wilcox, a wonderful and well-known institute teacher, taught that desire carves out depth of soul. Whatever depth we carve out through our desire, God stands ready and able to fill. The sons of Mosiah had "cavernous souls" because they desired so strongly the "*knowledge of the truth*" and the "*sound understanding*" that come from God (Mosiah 17:2; emphasis added). On the other hand, some people have "saucer lid souls" because they care so little about the things of the Spirit. I've seen prospective missionaries fit into both categories. Determine right now to be the former, not the latter.

One final thought on obtaining the word. This process means so much more than just studying your scriptures or *Preach My Gospel* to increase in knowledge and understanding. At a deeper level, obtaining the word is a beautiful metaphor and symbol for obtaining Christ—the Word of God (see John 1:1–4; D&C 93:8). When we obtain the Word, we come to know on a very personal and real level the Lord Jesus Christ. We learn of His attributes, His goodness, His care, and His love. We then seek to align our lives more fully with His. Thus the process of obtaining the word could be broken down into four simple steps:

1. *Learn* of Christ
2. *Apply* Christlike attributes, standards, and teachings
3. *Become* like Christ
4. *Repeat* steps 1–3

Learn, apply, become, repeat. Only when this process has occurred and is occurring will you be an effective gospel teacher.

Principle 3: Teach from the scriptures (see *Preach My Gospel,* 180–182)

Once you obtain the word, you are now equipped to use the word. *Preach My Gospel* states that "it is vital to use the scriptures as the basis for your teaching" (180). I know this principle may seem obvious, but I'm amazed when I go out with the missionaries how sparsely they use the scriptures in their lessons. Now I'm not suggesting you overwhelm your investigators with nine million references, but you should turn often to the scriptures to support the doctrines you teach. Missionaries who use the scriptures to help explain doctrine and answer questions teach with greater validity and power. They realize that God's word is mightier than their own explanations. On the other hand, missionaries who neglect the scriptures produce teaching that is hollow and unconvincing.

When you share a passage of scripture, give the investigator the opportunity to read. This gets them involved in a meaningful way and in some cases helps them become more comfortable with scriptural language. Before having an investigator read, always remember to do two things. First, provide the basic context of the verse. This doesn't mean you need to give a ten-minute soliloquy on the plot and subplot of the text or go into the Hebrew or Greek derivatives. Providing context simply means giving a brief explanation that sets up the verse. Second, make sure you give them something to look for to help focus their reading of the verse. The following are some examples of giving appropriate context:

Amos 3:7—Amos was a prophet to the nation of Israel, and in this verse he teaches how God reveals truth to His children.

John 14:26—In this passage, Christ and His apostles are at the Last Supper, and He's teaching them about the role of the Holy Ghost.

Moroni 10:3–5—Moroni is the last prophet in the Book of Mormon. Before he hid up the plates he issued a challenge and promise to the future readers of this book.

D&C 89:18–21—In these verses the Lord outlines the blessings associated with the Word of Wisdom. Look for the promises God makes if we will obey this commandment.

Mastering this simple technique will improve the quality of your teaching and facilitate many meaningful experiences with God's word.

It would be comically ironic if I didn't include a scripture to support this principle. While there are dozens to choose from, the following passage from the book of Helaman gives several reasons to teach from the scriptures: "Yea, we see that whosoever will may lay hold upon the word of God, which is quick and powerful, which shall divide asunder all the cunning and the snares and the wiles of the devil, and lead the man of Christ in a strait and narrow course across that everlasting gulf of misery which is prepared to engulf the wicked—And land their souls, yea, their immortal souls, at the right hand of God in the kingdom of heaven" (Helaman 3:29–30).

Principle 4: Testify often

The importance of testimony in gospel teaching cannot be overstated. From *Preach My Gospel*, we learn that "sharing your testimony often is one of the most powerful ways of inviting the Spirit" (198). Elder Holland has taught why testimony is so integral in the teaching process. He explained that when a missionary bears testimony, it stirs up a divine echo within the souls of those who hear it, for surely they possessed and bore that same testimony when they chose to follow the Savior in their premortal life ("Missionary Work and the Atonement," 15–16). When you have the privilege of teaching someone the gospel, imagine the testimony they once had and do all you can to reawaken that testimony.

The power of a simple testimony may be the key that unlocks a person's heart. Brigham Young investigated the Church for an extended period of time but wasn't convinced of its truthfulness until he came under the influence of a humble missionary's testimony.

The prophet Alma relied on the power of testimony to save an entire nation. During a period of Nephite wickedness and idolatry, he relinquished the judgment seat so he could spend his days crying repentance. As you read the following passage, look for the role of testimony in his teaching: "And this he did that he himself might go forth among his people, or among the people of Nephi, that he might preach the word of God unto them, to stir them up in remembrance of their duty, and that he might pull down, by the word of God, all the pride and craftiness and all the contentions which were among his people, *seeing no way that he might reclaim them save it were in bearing down in pure testimony against them*" (Alma 4:19, emphasis added).

Pure testimony is testimony borne of the Spirit. Never forget that the people you teach are literally spirit children of our Heavenly Father and that the spirits housed within their mortal bodies long to learn and do that which is pleasing unto Him. This is another reason bearing testimony has such a powerful effect in gospel teaching.

Newly called missionaries should not worry about their inexperience and inadequacies or, in many cases, the daunting language barrier. They should focus instead on seizing every opportunity to bear straightforward, humble, pure testimony. Doing so will allow them to make a significant contribution to the work of the Lord. It will make them effective teachers.

Principle 5: Too much/Too little/Just right

Let's see if we can get a little more practical with our last few principles of effective teaching. When preparing to teach, many missionaries wonder what and how much to say about the various doctrines of the gospel. The easy answer is to stick with the content outlined in *Preach My Gospel*. However, considering that missionaries are now trained to take the content and then make it their own, a discussion on this topic might be helpful.

Teaching the doctrines of the gospel is like seasoning a meal. Too much information and the experience is overpowering and unpleasant—like the dinner where your older brother unscrews the salt shaker lid so when you go to put some on your mashed potatoes the whole thing dumps out.

Conversely, missionaries who teach too little produce outcomes that are bland and unsatisfying, like a meal with no flavor or where the portion sizes are ridiculously small. This type of teaching lacks substance and leaves those being taught with an incomplete and hazy understanding of the gospel.

Let me give you an example of what I'm talking about. The following scenarios portray a missionary teaching about the Apostasy from the first lesson:

Too much: "After the resurrection of Christ, the apostles went out and tried to build the Church, but they were rejected and even killed. Many of the essential truths of the gospel were abandoned or changed, and the priesthood (or authority to act in God's name) was lost. The Christians were hated and persecuted until the emperor Constantine chose Christianity as the vehicle to unite the Roman Empire. In the year 325 AD, he convened a council at Nicea, where the leaders of the different Christian factions were brought together to discuss and debate what the official doctrines of the church would be. From this council originated many errors that still exist today, most notably a belief in the Trinity . . . "

Too little: "After Christ's resurrection, there was an apostasy, and that's why the Church needed to be restored by the Prophet Joseph Smith."

About right: "After Christ's resurrection, the apostles went out and tried to build the Church, but they were rejected and even killed. Many of the essential truths of Christ's gospel were abandoned or changed, and the priesthood (or authority to act in God's name) was lost. This falling away from the truth resulted in an apostasy. An apostasy is a period of time when the fullness of God's truth is not on the earth. For many centuries the world lay in darkness, but in the year 1820, God again reached out to the world through the Prophet Joseph Smith." (The missionary would then proceed with the Joseph Smith story.)

Hopefully you can see the problem with the first two scenarios. One gets off track at the end and overwhelms the investigator with unnecessary information. The other skips over or speeds through vital doctrines that need to be fleshed out in greater detail. An investigator who is taught in this manner will be completely lost about the meaning of your message.

Every effective teacher must master this principle. It comes with experience and will develop more quickly as you practice and seek the feedback of others. More importantly, the Spirit will clue you in on how much and what to say. Remember, not too much, not too little.

Principle 6: Sequence

Our Heavenly Father is a God of order. He is not random, haphazard, or unpredictable. Naturally, this divine attribute is mirrored in the restored gospel. The gospel of Jesus Christ is a divinely designed, step-by-step tutorial on how to find joy in this life and return home to our Father in the world to come. The scriptures use the phrase "line upon line, precept upon precept" to describe how the doctrines of the gospel build upon and complement each other, each concept coming in its due time and place (2 Nephi 28:30).

Effective teachers understand that sequence is an essential component of gospel teaching. There must be a natural and logical flow to the doctrines being taught. For instance, the Restoration of the gospel will be confusing if you have not established the Apostasy of the original Church. Likewise the Atonement of Christ takes on greater meaning when the Fall of Adam is understood. These are just a few examples of doctrines that need to be taught in proper order.

Now for the caveat. While God is undoubtedly a God of order, He is certainly not rigid, mechanical, or aloof. As a loving, mindful Father, He alone understands the different questions and needs of each of His children. For this reason God serves as an active participant in the conversion process. Isn't it incredible to think that you are literally partners with Him as you share the message of salvation with His children?

While teaching, there will be times when the Spirit directs you to skip ahead to a later principle or go back to something that has already been taught. Don't become so inflexible that the Spirit can't guide you. Yes, sequence is important, but nothing supersedes the whisperings of the Holy Ghost.

Principle 7: Questions

Questions play a major role in the teaching and learning process. Effective teachers create a climate in which those being taught feel comfortable asking sincere questions. Always remember that you don't teach *lessons*, you teach *people*. An investigator should never feel hesitant, embarrassed, or unable to interrupt at any point to ask a question. Make it very clear that you encourage and welcome questions that may arise during the teaching process, especially if the investigator is confused about something that has been taught. Establishing this open climate will greatly accelerate the learning that takes place.

As missionaries seek to answer investigators' questions, two challenges may arise: First is the investigator who lacks sincere desire to be taught and asks questions solely to tear down the faith and beliefs of the missionaries. In these instances, the missionaries should not become defensive or combative.

Instead, they might consider answering the questions the investigator *should have been asking.* For example, an investigator may accusingly ask how many wives the Prophet Joseph Smith had. Obviously the purpose of this question is to dredge up the old polygamy debate and challenge the claim that Joseph Smith was a true prophet. Thus, answering that specific question would be pointless, even counterproductive. The better option would be to answer the question they should have asked, which is *How can I know Joseph Smith really was a prophet called of God?*

The second challenge a missionary may encounter when answering questions is the "stumper." A "stumper" is a question to which you and your companion have no answer. That doesn't necessarily mean there isn't a good answer; it just means you don't quite know what that answer is. In situations like this, you shouldn't feel stupid or embarrassed. Simply admit that you don't know the answer to that particular question and promise to do some research on it. You might also take the opportunity to explain that faith is the foundational principle of the restored gospel and that some things have not yet been revealed.

Finally, when it comes to answering questions, missionaries should remember the following promise from the Lord: "Speak the thoughts that I shall put into your hearts, and you shall not be confounded before men; For it shall be given you in the very hour, yea, in the very moment, what ye shall say" (D&C 100:5–6).

Effective gospel teachers not only know how to answer questions, they also know how to ask the right questions. The questions they ask provoke thought and provide opportunities to build and strengthen testimonies. Considering that questions can make or break the teaching experience, let's evaluate some guidelines that will help you in this regard.

The first thing you need to understand is the purpose for asking questions in gospel teaching. The purpose is *not*:

1. To find out what they already believe about various religious principles *(What do you believe about God? What do you think is the purpose of life?)*

These types of questions are misguided and serve little purpose. The hope is that the investigator will respond in a doctrinally accurate way so you can build on common beliefs. The reality is that this rarely happens— so right from the beginning you've needlessly put yourself in a sticky situation where you have to correct their erroneous beliefs. This pits you versus them and makes you an adversary rather than a guide. The Lord has clearly warned against this method of teaching. In the Doctrine and Covenants He gave the following instruction to the elders: "Ye are not sent forth to be taught, but to teach the children of men the things which I have put into your hands by the power of my Spirit" (D&C 43:15).

Can you imagine going to your doctor when you are ill, explaining your symptoms, and then having him turn to you and say, "So what do *you* think is wrong with you?" You'd probably respond, "Uhhh, I don't know, Doc. You're the one who went to medical school for 5,000 years." Don't be so concerned about finding common beliefs to build upon; they will emerge naturally throughout the teaching process. As one who possesses a fullness of the truth, your responsibility is to teach, not to be taught.

2. To quiz them about facts pertaining to the gospel

(What was the name of the prophet who built the ark? Do you remember from John 3:16 how God showed He loves the world? What happened to the apostles after Christ died?)

Nothing drives me crazier than teachers who do this and think they're using questions effectively. Fact-based questions are absolutely pointless. They are nothing more than a gimmicky way for the teacher to assert control and in some cases to display their own knowledge. No matter how simple or harmless, these questions destroy the climate of security and comfort that learning requires. No one likes to be put on the spot or feel like they are being quizzed or interrogated. *Preach My Gospel* points out that such questions "turn a good teaching environment to a game of guessing" (184). As a missionary teaching investigators, avoid these questions like the plague.

3. To have the investigator regurgitate exactly what you've just said

(Any question that begins, *From what we've just taught . . .)*

Teaching and learning should never become an exercise in regurgitation with investigators mechanically spitting out exactly what you've just said. In the legal world asking questions of this nature is referred to as "leading the witness" and will rightfully raise an objection. When a question blatantly points to a specific answer, then the investigator serves as little more than a mimicking parrot. This quickly gets annoying and sours the learning experience. Instead, ask questions that prompt genuine thought and evoke sincere and real answers. This type of interaction greatly enriches the teaching process.

These are some of the purposes *not* to ask questions. Now let's flip things around and take the opposite view. The purpose of asking questions *is*:

1. To see whether the investigators understand what is being taught

(*What is the role of prophets? What does it mean to have faith in Jesus Christ?*

Why did the Church have to be restored? What questions do you have about what we've taught thus far?)

After teaching key principles, it is important to see if the investigators have understood what's been taught. Asking appropriate questions is the natural way to do this. As a missionary you've got to be perceptive because every situation and investigator is different. Some people are naturally shy or reserved and will feel uncomfortable if they are required to answer specific questions. In these situations simply ask: "Do you have any questions about what we've taught so far?" after important principles during the lesson. This will allow them to dictate how much or little they choose to participate. Other people will want to take a very active role in the lessons, and you should ask frequent questions to provide them this opportunity.

No matter the situation or person, keep your questions simple and to the point. Be careful never to make an investigator feel awkward or embarrassed. If they don't know how to respond or if they answer in a way that is somewhat incorrect, be quick to shift the blame to yourself. Phrases like "I apologize, I probably didn't explain that as well as I should" or "We realize that what we're teaching is new, so it's kind of hard to understand" may help you go a long way toward diffusing uncomfortable situations. These phrases also provide a natural segue to reteach the principle that has been misunderstood.

2. To help investigators analyze the principles being taught

(What difference would it make if there was a prophet in the world today? Why is it important that we have faith in Jesus Christ? What difference would it make in your life to know God has a plan for you?)

After it's clear that an investigator *understands* the gospel principle you are teaching, help them *analyze* why that principle is important. "Analyze" questions help investigators find deeper meaning in the truths you have taught and will make your lessons more powerful. For instance, it's one thing to understand what faith in Christ means; it's entirely different to see why faith in Christ is important. Thus, this second tier of questions is designed to build upon and expand an investigator's newly acquired knowledge.

3. To help investigators apply the truths in their lives

(When have you felt God's love? Have you ever felt confused about religion? What are some things that you love about your family?)

When an investigator understands gospel truths and has analyzed what they mean, they are now in a position to recognize experiences from their life when they've seen these truths manifest. Most of the investigators you teach will have a vast reserve of spiritual experiences they aren't even aware of. As a missionary you must give them the key and help them unlock this treasury. Questions that allow investigators to share past experiences prepare the way for questions that will invite them to apply the doctrines in the future. As discussed at the outset of this chapter, applying truth is the ultimate aim of the teaching process.

So to quickly review, level 1 questions help you, the missionary, see if an investigator *understands* what's being taught; level 2 questions help the investigator *analyze* the meaning of these truths; and level 3 questions help the investigator identify past experiences, giving them confidence to *apply* these truths in the present and future.

When used together, these different levels of questions reinforce each other; however, you don't need to ask three separate questions about every principle you teach. This would be time-consuming, redundant, and ineffective. In fact, there are lots of principles where you either may not ask any questions at all or you might ask a question from only one of the levels and that will suffice. Sometimes the Spirit may direct you to spend less time on one principle in order to have more time to emphasize a different part of the lesson. Other times it will be evident from the investigator's facial expressions and body language that they understand and are ready to move on. But a teacher who can effectively use the three levels of questions will facilitate many sweet moments of depth and insight. As in all things, let the Spirit be your guide.

Principle 8: Listening

Lastly, if missionaries are to become effective teachers, they must learn the skill of listening. Truly listening to someone means much more than just paying attention to what they say. It involves the ability to make a person feel both valued and validated. Moreover, listening allows missionaries to understand those they teach. When a missionary comes to really understand an investigator—their questions, concerns, background, strengths, weaknesses, hopes, and desires—love and trust is built between them. Always remember that when an investigator opens their mouth during a lesson, they may also be opening their heart.

The Master Teacher

As we began this chapter, we established that Jesus Christ is the Master Teacher. Throughout His ministry, Christ modeled every principle of effective teaching. He gave adequate time to preparation and regularly used scripture to support His words. He knew His audience and tailored His message appropriately. He asked and answered questions. He told stories to illustrate the doctrine and used objects from His surroundings to make His lessons more relatable. In sum, His life served as the ultimate course in teaching improvement.

Take, for instance, the following story from the life of Christ, recorded in John 4, that illustrates what a powerful teacher He truly was.

After observing the Passover at Jerusalem, the Savior and His apostles begin the return journey north to Galilee. Instead of taking the more common route east through Jericho and up the Jordan riverbed, Christ leads them directly into the heart of Samaria. This unusual deviation had to leave the apostles scratching their heads. Culturally, the Jews have no dealings with the Samaritans and go out of their way to avoid entering their territory. Geographically, Samaria is dotted with hills and more difficult and time-consuming travel. But despite all this, where Christ goes, His apostles dutifully follow.

Arriving at the outskirts of a village, Christ sends the apostles to get provisions while He sits down at a nearby well to rest. Soon a woman approaches, and Christ asks her for a drink of water. She's surprised by the request and probably a little wary. "How is it that thou, being a Jew, askest drink of me, which am a woman of Samaria?" she responds (John 4:9). Jews don't normally speak to Samaritans, and men certainly don't speak to unfamiliar women. With one simple question Christ has bulldozed several cultural barriers. Suspicious, she snubs His request and resumes her task. Undeterred, Jesus remarks that if she knew who He was, *she* would be asking *Him* for water (see John 4:9–10).

Well, now she's amused. Assessing the situation she can clearly see that this man doesn't even have a bucket. How could He possibly retrieve the cool water from the depths below? She bluntly expresses her doubts in his ability to provide a drink then is stunned when Jesus goes further and promises her a source of water that will never run dry: "Whosoever drinketh of this water shall thirst again: But whosoever drinketh of the water that I shall give him shall never thirst; but the water that I shall give him shall be in him a well of water springing up into everlasting life" (John 4:13–14).

This gets her attention. Anciently it was the woman's job to retrieve water from the well and carry the pot back to the home. This is most likely the domestic chore she detests the most. It's hot outside, the pot is heavy, and, as we'll see in a moment, this woman is harboring a major secret that makes this unpleasant chore even more dreadful.

From the depths of desire she pleads with Christ to supply this water so she will never have to come to the well again. Strangely, he requests that she call her husband and have him join in the conversation. She tersely answers that she has no husband, which is a half-truth designed to conceal unpleasant facts about her past. Christ sees through her response and then shocks her by stating that in reality she has had five husbands and that the man she is currently living with is not her husband.

So finally we learn the truth. She has been abandoned by five different husbands. In today's world this woman's life would be tragic, but at least our modern society protects a woman's rights and assigns equal or greater blame to the husband. In contrast, divorce in the ancient world was brutal on women. The process was extremely biased toward men and humiliating and dehumanizing to women. The man could basically walk out on his wife at any point and for any reason.

So consider for a moment the circumstances of this woman's life. While we don't know the specific details of her past, it's very likely that she has been betrayed, used, and hurt beyond comprehension. She has probably been labeled a woman of loose morals and treated as an outcast in society. How many times has she come to this well and found the other women speaking or gossiping about her? How much loneliness and pain has she endured day after day for all these years?

But there sits Jesus beside her. She now realizes He's no ordinary man, for how could He possibly know such private and intimate details of her life? Staggered by His discernment, she responds, "Sir, I perceive that thou art a prophet" (John 4:19).

They are no longer talking about water. Jesus immediately takes the opportunity to prepare her for the day when the Samaritans will receive the fullness of His gospel. He teaches her of God's desire to bless all His children. He teaches her of light and truth.

Suddenly, this woman has a flash of insight that must have been electrifying. She turns to Him and says, "I know that Messias cometh, which is called Christ: when he is come, he will tell us all things" (John 4:25), to which the Savior responds, "I that speak unto thee am he" (John 4:26).

At this point the apostles return, essentially ending their discussion. The woman is so excited about her experience that she leaves to share the news with others in her village. Skeptical, the people follow her to Jesus, where He teaches them for the space of two days. Many believe and gain their own testimonies of Christ's divine identity.

Let's take a step back and evaluate what happened over the span of this brief conversation. When Christ began talking to this woman, she was annoyed and suspicious. I'm sure she just wanted to get her water and be left alone. As He persisted, she became slightly amused and a bit curious. And finally, she became interested and desirous to hear what He had to say. Simplified, her change in attitude looks like this:

Annoyed → Suspicious → Amused → Curious → Interested → Desirous

The connection to missionary work is obvious. Most of your experiences with investigators will follow this same pattern. At first they might be annoyed and suspicious, wondering why you knocked on their door or stopped them on the street. If they give you a chance and hear you out, they often become curious about who you are and what you're doing. Almost always, they are amused by your youth or your funny accent or how you and your companion just happen to share the same first name, *Elder*. Then something you say or testify of sparks an interest deep inside of them. They feel something they can't quite describe, and their spirit begins to desire the nourishment only your message can bring. Consequently, an effective teacher must be patient enough to see an investigator through each phase until they become desirous to learn the truth.

Returning to the story, not only do we see a drastic change in this woman's attitude toward Jesus, but also her *perception* of Jesus. At the beginning, she refers to him as "a Jew" (v. 9). In other words, Jesus is no different to her than a million other guys. Then comes the pivotal moment where Christ gives the details from her past, and her perception instantly changes. She now sees him as "a prophet" (v. 19). By the end of their visit, she comes to the realization that Jesus is the Christ, the promised Messiah (see v. 25).

It's interesting to note that a similar progression often occurs in the way investigators perceive the missionaries. At first investigators view missionaries as "just kids" or "young American boys" who are no different from millions of others. Then, as they begin the lessons and observe the missionaries up close, they start to notice that these are no ordinary nineteen- and twenty-year-old boys. There is something very special about them. Eventually they come to recognize the missionaries for what they truly are: representatives of the Lord Jesus Christ and messengers sent from God.

While our discussion of this beautiful story has hopefully been insightful, we haven't really identified any principles of effective and powerful teaching. Let's quickly do so.

Go back to the very beginning of the story with Christ sitting at the well and the woman approaching. Because Jesus is a God, He knows everything about her. He knows that she has experienced unimaginable pain, humiliation, betrayal, and sorrow and has now given her life over to sin. He knows how desperately she needs the power of His Atonement to repent, heal, forgive, and find peace and happiness in her life. So knowing all this, with her very soul at stake, what does He choose to talk to her about?

Water.

Why does Jesus do this? Why would He talk about something so trivial and fleeting? I've drunk a lot of water in my life, and I don't ever remember it being a spiritual experience. Why doesn't He introduce himself right away as the Son of God and start teaching her what she needs to know?

The answer is easy.

In that moment, *water* is what she's focused on and cares about the most. Jesus, the Master Teacher, recognizes this and uses it to spark a conversation and show genuine interest in her. Brother Scott Anderson, an incredible institute teacher and well-known speaker, has used this story to coin the phrase "finding someone's water level" (Utah Valley North Area Inservice, 2009).

Developing the ability to find and go to someone's water level is crucial. Most of the people you approach as a missionary will initially be skeptical, indifferent, apathetic, or even angry. But you know the truth: *they just don't know that they care about or need your message.* Finding their water level helps them come to this important realization.

Now please do not misunderstand; "finding someone's water level" is not making small talk or engaging in superficial chitchat. Doing so usually repels most potential investigators. Your initial conversations with people should never feel fake, unnatural, or rehearsed. Unfortunately, there isn't a magical question or surefire way to instantly get to an investigator's water level. However, I can tell you that the water level is usually found when you genuinely care about people and take an interest in their lives.

Isn't that what we see Christ doing with this woman? If at the beginning He would have declared who He was and immediately launched into a sermon on repentance, the entire focus of their conversation would have been on Him and what *He* was interested in. Instead, we see Him sincerely focused on her cares while patiently waiting for the opportunity to share His message.

This leads us to the next principle, which I call the "pivot." Most casual interactions with people have a moment that provides an opening to introduce who you are and why you're there. This is the pivot. The pivot is the moment where you start to leave the water level behind in order to lead someone to higher ground. In this story, the pivot occurs when Jesus asks about her husband and discloses the details from her past. That's when she realizes there is something special about Jesus and they stop talking about water. Now, the obvious challenge you face as a missionary is that, unlike Jesus, you are not a god and will not know the background and life details of the people you contact.

Or will you?

Let's really think about what Jesus did in that pivotal moment. He basically said, "Even though we are total strangers, I know something about you that is really important." So what do you, the missionary, know about your investigators that falls under this category? You know they

- love their family and want to be with them forever. They've even wondered what will happen to their family relationships after they die.

- have felt guilt and shame for past actions and wondered how they can move forward and find peace of conscience.

- have felt confused about religion—wondering if there even is a God and if any churches are true.

- have asked themselves what the purpose of life is, where they came from, and where they are going.

- have wondered how to get answers to the questions they have.

As you can see, missionaries know a lot more about investigators than they might think. Guided by the Spirit, you will receive insight into the specific circumstances of those you teach. Pray and plead for the ability to speak the words that will open their spiritual eyes to see clearly who you really are.

The last principle is my favorite. As I've studied this story more closely, a phrase has jumped out at me that I've never noticed before. It comes in verse 28 and reads, "The woman then left her water pot and went into the city." Isn't that phrase symbolic of the profound impact Christ's teaching has made? Filling that water pot was the reason she had come to the well. Now, because of this unplanned and unexpected encounter with the Savior, her priorities and perspectives have completely changed. The water pot that just moments earlier meant so much now means so little.

The metaphor is clear. Every person in this world has their own "water pot" that he or she carries and tends to. These water pots represent the worldly cares and concerns that occupy and dominate people's lives. When missionaries teach effectively they will help investigators see these temporary and worldly water pots for what they truly are. They will then help them leave their water pots behind in order to begin new lives as disciples of Jesus Christ.

In order to be an instrument in the hands of God you must become an effective teacher. Through proper preparation and diligence, you can become what was said of the Master, even "a teacher come from God."

Chapter 8
A Living Sermon

"Along with your authority comes a responsibility to live worthy of your calling. As the Lord's representative, you are to be 'an example of the believers' (1 Timothy 4:12)." —Preach My Gospel, 4

WHEN I WAS A MISSIONARY in Romania, it was easy to feel obscure. We had 130 missionaries and 2,000 members in a country of 26 million. In case you're no math guru, that's not a lot of Church membership. Early on in my mission I was constantly nagged by a feeling of insignificance. Going from Utah, where LDS chapels pop up seemingly on every other block, to a Romanian city, where our nine members met in a hotel room, was jarring, to say the least. How could we possibly make a difference or even be noticed when so few in number?

During this period, my zone leader came to visit and shared with us a story that completely changed my attitude and perspective. His first area had been the capital city of Bucharest, and one day he and his companion were out proselytizing next to a major city landmark. They soon stopped to contact a passing gentleman and exchanged pleasantries. This elder then asked the man if he was familiar with our church or our missionaries. His answer was surprising. "Oh yes," he replied. "Everyone knows who you are." After parting, these elders couldn't stop thinking about that definitive statement: *Everyone knows who you are.*

Throughout my own mission, this phrase resurfaced again and again in my mind as I found myself in a variety of situations. *How should I treat this persistent gypsy beggar? Do I really have to pay for a bus ticket when we're only going half a mile? What type of sportsmanship should I display when playing soccer on preparation day? How should I act as I negotiate the price for a taxi fare? What do I do when a group of very attractive girls yells provocative invitations to us?* Every missionary in the world could benefit from this mental reminder: Be careful what you do because everyone knows who you are—and they are watching!

As a full-time missionary, your level of conduct must be above reproach. Think of all the people whom you represent as you go into the world: your parents and family; the Church, including your bishop and stake president, who recommended you; the prophet and apostles who issued your call; and most importantly, the Savior Himself. All are counting on you to conduct your labors with dignity, honor, integrity, and purpose.

So what is the best way to accomplish this? It's actually quite clear: as a representative of Jesus Christ you try your very best to follow in His mighty footsteps. His life was spent serving, so you should serve. His life was spent teaching, so you should teach. His life was spent building others, so you should build all around you. His life was one of complete obedience to our Heavenly Father's will, so you should be obedient. In every aspect His life becomes the ultimate blueprint for yours.

I believe Ammon patterned his mission after this divine blueprint. In fact, a close study of Ammon's life reveals many striking parallels to the life of the Savior. Both left kingdoms behind in order to save souls; both were willing to live and dwell among those whom they sought to save; both assumed the humble yet symbolic role of shepherd; and both were perfectly obedient to the instructions and commandments of their respective kings. But perhaps the greatest way Ammon reflected the life of Christ was in the righteous example he set for all around him.

Take, for instance, the moment when King Lamoni received the report of Ammon's courage and devotion in defending his sheep. The scriptures say that the king was "astonished exceedingly." Then follows one of the coolest lines in scripture as King Lamoni turns to his guards and says, "Surely, this is more than a man" (Alma 18:2).

Isn't that amazing? Ammon hadn't even opened his mouth about the gospel, yet Lamoni thought he was a god. I find it fascinating that "godliness" is one of the attributes outlined for missionaries in Section Four of the Doctrine and Covenants (v. 6). While you serve, your conduct must always point to Him who called you, thus making it possible to say of you what was said of Ammon: "Surely, this is more than a man."

Over the course of my mission I marveled at the Christlike examples of fellow missionaries. An experience in particular comes to mind. One morning we woke up to the sound of steady rainfall splattering against our window. When it came time to leave the apartment the rain had only intensified, so my companion and I decided to stay dry and do some block knocking. After a few hours, the storm moved on, and the rain stopped. With the sun now shining we left the blocks to go contact people on the street. We promptly headed toward the city center and within a few minutes ran into the other companionship of elders. We stopped for a moment to say hello and were amazed at the story they had to tell.

Instead of having the sense to avoid the rain by tracting indoors, these elders had stubbornly insisted on their morning ritual of street contacting. After only a few minutes, they were soaked and looking for a dry refuge. A large shopping mall was located nearby so they headed that direction. Attached to the entrance of this mall was a massive canvas overhang that, by this time, sheltered a large group of people underneath. These elders joined the crowd and began to share their message with those around them. Soon they had a growing number of interested listeners, prompting one of the missionaries to get a crazy idea. Why not get the attention of everybody and teach the entire group? He pitched the idea to his companion, who was immediately on board. They quickly relocated to a more prominent location, let out a few loud whistles, and then announced to the people that they had something to say.

"Hey, everybody," they began, "we're missionaries from America, and we have a really important message that we want to share with all of you. You're stuck here waiting for your buses, so you may as well listen to us!"

With that, they began the message of the Restoration. They had been teaching for nearly ten minutes when a newcomer joined the crowd. After listening for a moment, this newcomer made his way up to the front of the group and demanded that the missionaries stop preaching. He accused them of bothering the people and claimed that no one was interested in what they had to say. The missionaries pointed out that they had already been speaking for nearly ten minutes and not one person had objected or complained. One of the elders even turned to the crowd and asked if anyone else was bothered or considered them a nuisance. To his delight, not a soul responded negatively; instead, many voiced support for their message and encouraged them to continue.

They immediately began doing so but were interrupted yet again by the same man. This time he charged up to them and began screaming obscenities and threats if they didn't leave. The missionaries tried to defuse the situation, urging him to calm down, but the confrontation quickly escalated as the man got face-to-face with one of the elders, cleared his throat, and spit right in the missionary's face.

Now at this point I must interject an important piece of information. This elder was not small. He was a star football player in high school and was as solid as a rock. The man who spit in his face was half his size, and this elder could easily have destroyed him with one punch. (In fact, as his companion later related the story to us, I was certain that the elder had probably snapped and that the Romanian guy was lying in a coma at some local hospital.)

Back to the story. With the mucus running down his face and the impish man standing there taunting him and with a large crowd witness to this despicable and humiliating act, the elder stepped back, closed his eyes, took a deep breath, and then said to the crowd, "It's obvious that we're bothering this man, so we'll leave."

As the missionaries began to walk away something incredible occurred. Several large men who were part of the crowd rushed up, instructed the elders to wait for a moment, and then cornered the man who had attacked them. They then proceeded to chew him out, yelling something like the following:

"What do you think you're doing? Here these nice boys come from America to share a message from God and this is how you treat them? You swear at them and threaten them and then spit in their face. What kind of opinion do you think they're going to form about us Romanians? Oh, and by the way, *they're* not going anywhere! It's *you* that's going to leave, and if you won't go, then we'll just have to help you on your way."

Sensing the rising anger of the crowd and the ill intentions of the men standing before him, the spitter quickly departed. Those who had come to the missionaries' defense apologized for the incident and pleaded for them to finish their message.

I heard this story only minutes after it actually occurred. Even though the elder's suit coat was still peppered with spit, he was already laughing and joking about the encounter. As I listened to him shrug it off, I couldn't help marveling at his positive attitude and self-control.

Throughout the rest of that day I kept thinking about what had happened, and in so doing received the following insight: On that morning these missionaries had stood before a group of people and taught the gospel, but the true sermon was not in the message they shared or the words they said; the true sermon was in the Christlike manner in which they responded to an extremely unpleasant situation. Through their actions, these elders became a *living* sermon, as should all who go forth as representatives of Jesus Christ.

The power and impact of living sermons are almost always greater than those that are spoken. The things we *hear* are easily forgotten, while the things we *see, feel,* and *experience* remain long with us. Going back to that story, I've often wondered if the events of that day long ago may still be bearing fruit today. In my mind's eye, I see a pair of missionaries contacting people on those same beautiful streets in Iasi, Romania. I see them stop a family on a Sunday afternoon and hear the following exchange:

Missionaries: "Hello. We are representatives of The Church of Jesus Christ of Latter-day Saints. We're here sharing a message about the eternal nature of the family and how we can strengthen our family relationships. Would this message interest you?"

Father of the family: "You know, I normally wouldn't be. But a few years ago on a rainy morning I was waiting for my bus to go to work, and two of your missionaries stood up and began addressing the crowd. I know they must have been from your church because you're dressed exactly the same. Anyway, I wasn't even really paying attention until a man went up to them and began treating them very rudely. It got so bad that he threatened them and then spit in one of their faces. I thought for sure that the missionary would strike back but was amazed to see the way he responded. He didn't get mad or lose his temper. He just took it in the most calm, measured manner. It was one of the most incredible acts of self-control and discipline I have ever seen. I was really impressed and wanted to go talk to them to find out more, but my bus came and I had to leave. I promised myself that the next time I saw you guys I would find out who you are. All these years have passed, and this is the first time I've run into you. Like I said, normally I wouldn't be interested, but I guess I'm kind of curious about a message that gives you such perspective."

An instrument in the hands of the Lord understands the importance of every act. They understand that unspoken sermons shout louder than words. People do know who you are, and they are watching. They will form their opinions and ideas about the Church based solely upon what they see. Each morning when you put on the missionary name badge, be committed to represent everything it should stand for. In all you do, remember the wise moral of the following poem:

EXAMPLE

*Someone is watching and
this is a fact,
Someone will copy the way that I act.
So make this your motto
and put it to use,
Be someone's example,
and not their excuse.*

—Author unknown

Chapter 9
Stratego

"Your success as a missionary is measured primarily by your commitment to find, teach, baptize, and confirm people and to help them become faithful members of the Church." —Preach My Gospel, 10

I LOVE BOARD GAMES. IN junior high I became friends with the son of an army captain and was introduced to some great war simulation games. My favorite of these was *Stratego*. *Stratego* pits two players against each other acting as generals of opposing armies. Each player's army consists of forty soldiers (pieces), and the soldiers are ranked from one to twelve, with one being the strongest and twelve the weakest. The ranks are displayed on only one side of the pieces so your opponent doesn't know where you've positioned your various soldiers on the board. To play, each person takes turns moving one piece at a time. If a piece is moved to a square occupied by your opponent, both pieces are turned around and the stronger piece wins. The weaker piece is removed, and the game continues. The first player to capture the other's flag wins.

Perhaps the most intriguing and important aspect of *Stratego* occurs before the game even begins. The strategy each player employs in arranging their pieces usually determines the outcome of the game. This arranging takes a little bit of time, and the more you play the more you start to notice something. Positioning the weakest pieces is extremely difficult and annoying. No matter where you try and put them you know they're just going to get wiped out anyway. They are a complete liability. In contrast, placing your strongest pieces is awesome. You know you can put them anywhere and have confidence that they'll help you dominate the battle.

So what does any of this have to do with missionary work?

The last eight months of my mission I had the opportunity to help the mission president with transfers. Every six weeks we would meet together in his office and gather around the transfer board. The transfer board was a huge map of the mission with pictures of all our missionaries in their current assignments. As I worked on transfers for the first time and we began moving pictures around, I kept having the thought that the whole process was vaguely familiar, but I couldn't place it. Finally, at the end of the two days, it hit me like a bolt of lightning: It was like setting up my *Stratego* board!

The parallels between the two were uncanny. Looking up at our board, I immediately noticed how many powerful number one and number two ranked missionaries we had serving in our mission. These were the elders and sisters who were unfailingly obedient, diligent, happy, hardworking, self-motivated, and easy to get along with—missionaries who in every way lived up to the dignity of their calling as representatives of Jesus Christ. We knew we could literally put them anywhere and ask them to do anything and they would do it and do it well.

Sadly, I also noticed that there were a few number eleven and number twelve ranked missionaries bogging down the process. These were the missionaries who were disobedient, lazy, and unmotivated—missionaries who were never content with their companions, cities, or assignments. I quickly learned that an overwhelming majority of our time doing transfers was consumed by this small handful of missionaries.

I recall one transfer in particular where we stared at the picture of an elder for nearly four hours, wondering what to do with him. He definitely needed to be transferred, but each time we would propose a new companion or city there would always be an issue of some sort: "If we put him with that missionary they'll be disobedient"; "If we put him with that missionary they won't work"; "If we put him in that district, he'll flirt with the sister missionaries"; "We can't put him there—it's too far from mission headquarters." After four hours we knew we had to move on, so we finally put him in a place where we hoped he would do the least amount of harm. While this was happening, I remember feeling angry and resentful toward this missionary. Here I was, wasting four hours of my mission because he was such a problem. But soon these feelings gave way to a deep sadness—sadness that this elder was squandering his one shot to serve the Lord, that he was missing out on the boundless joy that comes from giving all your heart, mind, and strength to the work.

Participating in the transfer process and having experiences like these always caused me to look inward and reevaluate how I was doing in my own missionary labors. I certainly wasn't perfect and constantly saw areas that needed improvement. I knew more than anything I wanted to be like the missionary number ones and number twos that I admired so much. Helping with transfers always provided motivation to do so.

Another "transfer board" experience highlights the point I'm trying to make. There was a city in our mission that had been struggling for a long period of time. The missionaries had not baptized in months, the branch was stagnant, and enthusiasm for the work was low. In the upcoming transfer my mission president was determined to address the problem and turned to us for ideas. My companion and the mission president brainstormed for a few minutes but were unable to come to a consensus on what course of action should be taken. Seeing my silence, President Jarvis asked my opinion. I had been gazing at the transfer board and couldn't help but focus in on a few of our strongest missionaries. Finally I spoke up: "If we wanted to jump-start the work in that city, all we'd have to do is put Elder _____ and Elder _____ there. I bet that if we put those missionaries there, they'll be baptizing within a month."

The experiment was on. President Jarvis immediately gave his approval, and we made the transfers. Three weeks later I called these missionaries. I was curious to see how things were going and was not surprised to hear the following report: "Elder Christiansen, this city is awesome! There are so many people here who are ready to receive the gospel." The elder proceeded to list off the names of investigators they were teaching and then broke the news that an entire family had just committed to baptism. He was practically giddy with excitement.

As I listened to this elder, I wished so badly that I could record the conversation and play it for all the missionaries who had previously served in that city. How many times had I heard phrases like "There just aren't a lot of people here who are interested," "This city is dead," or "I can't wait to be transferred from here." This "experiment" confirmed what I knew all along: the problem was never the city or its inhabitants; the problem was the attitude of those who labored there.

Just as a person playing *Stratego* quickly comes to appreciate how valuable the number ones and number twos really are, surely the Lord must feel the same way about His strong and valiant servants. There are many reasons why the Lord needs and relies on His spiritual number ones and number twos. When times are good it's easy for everyone to be on board and moving in the right direction. But when things get hard and opposition mounts, it's always the number ones and number twos who take command and rally others to press forward. In moments of crisis, these select few can be counted on to provide unwavering strength and leadership.

Joseph Smith taught this principle using the following metaphor: "You know, brethren, that a very large ship is benefited very much by a very small helm in the time of a storm, by being kept workways with the wind and the waves. Therefore, dearly beloved brethren, let us cheerfully do all things that lie in our power; and then may we stand still, with the utmost assurance, to see the salvation of God, and for his arm to be revealed" (D&C 123:16–17).

In your mission, commit to being a "helm" for others around you. Be the type of missionary who provides strength and support to members and missionaries alike. And do so in a cheerful manner.

My trainer was this type of missionary. He approached every day of his mission like it was a rare gift to be treasured. I never saw anyone genuinely enjoy missionary work as much as he did. His enthusiasm was infectious. Even on days when we had absolutely nothing set up on our planners, he couldn't wait to leave the apartment in the morning. He was convinced that some spiritual experience, adventure, or memorable event was out there just waiting to happen—and most of the time he was right. I didn't even know that there was such a thing as "mission drudgery" because I never experienced it with Elder Hale.

While serving as his companion I remember thinking, *If all 65,000 missionaries in the world were like Elder Hale, Satan and his forces would be in serious trouble.* He truly was a modern-day Captain Moroni, of whom Mormon wrote the following tribute: "If all men had been, and were, and ever would be, like unto Moroni, behold, the very powers of hell would have been shaken forever; yea, the devil would never have power over the hearts of the children of men" (Alma 48:17). Is it any wonder that Mormon named his own son after his ultimate Nephite hero?

Another elder in our mission was a number-one missionary. He had recently been assigned to be the zone leader in Chişinău, Moldova, when he slipped on an icy sidewalk and broke his leg. My companion and I were the first to receive the frantic phone calls from the members of his zone. He had been transported to the hospital, but the missionaries were concerned about the quality of treatment he would receive there. We relayed the news on to our mission president, who was obviously concerned and instructed us to keep him apprised of any new information.

Throughout the night we kept getting phone calls, each with a panicked update of what was happening. This elder had been sedated and prepped for surgery, but the doctors were shuffling their feet and demanding bribes. The conditions at the hospital left much to be desired, and the operating room looked primitive. With each update we promptly passed the news along to President Jarvis.

Finally he had heard enough. He wanted this elder on the next train out of Moldova so that we could personally monitor the situation. Hesitantly I voiced the question that everyone had been speculating about: Would this elder have to leave the country to receive medical treatment? If so, the writing was on the wall; he would not be returning to Romania but would most likely be reassigned stateside after his recovery.

My mission president sighed and admitted that, depending on the severity of the injury, he would probably have to leave. I was deflated. This was one of our best missionaries, and now we were going to lose him.

The next morning we were finally able to get ahold of this elder. The doctors had opted not to perform the surgery but had put the leg in a cast and released him in a wheelchair to recover at home. We spoke for a moment, and when I was certain that he had his wits about him I broke the news: "Elder, President has asked that you get on the next train to Bucharest."

The phone went silent. All he could say was, "Why?"

I explained that we just wanted our doctors to be able to check him out and make sure that everything was okay.

This missionary was street savvy and saw right through me: "Oh, c'mon, Elder Christiansen, you know it's not just that. If I go down to Bucharest I guarantee they'll say they want to do some precautionary stuff and send me home. If I go back to the States then there's no way they'll let me come back to Romania. I'm not leaving Moldova!"

I was stunned and a little irritated. "But President Jarvis says you have to. It wasn't a request; it was an order."

He wouldn't budge. "Elder Christiansen, ever since I got to Romania I've dreamed about serving in Moldova. My dream finally comes true, and then after only two days I have to leave? Sorry, can't do it! Besides, I received a blessing at the hospital, and I have faith that I'll recover just fine."

The phone clicked and the line went dead.

I reluctantly called the mission president. "Uhh, President, we have a problem. Elder Robinson, he won't, umm, leave."

At first President Jarvis was clearly annoyed at both Elder Robinson and me, but after discussing possible courses of action (one of which was traveling up to Moldova and taking him by force), he paused for a moment, let out a laugh, and said, "I knew he wouldn't come." He was silent again and then began brainstorming out loud: "We need to see the X-rays of the break. Have the missionaries up there get them and fax them down immediately. We'll have our doctors here check them out, and if they feel comfortable with his treatment and if Elder Robinson's recovery goes well, maybe we can let him stay up there."

Elder Robinson was indeed permitted to stay up in Moldova. Part of the agreement was that he would obey the strict orders to stay off his leg during the long period of recovery. I knew that the following weeks would be extremely difficult for this missionary. He was one of our hardest workers and would absolutely hate being cooped up in the apartment. After a week I called to check up on him and see how things were going. As we talked he sounded really discouraged: "Yeah, things are kind of hard right now, and we're struggling a little bit. We didn't even meet our goal for 'number of discussions taught.'"

Number of discussions taught? I was confused. He wasn't supposed to be teaching discussions; he was supposed to be staying inside off of his severely broken leg. "What do you mean you didn't meet your goal for discussions taught?" I asked.

"Weeeell," he started apprehensively, "I stayed inside for about a day, but then I saw my companion getting way too comfortable in his pajamas so I told him to get dressed. I figured if I'm sitting *inside*, I may as well be sitting *outside* sharing the gospel. So I had my companion push me in the wheelchair down to the main plaza, and we just started talking to people who passed by. You should see how many people will talk to us because of my wheelchair; it's a sweet ice breaker.

"We did that for a few hours, but it started getting a little old. Then I got another idea. There was a bus stop nearby, so I had my companion wheel me that direction. When we got there we recruited some men to help load me on. We spent a couple of hours just going back and forth on the bus route contacting all the new people who would get on. We became good friends with the bus driver and are teaching him now. Anyway, I'm disappointed because we only were able to teach seventeen discussions and we set a goal to teach twenty."

I couldn't believe what I was hearing. Not only had he refused to leave the country, but he was also refusing to take any days off. I advised him to be wise and not do anything that would hinder his recovery, but inside I was brimming with pride and admiration for this elder.

Pretty soon we were getting calls from the other missionaries in his zone. "Do you know that Elder Robinson worked more hours than any other companionship this week?" "Elder Robinson is incredible! How can we not be motivated by him when he works harder than we do with a broken leg?" "The members absolutely love Elder Robinson; he's like a hero to them."

The legend of Elder Robinson could not be confined to his little Moldovan zone. Soon word of his incredible devotion spread like wildfire throughout the entire mission. The following month we witnessed firsthand the impact of his faithfulness as we traveled up to Moldova for zone conference. This zone had many candidates set up for baptism, morale was at an all-time high, and every companionship was contributing and experiencing success. As Elder Robinson hopped up to the podium to address the members of his zone, the admiration and respect that filled the room was overwhelming. It was one of the most powerful zone conferences I ever participated in.

Between meetings I pulled Elder Robinson aside, and we chatted for a moment. We laughed as we recounted the dramatic events of the past month. Then he got quiet for a moment and said, "You know, when I received the call to be the zone leader in Moldova I was obviously excited, but I was also really scared. I looked at the missionaries who were up here and saw that almost everyone had been serving longer than me. It might sound stupid, but I was worried how they would respond to a younger missionary being their zone leader. It was then that I prayed to Heavenly Father and asked him to help me earn the respect and support of the members of my zone. Even though it's kind of a painful way to have a prayer answered, this broken leg has been the answer."

That is the attitude of a number-one missionary.

Just as I learned powerful lessons from missionaries like Elder Hale and Elder Robinson, you should make it a practice to observe and learn from the positive examples around you. Doing so will provide inspiration to stretch higher, as well as supply ideas for growth and improvement.

The scriptures contain the ultimate collection of spiritual number ones and number twos. Think of Lehi, Nephi, Abinadi, Alma, Ammon, Helaman, the stripling warriors, Captain Moroni, Samuel the Lamanite, the brother of Jared, Mormon, and Moroni, and on and on it goes. While you were familiar with every name on that list, you probably haven't heard of one of my favorite scriptural number ones: the Old Testament warrior Caleb.

Caleb represented the tribe of Judah as one of twelve men sent to spy out the promised land. Upon returning to the camp the twelve spies gave their report. Ten of the men stood before the congregation of Israel and delivered ominous news. Their "promised land" was occupied by fierce-looking inhabitants, fortressed cities, and even a clan of warrior giants (see Numbers 13:26–29).

Needless to say, this grim report rattled the psyche of the exiled people, spawning doubt and fear. In the midst of the ensuing tumult, Caleb (one of the other two spies) arose and silenced the people with the following admonition: "Let us go up at once, and possess it; for we are well able to overcome it. . . . The land, which we passed through to search it, is an exceedingly good land. If the Lord delight in us, then he will bring us into this land, and give it us; a land which floweth with milk and honey. Only rebel not ye against the Lord, neither fear ye the people of the land; for they are bread for us: their defence is departed from them, and the Lord is with us: fear them not" (Numbers 13:30; 14:7–9).

The Israelites refused to rally around Caleb and even sought to put him to death. The Lord intervened and breathed out indignation and wrath upon his faithless and stiff-necked people. As punishment for their rebellion, this generation of unbelievers was forbidden to enter the promised land. Only Caleb and his counterpart, Joshua, would be granted that privilege.

After forty years of aimless wandering, a new generation was primed to inherit the promised land. Beginning with the miracle at Jericho, campaign after campaign brought incredible triumph as the Lord fulfilled long-standing covenants. The time soon came for the prophet Joshua to divide the conquered land among each of the tribes; but in the process he ran into a hiccup. The hill country that would serve as Israel's southern border was yet to be cleared of its native inhabitants. This region would be vital to the strategic defense of the new nation. But what tribe would want to settle there with much safer and comfortable alternatives available?

As I read the account, I picture the prophet Joshua convening the leaders of the various tribes and counseling with them regarding this pressing matter. I imagine a long moment of silence as each tribal leader considered the ramifications of such an assignment. Then in an instant, I see Caleb, the patriarch and spokesman of Judah, step forward and declare the following:

> Forty years old was I when Moses the servant of the
> Lord sent me from Kadesh-barnea to espy out the land;
> and I brought him word again as it was in mine heart.

> Nevertheless my brethren that went up with me made the heart of the people melt: but I wholly followed the Lord my God. . . .
>
> And now, behold, the Lord hath kept me alive, as he said, these forty and five years, . . . and now, lo, I am this day fourscore and five [eighty-five] years old.
>
> As yet I am as strong this day as I was in the day that Moses sent me: as my strength was then, even so is my strength now, for war, both to go out, and to come in.
>
> Now therefore give me this mountain, whereof the Lord spake in that day; for thou heardest in that day how the Anakims were there, and that the cities were great and fenced: if so be the Lord will be with me, then I shall be able to drive them out, as the Lord said. (Joshua 14:7–8, 10–12)

What a soul-stirring speech. Do you see how Caleb was truly a mighty number one for the Lord? If anyone had excuses to avoid such a heavy duty, it was him. For starters, he was nearly a hundred years old. Half of his life had been spent as a slave in Egypt; the other half had been wasted wandering in a harsh and desolate wilderness. In his old age, he had joined the warriors of Israel in battle to prepare the land for his people. Finally, he was at a point in his life where he could enjoy the fruits of his labors. Surely he had already done enough! But none of these things mattered to Caleb. As a number-one-ranked servant of the Lord, he would make no excuses; if God needed a task done, Caleb would find a way.

Another figure from the scriptures who was a mighty number one is the prophet Ether. Ether was the last prophet called to preach repentance to the Jaredite nation. Sadly, this call came at a time of deep apostasy and gross wickedness. In fact, Ether would eventually witness the fratricide (or self-annihilation) of his entire people. Before this tragic end, however, Ether carried the heavy burden of serving as the Lord's messenger. The account of his labors is recorded in the concluding chapters of the book that bears his name: "And Ether was a prophet of the Lord; wherefore Ether came forth in the days of Coriantumr, and began to prophecy unto the people, for he could not be restrained because of the Spirit of the Lord which was in him. For he did cry from the morning, even until the going down of the sun, exhorting the people to believe in God unto repentance lest they should be destroyed" (Ether 12:2–3).

How much success did Ether have among his people? We learn in the very next chapter that the people "rejected all the words of Ether" (Ether 13:2) and that they "esteemed him as naught, and cast him out" (Ether 13:13). The scriptures clearly indicate that Ether enjoyed little or no success. Every person he stopped on the street, every door he knocked on, every effort to share the gospel was met with apathy and anger, rejection and ridicule.

Anyone who has served a mission can attest to hard days, days filled with unmet expectations, dashed hopes, severe rebukes, and deep disappointment. But invariably such days are balanced out by others that brought unspeakable joy. It's much easier to cope with difficult days when you can draw upon the memory of successful days past and exercise hope for joyful days in the future. Now consider the circumstances of the prophet Ether. He had no such days to draw upon from the past; he would have no such hope for the future. Ether didn't have hard *days*; his *entire mission* was hard.

Yet from Ether we get some of the most powerful and profound descriptions of what it means to be a true representative of Jesus Christ. How can we not stand in awe at the phrase "He could not be restrained because of the Spirit of the Lord that was in him"? I'm sure there were moments when Ether wanted to quit. I'm sure there were times when he was completely overcome by the discouragement and frustration that accompany constant rejection and failure. But each time he considered quitting, each time he was about to give up, he couldn't because he was so filled with the Spirit of the Lord. Ether's determination to continue in the face of unrelenting discouragement places him squarely in the number one category.

The story and circumstances of Ether's mission are strikingly similar to those of the prophet Jeremiah. I'm convinced that Ether and Jeremiah must have been buddies in premortality and are probably swapping stories now in the next life. Just like Ether, Jeremiah was called to preach to an extremely idolatrous and hardened people—the same people, in fact, who would seek to murder the prophet Lehi and whose wickedness would usher in the destruction of Jerusalem by the Babylonians. And yet, Jeremiah was their missionary. He records that the people held him in "derision daily" (meaning they hated him) and that, in addition to their hatred, "every one mocketh me" (Jeremiah 20:7).

Apparently Jeremiah came to a point where he decided to "not make mention of [God], nor speak any more in his name" (Jeremiah 20:9). In other words, he was going to quit! I imagine his thought process went something like this: "Obviously no one cares about my message, so why even try? I'll keep living the gospel and being a good example to others, but as far as actively proselytizing, I'm through!" Then follows one of my favorite verses in all of the standard works: "But his word was in mine heart as a burning fire shut up in my bones, and I was weary with forbearing, and I could not stay [resist]" (Jeremiah 20:9).

What an awesome legacy to leave, to have the fire of testimony burning so brightly that you simply can't resist sharing the gospel with all around you! Surely it was this "bonfire" testimony that made Jeremiah a number-one-ranked servant in the hands of the Lord.

As you study the scriptures, learn all you can from the men and women who lived valiantly on the side of truth. Then go out each day and do likewise.

Similar to the game of *Stratego*, there is a battle raging in the world today between good and evil. Satan and his forces are mobilized throughout the earth spreading sin, darkness, despair, confusion, hatred, and misery. Their aim is the captivity and destruction of as many of Heavenly Father's children as possible. When they achieves their aim, the scriptures note that "the devil laugheth, and his angels rejoice" (3 Nephi 9:2). Opposing Satan is the Lord Jesus Christ, the Prince of Peace, the Light and Life of the World. He is our Captain and leads His forces of truth throughout the earth. Speaking of this conflict and the inevitable outcome, the Prophet Joseph Smith said: "The standard of truth has been erected; no unhallowed hand can stop the work from progressing; persecutions may rage, mobs may combine, armies may assemble, calumny may defame, but the truth of God will go forth boldly, nobly, and independent, till it has penetrated every continent, visited every clime, swept every country, and sounded in every ear, till the purposes of God shall be accomplished, and the Great Jehovah shall say the work is done" (*History of the Church*, 4;540).

So there we stand! The world needs you. The Lord needs you. The warrior Caleb has long since gone the way of the earth, as have Ether and Jeremiah. Elder Hale and Elder Robinson no longer pound the streets of Romania but are now raising up future missionaries of their own. The stage is set, and the time is yours. It is YOU who must now step forth and be counted. Your level of preparation and desire will determine your rank as you labor on the side of light and truth.

Let me conclude with perhaps the coolest Stratego verse in all of scripture. In a revelation to his elders the Lord said, "I call upon the weak things of the world, those who are unlearned and despised, *to thrash the nations by the power of my Spirit*; And their arm shall be my arm, and I will be their shield and their buckler; and I will gird up their loins, *and they shall fight manfully for me*" (D&C 35:13–14; emphasis added).

As you determine in your mind and heart to be a number-one-rank missionary, you will "thrash the nations" by the power of the Lord's Spirit. You will "fight manfully" for the Lord. You will be a powerful instrument in the hands of God.

Chapter 10
Boldness—The True Language of All Missionaries

"As you prayerfully and worthily exercise [your] authority, you will receive spiritual power, which is evidence of the reality of your call. Do not be afraid or shy about fulfilling this commission." —Preach My Gospel, 4

THE YEAR WAS AD 34.

Christ had been crucified but had triumphantly risen and ultimately ascended into heaven. The burden of carrying on the Church now lay solely on the apostles whom He had chosen and set apart. These apostles knew from firsthand experience the opposition they would face. While things appeared calm at the moment, any movement begun in the name of Jesus of Nazareth would immediately draw the attention and wrath of the elite Jewish classes. The apostles had seen the crowd of people whipped into a hate-filled mob. They had heard the heart-piercing cries of "Crucify Him!" and been witnesses to the horrific scene of torture at Golgotha. Furthermore, the Savior Himself had hinted that their futures would be hauntingly similar to His past. Their testimonies would be sealed with blood.

With the stage now set, we turn to the opening scenes of the book of Acts of the Apostles. Devout Jews from all nations had gathered to Jerusalem in observation of the Pentecost. The apostles were likewise participating when the promised endowment of the Holy Ghost occurred. In dramatic fashion the Spirit poured down upon the apostles, and they "began to speak with other tongues, as the Spirit gave them utterance" (Acts 2:4). The crowds marveled at the scene and reasoned among themselves about what the meaning behind it could possibly be. Sensing an opportunity, Peter stepped forth and began to speak:

> . . . Ye men of Judea, and all ye that dwell at Jerusalem,
> be this known unto you, and hearken unto my words: . . .

Jesus of Nazareth, a man approved of God among you by miracles and wonders and signs, which God did by him in the midst of you, as ye yourselves also know:

Him, being delivered by the determinate counsel and foreknowledge of God, ye have taken, and by wicked hands have crucified and slain:

Whom God hath raised up, having loosed the pains of death: because it was not possible that he should be holden of it. . . .

This Jesus hath God raised up, whereof we all are witnesses. . . .

Therefore let all the house of Israel know assuredly, that God hath made that same Jesus, whom ye have crucified, both Lord and Christ. (Acts 2:14, 22–24, 32, 36)

What incredible courage! Think of the risk incurred by not only asserting the divinity of Christ, but also by accusing this very group of murdering the Messiah. This is not the course of action you would expect from someone in such precarious circumstances. Would anyone have blamed Peter if he had been intimidated? Would anyone have criticized him if he had trod lightly and downplayed the event? Absolutely not. If Peter cares anything for self-preservation he should be defusing the situation, not fanning the flames further.

Studying this story provides a valuable lesson for prospective missionaries. Although missionaries go throughout the world preaching the gospel in numerous languages, there is one language common to all: boldness. Peter understood this principle and so must every elder or sister who would become a powerful instrument in the hands of the Lord. The miraculous epilogue comes as Peter's boldness yields a bountiful harvest of nearly 3,000 souls.

In subsequent chapters the saga only gets more compelling. Through the power of the priesthood and in the name of Christ, Peter and John heal a man lame from birth. The onlookers are astounded, and Peter again seizes the opportunity to preach (see Acts 3). Word of both the miracle and message reaches the Sanhedrin, and prompt action is taken to impede further momentum of the "rogue" apostles. Peter and John are arrested and brought before the ranks of this powerful ruling body—the same ruling body that plotted against Jesus and delivered Him over to the Romans to be crucified. If anyone should feel cautious, fearful, or worried, it's them.

Yet when given a chance to speak, this is their opening statement: "Ye rulers of the people, and elders of Israel. . . . Be it known unto you all, and to all the people of Israel, that by the name of Jesus Christ of Nazareth, whom ye crucified, whom God raised from the dead, even by him doth this man stand here before you whole. This is the stone which was set at nought of you builders, which is become the head of the corner. Neither is there salvation in any other: for there is none other name under heaven given among men, whereby we must be saved" (Acts 4:8, 10–12).

Can you imagine the shock that must have rattled this council? The power of the Sanhedrin was unquestioned and absolute. No one spoke like that before them. No one dared defy or challenge their authority. Yet here stood two men associated with Jesus who showed absolutely no fear or trepidation before their ranks. The Jewish rulers' bewilderment is registered in the following verse: "Now when they saw the boldness of Peter and John, and perceived that they were unlearned and ignorant men, they marvelled; and they took knowledge of them, that they had been with Jesus" (Acts 4:13).

In response to the boldness and defiance of Peter and John, the Sanhedrin decrees that all mention of Jesus of Nazareth must cease and breathes out all manner of threats if they are found in noncompliance (see Acts 4:16–21). The two apostles are permitted to leave and, undeterred, resume their preaching of the Master. Miracles follow everywhere they go, and their reputation and influence grows daily among the masses.

Soon the Sanhedrin can no longer ignore the problem, and they again have the apostles arrested and imprisoned. An angel of the Lord delivers them, and they immediately go to the temple complex and preach to all who will listen (see Acts 5:17–21). When the Sanhedrin learns that they have not only escaped the confines of the prison but are even at that moment teaching the multitudes, they take hold of them yet again and bring them before the council. Exasperated, the leaders demand, "Did not we straitly command you that ye should not teach in this name? and, behold, ye have filled Jerusalem with your doctrine, and intend to bring this man's blood upon us" (Acts 5:28).

Note how this mighty and arrogant council is almost begging the apostles to stop their proselytizing. Note also the power in Peter's response: "Then Peter and the other apostles answered and said, We ought to obey God rather than men. The God of our fathers raised up Jesus, whom ye slew and hanged on a tree. Him hath God exalted with his right hand to be a Prince and a Saviour, for to give repentance to Israel, and forgiveness of sins. And we are his witnesses of these things; and so is also the Holy Ghost, whom God hath given to them that obey him" (Acts 5:29–32).

This declaration of testimony and condemnation nearly costs these men their lives. After fierce deliberation, the Sanhedrin opts to release them once again but not before inflicting a more severe punishment. They order Peter and John to be violently beaten as a show of power and a future deterrent. With the cost of discipleship quickly escalating, notice how the apostles respond: "And they departed from the presence of the council, rejoicing that they were counted worthy to suffer shame for his name. And daily in the temple, and in every house, they ceased not to teach and preach Jesus Christ" (Acts 5:41–42).

Studying these chapters in the book of Acts never fails to amaze and inspire me. During this extreme period of persecution, the ancient apostles courageously fulfilled their callings as representatives of the Savior. In doing so they also exhibited the true principle of boldness.

Let's face it; the thought of knocking on doors or stopping strangers on the street can be scary and intimidating. Being a bold missionary means having the courage to open your mouth in spite of nervousness and fear. Boldness is constantly guided by the question *What would God think?* rather than *What would man think?* You never know whether someone will accept the gospel unless you give him or her that chance. For this reason, a bold missionary will take every opportunity to bear testimony of the Savior and His true Church. Whenever I was afraid as a missionary I would tell myself, *The worst that can happen is you get rejected; the best that can happen is you save a person's soul.* As you can see, the reward far outweighs the risk.

While the gospel message must be preached boldly, the Book of Mormon provides a caution associated with this principle. In counsel to his son, Alma warned, "Use boldness, but not overbearance" (Alma 38:12). The line between boldness and overbearance is very fine indeed, and many missionaries struggle to know where they are in relation to this line. Some— in the name of boldness—cause much harm through overbearing words or actions.

Early on in my mission I was this type of missionary. I not only crossed the line, I obliterated it with a jackhammer. In my personal study I had read the Savior's instruction to "say nothing but repentance unto this generation" (D&C 6:9) and took it upon myself to call every person I encountered to immediate repentance. My street contact went something like this: "Hi! We're personal representatives of Jesus Christ, and we are here to tell you that you need to repent. If you don't repent and change your life then you will not be prepared for the time when Christ will come again. Our message is the key to help you in this process. When can we come share it with you?"

As you can imagine, very few people responded favorably to this approach. Yet I was so proud of my "boldness" that I actually thought less of other missionaries for not sharing my zeal. All of this changed one day when a zone leader visited our city and took me out on an exchange. While heading toward the city center to begin contacting, he mentioned how he had heard that I was a bold missionary. In my mind I smugly thought, *He's never seen bold; I'll show him the epitome of bold.*

I told him that I would stop the first person, saw a man nearby, and approached him. I introduced who we were and then launched into an even brasher version of my contact. When I asked the man if we could come to his home and share our message, he angrily said, "No!" and stormed off.

My zone leader looked stunned. In my mind I thought, *He's just overwhelmed by seeing true boldness.*

Finally he spoke. "That's, um, an . . . interesting approach you're using."

Defensively, I stated my opinion that as missionaries we should be bold and preach nothing but repentance as the Savior had taught. I argued that such preaching leaves no room for ambiguity: either people choose to repent or they don't. He just stared at me, dumbfounded, not knowing what to say.

Finally he asked if he could stop the next person, and a minute later he approached a passing gentleman. He began with introductions and then asked a simple question: "Sir, how are you doing today?" This question spawned a dialogue that lasted nearly five minutes. Each question asked by this missionary was done with deep sincerity and love. In fact, he showed such genuine interest and concern for the man that after only a few minutes it was evident there was a high level of comfort and trust between them.

At this point the zone leader began to introduce the Book of Mormon. The sincerity that had previously been shown to the man was now accorded to the book in his hand. As he taught and bore testimony, I glanced up at the investigator and noticed that he was staring at the Book of Mormon like it was the most valuable treasure on earth. The missionary didn't even need to extend an invitation; the man actually interrupted and asked if he could have a copy. An appointment was set, and after further testimony, we parted ways.

I was stunned.

Everything this missionary had done seemed so opposite to my "bold" approach, yet the result had been undeniable. This elder could tell I was struggling to process what I had seen and didn't intrude on my thoughts. Finally I couldn't bear the silence and blurted out, "I'm wrong! You're right! My way is stupid! Your way rocks!"

I felt like such an idiot.

He just laughed, smiled at me, and motioned for us to sit down on a nearby bench. There he taught me a valuable lesson: "Elder Christiansen, your enthusiasm and desire and passion are awesome. Never, ever lose those. But you can't walk up to complete strangers, command them to repent, and expect them to want to hear your message. You've got to show people that you possess a genuine love and concern for them. Once they sense this, you can tell them *anything*."

From that moment on, I put this elder's advice into practice and saw that he was right.

As is the case with many gospel principles, problems occur when we venture into extremes. We have already discussed how too much boldness quickly morphs into overbearance. Now let us turn our attention to the problem of too little boldness.

In an effort to avoid overbearance in preaching the gospel, some missionaries cower to faithlessness and timidity.

I encountered this problem once while teaching at the MTC. There was a missionary in my district who simply refused to give commitments. His opinion was that missionaries shouldn't "push" people into doing anything. If his investigators wanted to do something, then that was up to them, but he wouldn't try to force them or change their mind.

His attitude was deeply troubling to all around him, but he simply refused to budge. Each time someone would try to explain the error of his thinking, he would cite his respect for God-given agency and then become defensive and stubborn. Week after week this continued, and he became more and more entrenched in his opinion. With only days remaining before his departure, I sat him down one last time to address this problem.

I began by explaining how his refusal to extend commitments actually *contradicted* the principle of agency because it failed to provide clear choices for those whom he would teach. I reminded him that a missionary's purpose was clear: (1) teach the gospel by the Spirit with love, clarity, and power; and (2) invite those who have been taught to conform their lives to these truths. Only under these conditions could an investigator properly use the gift of agency to accept or reject the message. I then showed him several scriptural passages where the Savior Himself extended invitations to prospective disciples.

Although unable to disprove anything that I was saying, he still refused to yield. It was then that I realized what was truly plaguing this elder. He was afraid! He was afraid to give commitments; he was afraid to have expectations. In sum, he was afraid of taking the leap of faith that so often is required in missionary work.

I felt impressed to be blunt with this elder and told him that his approach had little to do with respecting the agency of others and everything to do with a lack of faith. He furiously denied it and stated in very clear terms that he no longer wanted to hear any counsel or advice from me. I issued yet another warning that his foolish approach would render him entirely ineffective in the mission field, and he abruptly stormed out of the room.

Over the course of the next few days I closely observed the Spirit working on this young elder. Finally, the night before he was scheduled to leave, he pulled me aside and asked if we could talk. We sat down, and in a very contrite manner he confessed that I had been absolutely right in my assessment. It was fear. It was a lack of faith. He promised that he would change and that he would preach the gospel message with courage and boldness. I immediately took the opportunity to express love for him and confidence in his ability to do much good as a representative for the Lord. This indeed came to pass as he went on to serve an honorable and successful mission.

Although previously mentioned, I believe it deserves repeating that true boldness must be motivated by love and is always inspired by the Holy Ghost. The Book of Mormon provides essential insight on the role of the Spirit in relation to boldness. When Father Lehi gave his sons Laman and Lemuel a final blessing, he explained the following: "And ye have murmured because he [Nephi] hath been plain unto you. Ye say that he hath used sharpness; ye say that he hath been angry with you; but behold, his sharpness was the sharpness of the power of the word of God, which was in him; and that which ye call anger was the truth, according to that which is in God, which he could not restrain, manifesting boldly concerning your iniquities" (2 Nephi 1:26).

What precedes this passage is obvious. Laman and Lemuel complained to Dad that little brother Nephi was bugging them again about their righteousness, or lack thereof. In a word, they think he's being overbearing. They have never liked the message and have long projected their frustration and wrath on the messenger. To this, Lehi teaches his sons a powerful truth: the source of the message was never Nephi; the source was God Himself.

As a missionary you will often be called upon to wield the "sharpness of the power of the word of God." As with Nephi, doing so will occasionally draw the ire and disfavor of those whom you seek to help. In such moments, be steadfast in your message but show an increase of love.

In this chapter we've established that boldness must be the true language of all missionaries. If this language is spoken too harshly and untempered by a spirit of love, it is overbearing. If this language is spoken too timidly, in weak tones and cowardly compromises, it is faithless. Oh, what a difference it would make if every missionary's prayer would echo that of Peter and the early apostles: "Lord . . . grant unto thy servants, that with all boldness they may speak thy word" (Acts 4:29)!

Chapter 11
Missionary Black Holes

"You will . . . be expected to devote all your time and attention to serving the Lord, leaving behind all other personal affairs." —Preach My Gospel, 137

As a kid I was always fascinated by space. On warm summer nights my brother and I would sleep outside on the trampoline and stare up into the endless sky. Somehow the night sky always seemed to spark feelings of awe and wonder. Years later in college I had the chance to take an astronomy class and absolutely loved it. To this day I remember one lecture very distinctly. The professor instantly hooked our attention by proposing the existence of alternative or parallel universes. He then hypothesized on possible entry portals between such universes. In this discussion the topic of black holes was introduced.

A black hole is a concentration of mass so dense that its gravitational pull sucks in all nearby objects. Each black hole contains an event horizon (or "point of no return"). Basically, once something enters a black hole and moves past the event horizon, it's gone.

Similar to the black holes that occur in space, there are also missionary black holes. These black holes threaten to devour a missionary's most valuable resource: TIME. At the outset of a mission two years or eighteen months may seem like a very long time. Yet as missionaries begin to lose themselves in the work, time often seems to be playing cruel tricks. After serving for six months it will feel like only yesterday that you entered the MTC—nonetheless a quarter of your mission is complete. At the year mark missionaries will have to use their fingers and count out loud the months to convince themselves that they really have been out that long. Finally, the tears will flow freely as you leave the soil of your mission and board the plane for your departure home.

Once you return, you'll be welcomed home by family and friends. Hours will be spent enjoying sweet reunions until your body crashes from the strain of traveling home after two years of devoted service. You'll sleep for a long time, maybe even days, and then you'll wake up in your old room. This moment will bring a feeling of disorientation and confusion like none other you've ever experienced. In the daze of having slept so long and waking up in such familiar yet unfamiliar surroundings, you'll have the strangest thought enter your mind: *Was it all a dream?* For a brief moment you will literally wonder if your mission ever happened. That is how short the two years of missionary service truly are.

"Little Jonathan's Race"

My mission president shared a story with us that completely changed the way I viewed the two years of a mission. He was raising his family in Western Canada, and the town in which they lived held an annual race for the boys and girls. His youngest son, Jonathan, begged to enter, and so on the scheduled morning he went and signed him up. Soon it was time for the race to begin, and the starting gun sounded. The parents yelled and cheered for their children as the huge pack of racers took off. Once the youngsters had vanished from sight, the adults made their way over to the finish line to position themselves for the end of the race.

After a few minutes, a pack of racers came bolting around the corner toward the home stretch. Parents strained to spot their children as the lead group sprinted toward the finish line. My mission president looked for Jonathan but didn't see him among the finishers in this first group. A little disappointed, he continued to watch as racers trickled in. By this point he was getting a little worried and was about to jog the race course in search of his son. Suddenly, a surge of excitement came from the crowd, and he noticed other parents motioning toward the distance. A little boy was flying toward the finish line at a blinding speed. Sure enough, it was little Jonathan. Passing several fellow racers as if it they were standing still, Jonathan burst through the finish line as the crowd cheered his extraordinary effort.

On the drive home my mission president listened to his son as he talked excitedly about the race. Finally he couldn't resist asking the question on his mind: "Good job, buddy," he began, "but what happened out there? That last part of the race you were running twice as fast as the boy who won."

Jonathan nodded his head and responded, "Yeah, if I would have known how short the race was, I would have turned on the jets a lot faster!"

To any prospective or new missionary I would echo the wise words of little Jonathan. If you only knew how short the race actually is, you would turn on the jets a lot faster.

Hopefully the point has been made, but it can't be overstated: TIME is a missionary's most precious resource. With that concept properly emphasized, let's turn our attention to some of the missionary black holes that could waste your precious time.

Missionary Black Hole 1: Contention within a Companionship

There is great wisdom in the two-by-two approach to preaching the gospel. It is divinely inspired and wisely implemented in the missionary program of the Church. A missionary companion provides support, protection, and above all, companionship. Isn't it comforting to know that no matter how far you are from home, you will never be alone in the service of the Lord?

Having a companion also brings some inherent challenges. Just as you do not pick the mission to which you are called or the area in which you'll be assigned, you likewise will not have the luxury of selecting the companions with whom you serve. Over the course of your mission you will work with approximately eight to twelve different companions. Many of these companions will probably be very different than you. They'll have different personalities, different interests, different opinions, and different ways of doing things. And yet the Lord's instruction is unyielding: "Be one; and if ye are not one ye are not mine" (D&C 38:27).

Contention within a companionship is an enormous black hole that depletes time and energy and renders a companionship virtually useless. Why is contention so debilitating? Because the gospel message can only be taught by the power of the Spirit. The Savior left no room for debate when He declared, "If ye receive not the Spirit ye shall not teach" (D&C 42:14). Notice how He doesn't say, "If ye receive not the Spirit ye probably shouldn't teach," or "It's not a good idea to teach." This is not a suggestion; it's a commandment. Tied to this commandment is the doctrine taught so clearly by Christ to the Nephites. To them He said, "The spirit of contention is not of me, but is of the devil" (3 Nephi 11:29).

So think about it. If Satan can get you and your companion to bear grudges against each other, he wins. If he can stir you to anger and harsh words, he wins. If he can sow feelings of resentment through small irritations and annoying quirks, he wins. If he can get you to tear each other down or speak behind each other's backs, he wins. The smallest shard of contention between companions allows the adversary to rest easy, knowing such missionaries pose little threat. They simply lack the power necessary to accomplish what they are ordained to do.

Throughout your mission this black hole will swirl ominously around you, but you can avoid it. The following suggestions will help you to do so:

Look for the good in your companion.

When we meet someone and form an opinion about them, we often find exactly what we are looking for. If we are looking for flaws, weaknesses, and imperfections, chances are we will find them. But if we are *looking for the good*, then positive attributes will manifest themselves, and that's where our focus will be.

Consider for a moment the unique opportunity that lies ahead on your mission. You will be serving with many different companions, each of whom will possess different strengths, talents, and Christlike attributes that you may not have. If during your mission you look for the good in your companions, you can then seek to incorporate their strengths into your own character.

My own missionary companions taught me so much. From my trainer I learned incredible love for the people. From another companion I learned the power of true, sincere prayer. Yet another taught me the value of increased organization and planning. From a brand new missionary I learned amazing persistence and faith. All of these helped me grow and become a much better servant in the hands of the Lord.

Communication

Food is essential to the survival of the human body. In terms of human relationships, *communication* is the food that brings life. Where communication is lacking or insincere, relationships die. As a missionary, it is essential to communicate in healthy and constructive ways with your companion. When problems or issues arise (and yes I did say *when*, not *if*), it's important not to let them fester. I've heard it said that there's a time in the life of every problem when it's big enough to be seen but small enough to be solved. It is in this brief window of time that a missionary must act to counter any contention that might threaten a companionship.

The Natural Man or the Saint

Even in the best companionships, there will be times of disagreement, frustration, and conflict. In these moments, the pride-fueled *natural man* will assume he's right and hunker down for a long and perhaps devastating battle. The toll and cost don't matter, only the preservation of pride and ego. The *Saint,* however, takes an entirely different course. Governed by humility, he appeals to the Atonement of Christ for the capacity to love, forgive, change, and reconcile. In turning to the Savior, the saint is first made to focus on his own weaknesses and flaws, taking the focus off those of his companion. The saint's attitude then shifts to that displayed by the ancient apostles: "Lord, is it I?" (Matthew 26:22)

By choosing the response of the saint you will successfully avoid the black hole of contention. You'll realize that you are just as plagued by weaknesses as your companion and will be much more understanding and patient in your relationship together. As you keep lines of communication open and healthy, you will be better prepared when dealing with problems.

Be Loyal to Your Companion

More than anything else, *be loyal to your companion*. Once trust is betrayed, it is nearly impossible to regain in the short time you will be together. Do not say anything negative about your companion to other missionaries— ever! Doing so says more about you than the missionary you're degrading.

My trainer taught me this lesson early on. One preparation day I heard the other district members talking about the elder who had served with my companion before me. They were telling the wildest stories of what a jerk this missionary had been to my trainer. In not-so-subtle terms they expressed their dislike for him and relief that he was gone.

I couldn't believe it. I had been with my trainer for nearly a month and had never heard him say a word about any of this. Being curious, I slyly asked him about it the next day as we were walking to an appointment: "So Elder Hale, what was Elder _____ like?"

He smiled and let out a weak attempt at a laugh. I could tell he was choosing his words very carefully. Finally he looked at me and said, "Elder Christiansen, I'm very glad to be serving with you."

He put his arm around me and changed the subject. That's all he would say. I later served in the same district with his former companion and witnessed firsthand what a difficult missionary he actually was. But I always remembered the lesson from my trainer who had absolutely refused to speak ill of another missionary.

Missionary companionships will be the source of some of your greatest relationships, memories, and experiences. Hopefully the following story illustrates what I mean. Of the eight companions I served with in Romania, seven could have been my best friends from back home. I was incredibly lucky in this regard. But my experience with one companion was a little challenging. When it was announced in transfer meeting that this elder was my new companion, several missionaries came up and offered their condolences. Apparently I was in for a rough ride. During the five-hour train ride to our city, I immediately sensed that this companionship was indeed going to be different. I tried asking questions to begin the process of building a relationship, but my new companion responded with only one-word answers and we mostly sat in awkward silence. It was obvious we had nothing in common.

Arriving home late, we dumped our bags and got ready to go to sleep. We knelt beside our beds for companionship prayer, and after saying amen, I swooped over and grabbed my comp in a big bear hug. I had always done this with previous companions, and so it had become a habit. While hugging him, I said, "I'm really glad we're companions, Elder _____. Oh, by the way, you don't have any strange pet peeves do you?"

I'll never forget the annoyed look on his face as he gritted his teeth and replied with an emphatic, "I don't like to be hugged!"

That experience basically sums up what our companionship was like. This elder struggled with severe depression and anxiety and was constantly worried that his best efforts were somehow unaccepted by the Lord. When arriving at street intersections, he often felt it necessary to pray and wait for inspiration directing us which way we should go. We once waited at an intersection for nearly a half hour while he tried to discern whether to go right or left. I tried explaining to him that God didn't need to micromanage every trivial detail of our work, but he wouldn't budge.

As weeks went by, it became slightly disconcerting how little I knew about my companion. In spite of my incessant efforts to crack through his detached personality, he simply would not open up to me. Yet day after day I would pepper him with a string of never-ending questions. What did he like to do? What was something unique about him? What was the craziest thing he ever did before his mission? What was his family like? Did he have any pets? How did he feel about Einstein's theory of relativity? In response, he would either ignore these questions entirely or brush them off with a one-word answer.

One day I was going through my litany of questions when he abruptly stopped and then erupted: "Enough!!! Stop asking me these stupid, pointless questions! There's nothing special about me. I don't have any hobbies. I didn't do anything crazy before my mission—just leave me alone!"

I was shocked. He never showed any emotion, and now I could tell he was really mad. Unfortunately for him, I have this personality defect that when I know I'm annoying people, instead of relenting, I actually push harder and try to make it worse. So I kept going. "Oh, c'mon, Elder _____, just tell me one thing!"

He was fuming now. "YOU JUST WON'T QUIT, WILL YOU?"

By this point I was getting pretty worked up myself. "NO, ELDER, I WON'T QUIT! You only have four months left, so we're probably going to be together till the end of your mission. So from now until then just plan on me asking you these same stupid questions. But it won't end there. After you go home, I'll write you letters, and in the letters I'll ask you these same stupid questions, and then I'll get home and I'll look up your phone number and I'll call you every day asking these same stupid questions. Until the day you die I'll be asking you these same stupid questions, and even then I'll come to your funeral and hover over your casket and ask, 'WHAT'S THE CRAZIEST THING YOU EVER DID BEFORE YOUR MISSION!?!'"

He was stunned by my outburst and immediately became silent. To be honest, I was worried that I had gone too far and that he would never speak to me ever again.

After a moment he began to bargain. "If I tell you *one* thing, do you promise you won't bug me anymore?"

I quickly nodded my head, and he began to speak. "My dad grew up in the '70s and was kind of a free-spirited, artsy hippy. I remember when I was little he'd be in his studio painting or sculpting, and he would listen to the Bee Gees. I guess one thing about me is that I like the Bee Gees."

I was shocked. My companion was the most sober-minded, serious twenty-one-year-old I had ever met. And here he was confessing to me that he loved the flamboyant music of the band that personified the disco movement. I couldn't believe it. I tried to respond: "Y-y-you like the *Bee Gees?*" I knew I shouldn't laugh, but I couldn't hold it in.

"I shouldn't have told you!!!" he yelled. And our conversation was over.

Well, now I had some ammunition on my companion. He liked the Bee Gees. At random times throughout the day I would sneak up behind him and in my most prepubescent, high-pitched voice scream out, "Stayin' alive, stayin' alive, oh, oh, oh, oh, stayin' aliiiiiiiiiiiiiiiiiivvee, yeah!"

Of course, my companion would freak out and yell at me to be quiet.

The following week we had zone conference and our interviews with the mission president. When it was my turn, President Jarvis and I talked for a while, and then near the end our conversation, he hesitantly asked, "So how are things going with your companion?"

It was obvious that my answer surprised him. "Things are going really well. Elder _____ is the hardest-working missionary I've ever been with. He's vigilantly obedient, and he genuinely loves the people with all his heart. How can I complain or find fault with someone like that?"

He sat frozen for a moment, nodded his head, and let out a "hmmm" as he jotted something down on his notepad. My companion only had three transfers left, so I figured for sure that we would be together until the end of his mission.

You can imagine how shocked I was a week later when transfer calls came and my companion was being moved. When I told him of the transfer he showed absolutely no emotion and in the subsequent days was completely businesslike in his preparation to leave. The day of transfers came, and I accompanied him to the train station. Another missionary from our district was also leaving, so they would travel together down to Bucharest.

Heading toward the train station I was kind of nervous to see what parting with my companion would be like. With previous companions saying good-bye had been extremely difficult, with lots of emotion, hugs, and even a few tears. My gut instinct told me that this time would be very different.

When we arrived at the station, my companion went to buy tickets and returned just in time to hear the train whistle blow. He then turned to me, said, "Good-bye, Elder Christiansen," and promptly boarded the train without even a handshake.

Suddenly he stopped and called out, "Hey, Elder!"

I turned back, hoping he was going to express some sadness that our companionship was over, some token of affection. Instead he hurriedly commanded, "Make sure you go visit that family we met on the street yesterday." And with that, the train pulled away, and he was gone.

As I made my way back to our apartment I couldn't help feeling a little dejected. My companion had hated my guts—there was no doubt about that.

The remaining ten months of my mission seemed to pass by in an instant, and soon I was returning home. A few months later I was extremely excited to attend my first mission reunion. I traveled up to Salt Lake with some former companions and upon arriving formed a boisterous group of my closest mission friends. The nostalgia was palpable as we began reminiscing and swapping stories.

After about an hour I looked up and was mortified to see this former companion enter the backyard where the reunion was being held. He peered around as if searching for someone, and instinctively I kind of ducked, hoping he wouldn't see me. In my mind I thought, *He wouldn't be looking for me anyway. He hates my guts.* But sure enough, he soon spotted me and headed my direction. Approaching my large group, he said hello and we exchanged a few pleasantries. Then he grew serious and said, "Hey, I really need to talk to you sometime tonight."

I promised that I'd come find him, but inwardly I dreaded what might happen. I was sure he was going to tell me how badly he hated me and that my name was on a list of people for whom he wished a premature and painful death. After a second I shrugged it off and jumped back into the fun and enjoyment of the reunion.

Nearly three hours later the reunion was winding down. Most people had already left: however, my group of friends was just warming up as we made plans to hang out together that night. Out of nowhere, my companion appeared. I had kind of hoped he had forgotten about our impending heart-to-heart, but apparently he had not.

"Hey, I *really* need to talk to you," he said.

Well, I thought, *I may as well get it over with.*

So we started to walk.

As we walked he began to speak. "Elder Christiansen, there's something I need to tell you. During my mission I had fourteen different companions." In my head I quickly did the math and realized that equaled a new companion for nearly every transfer. "As a brand-new missionary I was so excited to be in Romania, but soon I could tell that my trainer thought I was weird and that he hated being my companion. This hurt me so much that I decided early on to put up barriers with each of my subsequent companions. I knew they weren't going to care about me, so why should I care about them? Instead, I'd devote all my love and attention to the Romanian people, not worrying about what my companions thought or felt about me."

My former companion then paused for a moment, looked me in the eye, and said, "Elder Christiansen, out of the fourteen companions I served with, *you* were the only one who I could tell really loved me. You were the only one who cared. You never made me feel like I was weird or a burden. You'll never know how much that meant to me." And with that, this companion gave me an awkward attempt at a hug (expressions of affection were not his thing) and then turned and walked away.

During my two years as a missionary I experienced mighty miracles, saw lives change, and felt the Spirit in powerful abundance. But I don't think I ever felt as good in Romania as I did after that talk with my former companion.

The adversary will try to poison your companionships, stirring you up to anger and contention. Do not let him win! As you look for the good in your companion, communicate effectively together, turn to the Atonement of Christ for help and humility, and are completely loyal, you will avoid this black hole.

Missionary Black Hole 2: "To Every Thing There Is a Season"

In the Bible, the book Ecclesiastes contains the famous passage, "To every thing there is a season, and a time to every purpose under the heaven: A time to be born, and a time to die; a time to plant, and a time to pluck up that which is planted" (Ecclesiastes 3:1–2). What is the underlying message in this poetic imagery? That there is an ebb and flow to our mortal lives, with different experiences each coming in their due and proper time. The next missionary black hole is eloquently put in a subsequent verse: "A time to embrace, and a time to refrain from embracing" (v. 5). Unless it's your mission president's wife, the two years of missionary service are definitely a time to *refrain from embracing.* Using the once-famous idea of Elder Spencer W. Kimball, every missionary needs to keep their heart securely locked (see "Lock Your Heart," Latin American Mission Tour, 1968, www.missionaryhelper.com/talks/lockheart.html).

Before your mission you are able to date and associate with members of the opposite gender in wholesome and enjoyable ways. After your mission such associations will not only resume but intensify as you begin to seek an eternal companion with whom you can be sealed in the temple. Yet sandwiched in the middle of these two life periods is a sliver of time when romantic thoughts, feelings, or relationships of any kind must not be kindled or acted upon. While the previous black hole threatened to rob you of your precious time, this black hole is capable of destroying much more than that.

Every missionary should pay close attention to the story of Corianton in the Book of Mormon. Corianton was one of Alma's sons who took part in the dream team of missionaries called to reclaim the apostate Zoramites. But instead of fulfilling his mission, Corianton lost control of his heart and was immoral with the harlot Isabel. This grievous sin not only stained Corianton's soul, but also brought other far-reaching repercussions. Of these Alma said, "Behold, O my son, how great iniquity ye brought upon the Zoramites; for when they saw your conduct they would not believe in my words" (Alma 39:11). Echoing the lament of Alma, President Kimball said the following to a group of missionaries: "One scandal in a community is enough to annihilate the work of all of you, maybe all the work you do cumulatively—for all your two years—neutralized by one scandal in the community!" ("Lock Your Heart")

Missionaries must be vigilant in preserving their reputation as virtuous, dignified, and honorable servants of God. Even the appearance of anything indecent or inappropriate must be avoided. Emphasizing this point, President Kimball tells a story of an elder who was seen by a neighbor being overly friendly with a female investigator. Word quickly spread, and the effect was devastating. This missionary was not committing immorality—nothing even close to it—but the damage that was done was irreparable. President Kimball described what happened: "That city was closed, absolutely closed to missionary work for 20 years! Do you think missionaries could go in that city? Why of course they couldn't! Because there was still the memory of this indiscretion!" ("Lock Your Heart")

So how can you protect yourself from this dangerous and devastating black hole? The following are a few suggestions:

Simply put, missionaries should not have time to get in trouble. They have too much work to do. In counseling Corianton, Alma observed, "Thou shouldst have tended to the ministry wherewith thou wast entrusted" (Alma 39:4). Section four of the Doctrine and Covenants contains the powerful phrase "with an eye single to the glory of God" (v. 5). An eye single to the glory of God is completely focused on the work and nothing else. Attaining this eye steers servants of the Lord far from temptation and entrapment.

In reference to the eye, President Henry B. Eyring counseled priesthood holders to be careful where they allow their gaze to linger (see "God Helps the Faithful Priesthood Holder," *Ensign*, Nov. 2007, 58). The world has increasingly become inundated with pornography, immodesty, and sensuality. The immorality of the world is designed to arouse curiosity and plant dangerous seeds within the human mind. A missionary must have the discipline to bridle his passions (see Alma 38:12) by shunning anything that would offend the Spirit. As you strive to do this, remember the simple but wise instruction of your kindergarten teacher: Stay on task!

The divinely inspired missionary program is structured to provide protection from this destructive black hole. Having a missionary companion is the ultimate safeguard against temptation and misconduct. President Kimball offered this prophetic perspective: "Through 137 years we have come to the conclusion that if two people will stay together the chances for sin or serious trouble are reduced about 98%. Once in a great while two companions will both go sour at the same time, but it isn't the usual thing" ("Lock Your Heart").

The words of a prophet four decades ago are just as valid and important for missionaries serving today. As a missionary, you must protect your companion and allow your companion to protect you. There is great wisdom in the mission rule to be within sight of your companion at all times. Missionaries cannot afford to be naïve. The adversary would love nothing more than to defame the elders and sisters of the Church and will do so even if by false accusation. Satan has never had qualms about lying, conspiring, scheming, plotting—and he certainly doesn't have any now. Having a companion constantly by your side provides valuable protection from false allegations and accusations. It also will discourage behavior or actions that might occur if you were alone.

Part of protecting your companion involves never letting him do anything that could jeopardize the cause for which you both serve. The adversary may try to get you to rationalize or justify small indiscretions. Don't! You demonstrate loyalty to your companion when you don't allow him to commit any improprieties. If an incident occurs that makes you feel uneasy, inform your mission president immediately. If you are unsure as to the seriousness of what happened, better to turn such matters over to someone who holds keys of discernment, releasing you from culpability should disciplinary action be necessary.

The following story illustrates the point I'm trying to make. At the beginning of my wife's mission in Italy she had a companion who would receive calls from a particular elder each night. This elder was not their zone or district leader but had previously served with this sister missionary and developed romantic feelings for her. Sensing the distracting and inappropriate nature of these phone calls, my wife sprang into action. Intercepting the nightly call, she firmly told this elder that if he ever called again she would immediately inform the mission president. She then hung up the phone, and that elder never called again. This infuriated her companion and their relationship was greatly strained, but my wife had the courage to do what she knew was right. Like my wife, you must remember that your ultimate loyalty is to the Savior and His Church. Nothing should be allowed to tarnish or threaten the area of the vineyard for which you hold stewardship.

When speaking of this black hole it must be understood that major acts of disobedience and sin do not simply occur on a whim. Most often they begin with small, seemingly insignificant actions. Corianton forsook the ministry by going "among the borders of the Lamanites" (Alma 39:3). Most certainly this was a location in which he did not belong. In other words, he was flirting with disaster. Before venturing into this nefarious locale, the scriptures note that Corianton had "[boasted] in [his] strength and [his] wisdom" (Alma 39:2). I wonder if his boasting went something like this: "Yeah, I know that Isabel has been able to bring down a lot of guys, but she said that she needed to talk to me and I'm sure I can handle it." My guess is that Corianton thought he was the exception to the rule. This false notion propelled him into a dangerous situation—a situation he was unable to handle.

As a missionary there are places where you don't belong. Remember, you are not the exception to the rule. Stay with your companion at all times, and together stay as far away from trouble and temptation as you possibly can. Keep your eye focused on the glory of God and the ministry with which you've been entrusted, adopting Nephi's prayer to "shake at the appearance of sin" (2 Nephi 4:31). By doing so, you will avoid this perilous black hole, causing "the gates of hell [to] be shut continually before [you]" (2 Nephi 4:32).

Black Hole 3: Disobedience

In chapter 5 we discussed how our level of faith is directly tied to our level of obedience. If obedience is the mechanism that opens the heavens, enabling the power of God to shower down upon missionaries in their efforts, disobedience certainly has an equal effect in sealing the heavens, depriving missionaries of the power they so desperately need. Truly the decision to bend or break mission rules is a black hole of dangerous proportions.

There are certain moments on a mission that gauge a companionship's level of obedience. Take for instance two elders who have just finished an appointment and are now returning home for the evening. Glancing down at their watches, they see that it's 9:25 p.m. If they continue to walk they'll be a few minutes late; but if they run, they can make it by 9:29 and be home before their 9:30 curfew. In this situation a missionary might wonder if it really makes that big of a difference whether they arrive home at 9:29 or 9:31. Let it be understood that the difference is not a matter of *minutes*; it's a matter of *mindset*—and this difference is not a small crevice but a gaping canyon.

In the Pearl of Great Price we learn that the entire plan of salvation hinges upon the principle of obedience: "And we will prove them herewith, to see if they will do all things whatsoever the Lord their God shall command them" (Abraham 3:25). In the Doctrine and Covenants, the Prophet Joseph revealed that "when we obtain any blessing from God, it is by obedience to that law upon which it is predicated" (D&C 130:21). Perhaps the most significant blessing missionaries receive through obedience is the constant companionship of the Holy Ghost. The Lord has clearly stated, "If you receive not the Spirit ye shall not teach" (D&C 42:14). Not only does the Holy Ghost play a central role in conversion, but the Spirit has the ability to guide and give life to the missionaries in all they do. Thus the stakes of disobedience are extremely high.

I had a rare experience that deepened my testimony of this principle. In one of my areas we had many inactive members. As a district we decided to coordinate our reactivation efforts by assigning specific companionships to focus on and reach out to specific people. My companion and I soon set up an appointment with one of our families and during this visit established a comfortable rapport. We asked if we could share a thought from the Book of Mormon, and the family members not only listened but also retrieved their own copies so they could participate. After the thought, the Spirit was so strong that I couldn't help asking why they weren't coming to church. They replied that the time just wasn't right but then added that we were welcome to come over whenever we wished.

So we began making weekly visits to the home of this family, and each time we would have powerful spiritual experiences. But they still wouldn't come to church. It was after one of these visits that I realized what was missing: service. We had *told* them dozens of times how much we loved them, but we hadn't done anything to actually *show* it. From that point on we began asking if there was anything we could do to help them, but each time they refused, insisting that our regular work was much more important than their odd jobs around the house. No matter how we phrased it, no matter how hard we pressed, visit after visit they declined our offers of help.

One Saturday evening we finished a teaching appointment around 9:00 p.m. Realizing we had nearly a half hour until curfew, we decided to stop by this less active family's home and invite them to attend church the following day. Approaching their house, we were surprised to see huge floodlights illuminating their front yard. We entered the gate, made our way to the open door, and then collided with the father, who was rushing out all covered in paint.

We asked what was going on, and ashamedly he confessed that, on a whim, they had decided to repaint their entire house. Stunned, we asked why they hadn't called us to help with the project. Again he rattled off the same excuse about not wanting to divert us from our usual work. A little irritated, we explained for the umpteenth time that such a request would not have been a nuisance but would have been welcomed. We entered their home to inspect their progress and saw that they had only just begun.

Suddenly I got an idea. They could quit for the night, rest on the Sabbath, and resume their project early Monday morning. I promised them a crew of six eager and hardworking missionaries if they would accept my proposal. They considered it for a moment and then declined. The husband had to work Monday morning and just wouldn't feel right having us do all the work without his help. They would paint late into the night, and they would finish.

Checking my watch, I saw that it was now 9:20 p.m.; we had to be home in ten minutes. We again expressed our regret that we couldn't help. They assured us that they knew about the mission rules and understood why we couldn't stay. "Besides," they said, "we should have called you earlier and asked for help."

After saying good-bye and leaving their home I felt extremely unsettled. Never on my mission had I felt so helpless. This was the exact situation we had been praying for, and now it was going to be squandered. Although it was unspoken, I could tell that my companion was wrestling with the same feelings.

Then, at the exact same moment, we looked at each other and took off running. The Spirit had confirmed to us separately the same message: *we* were supposed to paint that house.

Beyond the obvious difficulty of breaking a major mission rule, there was another factor that made this moment a true test for me. Our zone leader was visiting our city for a few days and was staying at our apartment. This was the first time I had met him, so naturally he didn't know my level of obedience and how strongly I felt about keeping the mission rules. His first impression of me was going to be a hurried note on the door briefly explaining the situation and promising that we would be home by 11:00 p.m. I had only recently been assigned as district leader and was certain this decision would make him doubt my ability to lead my district righteously. In fact, I figured that when we returned home he would be on the phone with the mission president and I would be in serious trouble. In spite of all these possibilities, I could not deny the prompting that both my companion and I had felt from the Holy Ghost. We had to obey.

We sprinted to our home, dressed down into gym clothes, and then sprinted back to the home of the family. This was the first time I had ever been out past 9:30 in my entire mission and nothing felt more unnatural. When we emerged through the front door of this family's home, they were shocked to see us. They insisted we go back home, but we explained that we had made our decision and that they only had us for an hour and fifteen minutes so they should at least not waste any time trying to get us to leave.

Then something happened that confirmed the prompting we had received: the mom started to cry and in an emotion laden voice exclaimed, "We were just wondering how we were going to paint the ceilings!"

My companion was six feet five inches tall, and I'm only a hair shorter. We didn't even need to go find a ladder; we just started at opposite ends and met in the middle. As we worked the most wonderful feeling of warmth, camaraderie, and love entered the home. The kids playfully splashed paint on my companion and me, and when we were almost finished we ceremoniously lifted up the youngest child to paint the last swipe.

With the job completed, we hurriedly explained that we had to go. They thanked us profusely and begged us to stay and eat with them, but we were already sprinting toward the door.

Then it happened. Lunging through the doorway the dad called after us, "Hey, Elders!"

We stopped and turned around.

"Elders," he continued, "we'll see you at church tomorrow."

The mom's eyes filled with tears, and the children cheered. My companion and I were so filled with joy and happiness at the events of the night that I think we floated home.

When we got back to the apartment, the reality of the impending awkward confrontation brought us back to earth. As expected, the zone leader was waiting up for us and demanded an explanation, but after hearing the entire story and all the unique circumstances, he was not angry at all. Instead, he expressed approval for what we had done and admiration for us as missionaries. His only regret was that we hadn't waited to bring him and his companion along so they could help.

That night as I fell into bed and thanked Heavenly Father for this sweet experience, I felt a very strong impression whisper to me the following: *Elder Christiansen, the only reason I was able to guide you tonight is because I've seen you run home so many times when it meant being a minute early rather than a minute late. If you were not an obedient missionary, you would not have received that prompting.*

Your mission experience will be greatly enhanced if you, like Nephi, adopt the mantra, "I must obey." There will always be excuses to bend the rules. Be the kind of missionary who simply finds a way to obey with exactness. By so doing, you will turn the key that unlocks a treasure trove of blessings, qualify for the priceless companionship of the Holy Ghost, and avoid a time-consuming black hole.

Black Hole 4: "Treabă"

The fourth black hole is difficult to understand unless you've served or are actually serving a mission. I went on my mission to Romania and was fascinated by the Romanian language. Romanian contains many words that have no English equivalent. One of my particular favorites is the word *treabă* (trah-buh). *Treabă* is a generic multipurpose word that, loosely translated, means "errands, things, or stuff." When missionaries find themselves spending most of their time doing *treabă*, they are falling into a black hole that may seem harmless but wastes time nonetheless.

There are missionaries in the world that spend too much time doing *treabă* and too little time building up the kingdom of God. Oftentimes when confronted, these missionaries cite the following passage in the Doctrine and Covenants as justification: "Wherefore, as ye are agents, ye are on the Lord's errand; and whatsoever ye do according to the will of the Lord is the Lord's business" (D&C 64:29). Somehow many missionaries misinterpret this verse, believing it provides a blank check for the way they choose to use their time. Their logic goes as follows: *I'm a missionary, so I'm on the Lord's errand, and whatever I do can be classified as the Lord's business.* This gross misunderstanding occurs when the phrase "according to the will of the Lord" is deleted or ignored.

Missionaries who labor *according to the will of the Lord* will not consume precious proselytizing time with activities that are unrelated to their calling as ambassadors of the Lord Jesus Christ. There is a day already set aside for such activities. Preparation day is the time to run errands including shopping, dry cleaning, getting haircuts, etc. This is also the day to visit the sites of the city or region, pick up souvenirs, and take and develop pictures.

While it is important to be vigilant and mindful about the way you use your time, you do not need to become Pharisaical or overzealous. There will most likely be days when you don't use every second in the most effective way possible. If such days occur you don't need to develop a complex or "stumble because of . . . anxiety" (see Jacob 4:18). Just be more aware of the way you use your time and try your best to please the Lord. When you fall a little bit short, repent and resolve to do better.

Black Hole 5: "Aspirers"

Black hole five is also difficult to understand outside of the actual mission field. Like the Church, missions are organized with clear structure and order. This organization provides direction and leadership and also coordinates specific tasks to specific assignments. For instance, a missionary may be called to serve as the mission secretary for a brief period of time. The secretary arranges appointments for the mission president and performs a number of other administrative tasks at the president's request. This allows the president to more effectively fulfill his responsibilities and enables the rest of the mission to focus on proclaiming the gospel.

Mission organization also entails many positions of leadership. The opportunity to serve as a mission leader *may or may not* occur during your mission. Such positions *are not* essential to fulfilling an honorable mission. The drawback to this leadership structure comes when missionaries begin to aspire to particular positions or assignments. Such aspiring may seem harmless, but if unchecked it can fester and expand until it becomes detrimental and distracting. Aspiring to positions or specific assignments becomes a black hole because it consumes precious time and energy and diverts the missionary's focus from things of greater importance. Getting caught up in mission gossip, rumors, or speculation is unwise and unfruitful. The weeks immediately before and after transfers are hotbeds of such idle talk. If a missionary is undisciplined and gets caught up in "the buzz" each transfer, a substantial portion of time could be spent serving below his or her potential.

An even more dangerous effect of this black hole occurs when missionaries lose focus of the actual purpose for serving. Instead of humbly laboring to build up the kingdom of God, ulterior motives can creep in, causing missionaries to labor instead to build personal kingdoms of self-promotion. Some elders even go so far as to measure the success of their mission by the positions to which they were called. The following story illustrates the foolishness of such thinking.

There was an elder in our mission who never served as a district or zone leader. He never even served as a trainer. Yet he was the missionary we would assign all of our "problem" elders to be with because he could somehow help them work and be productive. His ability to get along with these difficult companions was truly a rare gift.

One day, while scanning the transfer board, our mission president locked onto the picture of this elder and started speaking about him. He noted how this elder would never serve in any of the "premier" leadership positions but then praised him for his unique contribution. Finally he looked at us and said, "In my opinion, Elder _____ is the most valuable missionary we have." My companion and I couldn't have agreed more.

The Savior's life reinforces the importance of this principle. I find it interesting that Jesus chose to spend the bulk of His ministry laboring in the humble and obscure fishing villages of Galilee. In contrast, the Pharisees and Sadducees clamored for the attention, praise, and glory that accompanied their pageantry of self-righteousness in the capital city of Jerusalem. While the Savior sought out and dwelt with the outcast and the lowly, the Pharisees and Sadducees shunned such associations, preferring instead to vaunt themselves above the common man. Most telling perhaps is the Savior's swift and consistent penchant for redirecting any praise and adulation He received to His Father.

As a missionary, always remember, it's not where or in what position you serve that's important, but *how* you serve that truly matters to the Lord.

Black Hole 6: "Eternal Investigators"

In an ideal world missionaries wouldn't need to spend a great deal of time finding people to teach. The members of the Church would fulfill the role of "finders," allowing missionaries to focus on preaching the gospel. While we are working toward the ideal, the reality remains that most elders and sisters do a lot of their own finding.

Finding investigators to teach may be the most difficult and daunting endeavor associated with missionary work. It requires a lot of mental courage, emotional stamina, and physical effort to knock on doors, stop strangers on the street, or speak up on a bus. If we took a poll of every current full-time missionary and asked whether they'd rather be outside knocking on doors or inside a home teaching a family, I bet I could guess what 100 percent of them would choose.

However, sometimes this preference to teach and have appointments leads missionaries to spend their time with investigators who have stalled in their progress toward the baptismal commitment. In my mission we jokingly referred to such individuals as "eternal investigators." The time spent with or in pursuit of these investigators can quickly become a consuming black hole.

Eternal investigators usually come in one of two molds. The first mold is an individual or family who at one point may have been genuinely interested in the gospel message but has since lost interest and become flaky and noncommittal. Setting up appointments with these investigators is nearly impossible. They are never certain about when they can meet with you, and when appointments are scheduled, they often fall through. Missionaries working with this mold of investigator are made to feel like a burden more than a blessing. Each appointment is treated as an intrusion on the investigator's time. Continuing to work with this type of investigator is like a mosquito trying to suck blood from a mummy. Much time and energy will be expended, yielding little or no result.

At some point in my mission, I had an epiphany of sorts. I realized that the message I was called to bear to the Romanian people was the most valuable message on earth. I now saw my message for what it really was: a divine gift from a loving Heavenly Father to His children in that corner of the vineyard.

This new perspective changed my approach with investigators. No longer would I act like a desperate vacuum salesman, clinging to the microscopic chance that a customer who was clearly not interested would change their mind and buy my product. No longer would I beg, grovel, coerce, or try to manipulate in the hopes of extending my association with an investigator. God's message deserved a lot better than that. Yes, I would express love and concern for my investigators. Yes, I would declare the truth with boldness and invite them to conform their lives accordingly. Yes, I would bear pure testimony of the blessings that could be theirs. But I saw now that God's message deserved a dignified messenger.

Throughout your mission you will find yourself working with investigators of the first mold. You will arrive at an impasse where it is obvious that they are not progressing and that your efforts to help them are bearing little fruit. So what do you do? Above all, you must seek and be sensitive to the direction and whisperings of the Spirit, but such situations usually call for a frank and honest talk. This appointment should not be confrontational but should determine if the investigator is serious about the message and truly possesses a desire to continue your visits. This visit could go something like this:

"Mr. and Mrs. _____, first we want to say how much we've enjoyed meeting with you and your family. We appreciate you allowing us to share a portion of our message—a message that we love and know comes from God. We've noticed lately that it's been harder and harder to set up appointments with you and that our last few visits have actually fallen through. We realize that you are busy, and we have always tried to be respectful of your time. But just as we have been respectful of your time, you too must realize that as representatives of Jesus Christ, our time is not only extremely valuable, but also extremely limited. I only have ___ months left on my mission and am amazed how fast it's going by.

"If you remember back to our very first visit, we told you that you can't believe on our word alone but that you would have to find out for yourselves if the message we share is true. This requires real work and effort on your part. You will have to study and pray and ponder and act, but if you sincerely desire to know and are willing to do your part, we will always be here to help you along the path. But if this is not the case, you have got to let us know now so that we can focus our time and efforts on those who do have this genuine desire."

Such forthrightness will usually do one of two things. Occasionally it stirs the soul of the investigator, invigorating and renewing their desire to learn the message. More often than not, however, it leads such investigators to admit that they are no longer interested and would prefer discontinuing your association. When this occurs, it is extremely important to let them know that you still care about them and that if they ever change their mind, you or some missionaries like you will be more than willing to begin the process again. Leave them some reliable contact information, record a summary of your work with them in the area book, and move on in your labors.

The second mold of eternal investigator poses an even greater dilemma. This is an investigator who is not progressing but still invites you over and enjoys your company. The relationship and interaction with these investigators has taken a subtle or not-so-subtle shift from spiritual to social. They want you to come over, but during appointments it seems they want to talk about anything but the gospel message.

Well-intending missionaries often continue to meet with this type of investigator in the hopes that they will change, but doing so usually wastes a lot of time with little result. In sum, it's a black hole. Once you've entered this black hole it's quite difficult to escape. Regular appointments with people who enjoy your company are hard to give up, especially when the alternative is being out on the street or knocking on doors. A missionary may justify such appointments because the investigators are the ones who request that they continue. Surely this positive interaction is helpful to the Church, right?

When dealing with this type of investigator you must remember your purpose and commission as a missionary. You are not there as a public relations rep (although your daily interaction with the public should go a long way in this regard). You're also not there to spread goodwill (again, this should naturally occur). You are there to build the kingdom of God by administering the saving ordinances of the gospel to the people. An eternal investigator of the second mold has misunderstood your purpose for serving and needs to be reminded in a loving but clear manner.

Setting up an appointment with the second mold of eternal investigator will be easy. Having an honest discussion about the nature and purpose of your appointments will not. Over time you've probably become good friends with these people and will be saddened to discontinue your visits. Most likely they have become a mainstay in your missionary planner, and you'll realize that the time you were spending with them will now need to be spent finding others to teach. In spite of these challenging factors, you'll know you are doing what's right, and that can give you the courage to follow through. This visit could go something like this:

"Mr. and Mrs. _____, you know how much we have loved meeting your family and spending time in your home. You have made us feel welcome, and we truly do feel that we have become friends. The message we are called to declare is a message of great importance. This message is not about us but is about our Heavenly Father and our Savior Jesus Christ. As much as we love spending time with your family, if our visits are not centered on this message, then we are not fulfilling our purpose here. We hope you will still consider us your friends, and we will always be willing to help or serve you in any way. But if you are not serious in your interest about our message, we can no longer come to your home each week. If or when the time comes that you truly want to know whether our message comes from God, we will gladly resume our visits."

Missionaries who have been working with eternal investigators often wonder how long they should continue meeting with them. They may feel hesitant to drop such investigators from their teaching pool, fearing to give up on someone who might have joined the Church. They've heard stories or know members who investigated for a long period of time before finally embracing the gospel message.

It's true that the conversion process for some occurs quickly, while for others it takes much longer. In fact, Brigham Young investigated the Church for over two years before he finally became convinced of its truthfulness. Thankfully he wasn't taught by missionaries who gave up on him.

So how can you know whether to keep or drop investigators that have been regulars in your teaching pool? There are two questions that can help determine the proper course of action. One is for you, the missionary; the other applies to your investigators. The question for the missionaries is simple: Are you continuing to meet with this investigator mainly so you will have something to put in your missionary planner? If an honest evaluation reveals that such is the case, then the time has certainly come to set up the "frank talk" appointment.

The measuring stick for the investigators is also simple: Are they making and keeping commitments? If an investigator is making and keeping commitments, you should not drop them from your teaching pool no matter how long the conversion process seems to be taking. The simple act of them doing their part justifies continued visits. Yes, Brigham Young took a long time to join the Church, but during the lengthy span before his baptism he was studying, searching, praying, pondering, attending church services, keeping commandments, etc. While it took a long time, Brigham entered the Church with extremely deep roots of faith and testimony, roots that would serve him well throughout his lifetime of leadership in the Church.

Black Hole 7: Ineffective Appointment-Setting Practices

Every mission seems to have its own terminology for an appointment that falls through or fails to materialize. In Romania we referred to such instances as "being impaled." I distinctly remember a day on my mission when we had lessons set up at 11:00 a.m., 1:00 p.m., 3:00 p.m., 5:30 p.m., and 7:30 p.m.—the perfect day for a missionary, right? However, one by one each of these lessons fell through, and we ended up wasting the entire day. Returning to our apartment that night having accomplished nothing, I couldn't help letting out a pathetic laugh at our "impalement" slang, realizing it was right on. But it was days like this that got me thinking about and reevaluating the way we were setting up our appointments.

Conducting this honest evaluation of our methods, I began to see a glaring weakness. In Romania we spent a lot of time street contacting. We would stop seemingly hundreds of individuals each day, many of whom would allow us a few minutes to introduce our message. At the end of a brief "street pitch," we would testify of the truths we had taught and ask if we could visit their home and share the entire message. Several people would express further interest but were reluctant to commit to a home visit. The excuses were usually the same: they didn't think their spouse would allow it, their neighbors would get suspicious, they worked late and were rarely home, etc.

It was in this moment that we would usually make our fatal mistake. When the potential investigator seemed hesitant about a home visit, we would instantly jump in and suggest meeting at an alternative location, usually our church building. The person would almost always agree to the change of venue, and we'd proceed to set up the appointment. It always felt good writing these appointments down and seeing our missionary planners fill up with lessons. There was just one problem. People rarely showed up— and when I say "rarely," I mean less than 10 percent of the time.

I began to realize that in our zeal to have something scheduled in our planner, we were not practicing due diligence with our street contacts. We weren't asking the difficult questions to really decipher their level of interest. Basically we were setting up lots of appointments with people who never intended to come. They were only trying to be polite and didn't want to reject us and hurt our feelings.

So what do you do to avoid this?

When an individual expresses interest in your message but reservation at the prospect of a home visit, *do not be too quick to suggest an appointment at an alternative site.* Instead, explain that the standard procedure is to share the message in the homes of the people. It is more convenient for them and will provide a familiar and comfortable setting in which to hear the gospel message. Furthermore, testify that the message of the restored gospel is designed to bless and strengthen their entire family. If they have children, let them know that all family members will be invited and welcome to participate.

Even after you emphasize the advantages of a home visit, some people will still object and reecho their request to meet elsewhere. Yet again this presents a critical juncture in which forthrightness, governed by tact, is necessary. Before you agree to such an appointment, inform the individual that your purpose as a missionary is to seek out those who are *genuinely interested* in the message of the restored gospel. Let them know that they do not need to worry about hurting your feelings. You understand and have seen that many are interested but some are not. At this point a reminder of how valuable your time is as a missionary would certainly be appropriate. This should not be done with haughtiness or ego but with sincerity.

After explaining these things, ask them directly if they fully intend to honor their commitment. If they say yes, then go ahead and set up the appointment as well as a reminder phone call. If they still seem hesitant or noncommittal, invite them to your weekly church services and leave them with a pamphlet containing your contact information. Encourage them to get in touch if they ever have questions or desire to learn more. Then genuinely thank them for their time, perhaps taking the opportunity to leave one last chord of testimony.

Black Hole 8: "Don't Play with the Cat!"

During the last phase of my mission, I had access to our mission statistics and studied them to look for trends and patterns. One thing that instantly jumped out at me was the sizeable number of first lessons we were teaching in contrast to the scant number of subsequent lessons. I'm not a mathematician (far from it actually), but I started figuring some numbers and saw that only about 10 percent of our investigators were continuing to receive lessons after the first lesson.

That is a huge drop, and it made me feel uneasy. How could we be losing so much of the potential harvest? How could 90 percent of those who had been taught and exposed to the gospel message of truth and light reject it so instantaneously? Obviously I knew we weren't going to retain all 100 percent, but surely we could do better and narrow the gap. Even small improvements could bring about a considerable increase in the number of convert baptisms and growth of the Church. Yet again, the golden question arose: *So what do we do?* My recommendations fall under three distinct categories: (1) preparation before a teaching opportunity, (2) what to do during the lesson, and (3) don't "play with the cat" after the lesson.

Preparation before a Teaching Opportunity

Understanding the critical importance of the first lesson should influence the way you approach and prepare for these initial visits. You cannot take any first lesson for granted because statistics show it's the one shot you're going to get. Missionaries must have the mindset that each and every first lesson needs to provide the investigator with a powerful spiritual experience. Now don't get nervous or put any additional pressure on yourself. Yes, the stakes are high, but the Lord has always entrusted the preaching of His perfect message to His weak and simple servants. The more inadequate you feel, the more you will turn to the Lord for help. This humility will bring greater power in your teaching.

But humility must not be mistaken with laziness. There is never an excuse to be complacent or lackadaisical in your approach toward a teaching opportunity. Under the inspired direction of prophets and apostles, the introduction of *Preach My Gospel* has increased the amount of time allotted to missionaries to plan and prepare. Used wisely, these planning sessions provide the time necessary to focus on the day's teaching opportunities.

When planning, the first thing you should do is discuss with your companion what you remember about the family or individual whom you will be teaching. This allows you to tailor the message to meet their needs or answer their questions. After you decide what to teach, don't stop there— establish which missionary will be teaching each of the specific topics, then practice together to make sure that your transitions are smooth, questions are clear, and the presentation polished. Adequate preparation will ensure that the delivery of the message enhances rather than detracts from its power.

Thinking practically, you should also consider the address and location of the home or apartment of your teaching appointment(s). Punctuality is a sign of professionalism, so never be late to an appointment! Are you certain you will be able to find the address and arrive on time? If not, it would be wise to set aside some time in advance to become familiar with the area and locate the investigator's home or apartment complex. This can be done efficiently while contacting others in the area.

What to Do during the Lesson

As you enter the home of an investigator and begin sharing the message of the restored gospel, silently plead for the Spirit to assist you in your efforts. When you teach by the Spirit your abilities are magnified, giving you greater clarity and power. Additionally, the Holy Ghost will confirm the truth of your words, penetrating the minds and hearts of those you teach.

As you make your way through the first lesson, the influence of the Holy Ghost will gradually intensify. The spiritual pinnacle of this lesson usually comes during the Joseph Smith story—especially when it gets to the First Vision. As previously discussed in chapter 2, Satan must tremble when he sees missionaries introducing sincere investigators to the miracle of the Sacred Grove. Try as Satan might to interfere, the Spirit will pour down with great power as you recite in Joseph's own words what occurred that triumphant day.

Following the Joseph Smith story, you will introduce the investigators to the Book of Mormon. As you do so, the influence of the Spirit will remain powerful yet may diminish slightly from the apex reached when discussing the First Vision. After you explain the commitments and extend the proper invitations, you will probably be approaching the forty-five-minute mark, which is your signal to wrap things up. Someone will offer a prayer, and you'll stand up to leave. But at this point, a pleasant surprise might occur. They may want you to stay longer!

Don't play with the cat after the lesson!

Why does this happen? It's actually quite predictable if you think about it. The Spirit is extremely powerful in their home, and they've obviously made the connection between you and these wonderful new feelings. Now they want you to linger in order to prolong the experience. They'll beg to feed you. They'll beg you to chat about your family, your home, your hobbies. They'll beg you to help their schoolboy with his English homework. They'll beg you to play with their cat—*anything to get you to stay!*

This moment is extremely counterintuitive for the missionary. Every instinct in your body screams that this is a good thing. For starters, it shows that they enjoyed your message. Now you have an opportunity to get to know them better and deepen your relationship—not to mention the fact that remaining in their home an extra half hour sure beats being out on the street or knocking on doors. Besides, what could be the harm of staying?

Little do you know that this is actually a "make or break it" moment. When you make the decision to stay and socialize, the Spirit quickly departs. After all, the Spirit doesn't need to testify about the sumptuousness of the mother's cooking or your family at home or little Jimmy's English homework or their cat, Sparkles.

So, mistakenly thinking that you are aiding your cause, you remain at their home. When you finally leave twenty or thirty or sixty minutes later, something tragic occurs: they'll notice absolutely no difference in the way they feel with you gone compared to how they felt when you were there. The Spirit, which at one point had been incredibly strong, has long since faded, and they simply resume their domestic duties.

You will be excited and hopeful about these new investigators, but a few days later when you call them or stop by you'll receive disheartening news. They think you are nice boys, and it was really enjoyable to get to know you, but they're not really interested in your message. You'll ask them if they read the Book of Mormon and prayed about it, and they'll say they didn't get around to it. The phone call will end or the door will slam shut, and you'll sit in a stupor of confusion, wondering what went wrong. The result is just another first lesson that becomes a sobering statistic, never to be followed by subsequent lessons.

I've given a portrayal of what shouldn't happen; now let me depict what should. After teaching a powerful first lesson, missionaries need to leave the home of the investigators in a prompt and timely manner. If the family members object and express the desire that you remain, you simply use the standard excuse, "We want to be respectful of your time and also have another appointment we need to get to." Even if that "other" appointment is knocking on the doors of a neighboring apartment building, you have not been untruthful and have handled a delicate situation in a sensitive manner.

Before leaving, take a moment to identify the feelings of peace, joy, and comfort they experienced during the lesson, and help the investigator understand that these feelings have come from the Spirit which has been present in their home. Then testify and promise that when they fulfill their commitments by reading and praying about the Book of Mormon, the same feelings of the Spirit will return.

When you leave the home of an investigator promptly after finishing the lesson, an interesting phenomenon occurs. The Spirit that had been felt so powerfully quickly departs, making it impossible for the investigators *not* to notice the stark difference. They will link the sweet and desirable feelings to you, the missionaries, and will be excited to invite you back to hear more of the gospel message. They will also remember the promise you made before leaving and will be far more likely to fulfill their commitments.

There is one additional reason for leaving promptly after finishing a lesson. The modern world is extremely busy. Time is stretched, schedules are packed, and family and leisure time are at a premium. Chances are slim you will work with many investigators who enjoy a forty-hour, nine-to-five work week. Instead, fifty-sixty hour weeks are becoming the norm and are compounded by irregular and unpredictable schedules.

For this reason, missionaries must be extremely sensitive and respectful of their investigators' time. Even if the investigators are the ones who requested you stay an extra half hour or forty-five minutes, the fact remains that the visit occupied nearly two hours. When you call to set up a return appointment, this estimated time commitment will be at the forefront of their minds and could be a dissuading factor in not inviting you back. Very rarely should an initial visit exceed an hour. This doesn't mean that you rush the teaching process or brush off investigators' questions or concerns; it simply means that you prepare to teach in a timely and efficient manner. Make forty-five minutes your target, and you'll end up just about right.

A mission is too important to waste. Each day, hour, and minute presents a priceless opportunity to be on the Lord's errand in a literal and miraculous way. I doubt that any missionary in the history of the world has regretted working too hard, being too devoted, or giving too much of their heart, might, mind, and strength to the Lord. In contrast, I am certain that many missionaries have felt deep regret, sorrow, and even guilt at the thought that they have held back, wasted time that was not theirs to waste, and did not give the Lord an honest effort in their labors.

Now again for the reality. There will be times when you slip up, lose focus, or choose something that was "good" when "better" or "best" alternatives were available. In other words, you won't be perfect. But you can try your very best to honor and magnify your calling and by so doing qualify yourself to feel the Lord's approval for your efforts.

This brings to mind the beautiful passage, "Well done, thou good and faithful servant: thou hast been faithful over a few things, I will make thee ruler over many things" (Matthew 25:21). I worry that many missionaries make the mistake of waiting until the end of their mission to seek this divine stamp of approval. Somehow it's become a standard "flight home" procedure. A missionary boards an airplane, collapses into his seat, exhales for the first time after two years of diligent service, and then offers a grandiose prayer desiring to know if his mission was acceptable to the Lord. Angelic choruses sing praises, beams of light shine down, fellow passengers stand up and applaud, and the missionary knows that his mission was pleasing to God.

Now obviously I'm being facetious, but I do so only to make a point. Don't wait until the end of your mission to receive the Lord's approval when you can do so all along the way! I began a practice as a missionary that helped me give an accounting to the Lord for the way I had used my/ His time. In my evening prayer I would review the major events of the day, what I had done, and how I had gone about His business. Following this detailed report, I would ask if my day's work was acceptable and then listen for a moment to feel a response.

There were days when strong rebukes thundered down, with the Spirit pointing out clear areas for improvement. But more often than not, a sweet feeling of love would settle upon me, easing my mind and swelling my heart. When at the end of each day I could receive a confirmation that the Lord was proud of the way I had represented Him and carried His name, I felt rejuvenated and recommitted to carry on the next day. Also, knowing that I would be giving an accounting before the Lord each night provided much needed motivation on how I used my time each day.

The missionary black holes discussed in this chapter are just a sample of ways in which the adversary will try to squander your time and render you ineffective. But as you give your best effort to serve in a manner that is pleasing to God, His grace will be sufficient for you to overcome any obstacle that may stand in your path. You can go forth with confidence in the Lord that He will help you return with honor. You can be a mighty instrument in His hands.

SECTION THREE

Just for . . .

Chapter 12
Language Learners

"You are not alone in learning your mission language. Whenever the Lord gives a commandment, He provides a way to accomplish it." —Preach My Gospel, 128

IF YOU HAVE BEEN CALLED to a foreign language–speaking mission, I've got good news and bad news for you. The bad news is that learning a foreign language will possibly be one of the hardest things you do on your mission. It might be harder than the ACT, harder than AP Calculus, even harder than asking that good-looking girl out on a date. All right, maybe I'm being a bit dramatic, but you get the point. The good news is that God doesn't make mistakes, and He certainly doesn't call people to fail. If anyone on the planet can testify of God's ability to help with the language, it's me. So here's my story.

When I received my mission call to Romania, I knew it was right. Sure, there was a lot to be nervous about, but only one thing kept me up at night: *Romanian.* How in the world was I going to learn the language? I had taken three years of German in high school and had not fared well. In fact, during those three years I'd only managed to learn one phrase: *"gleich um die Ecke,"* which means "around the corner." Whenever my German teacher would ask me a question, my reply was always the same: *"gleich um die Ecke."* Everyone would laugh, and the teacher would remember that I was an idiot and promptly move on to more gifted students.

During the last semester of my senior year I really tried to apply myself and pay attention, but I quickly discovered that I genuinely lacked an aptitude for language learning. I just didn't get the various grammar components and how they all fit together. Concepts such as verb conjugations, nouns, pronouns, adjectives, adverbs, genitive and dative cases, prepositions, tenses, clauses, indicators, etc., were completely over my head. Add on top of that the seemingly endless stream of vocabulary words to memorize, and it was just too much for my stellarly average IQ.

But there I was, only a year later, called to preach the gospel in the Romanian language. As I mentioned, this really worried me. Somehow I had a hunch that a mission would entail much more than just carrying out a cheesy dialogue about bratwurst. I was going to have to explain complex gospel principles in a foreign language. I hardly felt comfortable doing that in English. I'd also have to carry on real conversations with people and answer their questions. I'd need to form deep and meaningful relationships with investigators and members. And to think, I didn't even know how to say "around the corner" yet in Romanian!

Exercising all the faith I could muster, I suppressed my fear and doubt and entered the MTC. After one full day of language learning I was completely lost. It was just like my German class but a thousand times more intense and for twelve hours a day.

Looking back I see how naive I was about the gift of tongues. I guess I kind of hoped that there was a magical "gift of tongues" vending machine in some secret chamber of the MTC and that upon arrival I would be given a Romanian token entitling me to one free gift of tongues.

Turns out it's nothing like that. I struggled with the language every single day at the MTC. The only thing I can compare it to is like trying to get a drink of water from a fire hydrant. I would study and work on a grammar principle, but by the time I finally felt comfortable with it we would have already moved on and learned five new ones. Most of the time I was confused; all of the time I was overwhelmed.

When my district's eight weeks were up and the time came to depart for Romania, I couldn't speak the language at all. Needless to say, getting on that airplane was a serious test of faith. Our itinerary took us from Salt Lake City to Chicago, from Chicago to Austria, and from Austria to Bucharest. On that final leg from Austria to Bucharest we flew on TAROM, which is Romania's national airline. As we settled into our seats I suddenly realized that the flight attendants were probably Romanian and that the preflight safety speech would be done in our mission language. This would be our first real chance to see how much we had learned.

The flight attendant stood up and said, *"Buna ziua"* (which is "hello" in Romanian), and then launched into her three-minute monologue.

After about five seconds, I turned to my companions and said, "False alarm; she can't be speaking Romanian."

But the others in my district were still listening intently to the woman. Then my genius Gordon-B.-Hinckley-BYU-Scholarship companion turned to me and said, "Uhhh, yeah, she is, Elder Christiansen."

I'll admit it; I panicked a little bit.

Actually, I panicked a lot. I immediately jumped to my feet and started for the aisle. All the other missionaries asked what I was doing, and I calmly informed them that I was getting off the plane and that they may or may not ever see me again. They quickly formed a human barricade and told me to relax, to which I responded that I was sitting on a plane that within the hour would deliver me to a country where I couldn't understand a word anyone would say to me! Finally, they persuaded me to sit back down, but by then I was physically ill and about to throw up. An hour later, we landed in Bucharest, and two hours after that, I found myself out on the street on exchanges.

It was even worse than I had feared. I literally couldn't understand a single word any real Romanian said. That evening we had our orientation, and one of the assistants to the mission president mentioned how we might be worried about the language. I was exhausted from jet lag and had almost fallen asleep, but when I heard him say this I sprang to attention and focused in like the NASA technicians bringing back Apollo 13. He continued, "I just want you to know that no missionary in the history of our mission has ever not learned the language."

Now, I understood that he was trying to be encouraging, but at that moment I remember having the distinct thought, *Great, I'm going to be the first. After six months of epic failure they're going to reassign me stateside and put a plaque in the mission office with my picture on it that says, "Elder Christiansen: The Only Missionary Ever to Not Learn the Language (currently serving in Pocatello, Idaho)."* I know it sounds pathetic, but that's how shaken my confidence was at that point. The next day I met my trainer and received my first assignment, and before I knew it, I was waking up in my new apartment heading out the door to do real missionary work.

I'll be honest. Those first few weeks in Romania were the hardest of my entire life. I have never felt so inadequate, helpless, useless, and frustrated. As you can probably guess, most of these feelings stemmed from my language struggles. Imagine having a two-minute lag to every conversation. I would try so hard to understand what people were saying, but by the time I processed it they would be two minutes further in the conversation and I'd have missed everything in between. So I would start all over again, picking out a word I understood and then trying to figure out what they were talking about. I did this for twelve hours a day, basically understanding about 5 percent of what people were saying. I remember going home at night and being so mentally exhausted that I couldn't even think. My brain literally felt like mush. I would take some Ibuprofen, plop down in a chair, and stare at the wall until bedtime.

Months passed, and my language woes continued. I was getting better at understanding people, but my ability to speak just wasn't coming. The only thing I could do was a one-minute memorized spiel that I used to contact people. When I got to the end of this spiel my trainer would always take over and do the real talking. I loved every other aspect of being a missionary in Romania, but the fear and doubt about the language always lingered in the back of my mind. *What if I never learned the language? Would I have to deal with this my entire mission?*

One Monday we got a call from our zone leader reminding us about the conference scheduled for the latter part of the week. He then broke the news that he had received permission to do a zone preparation day together. This was exciting because his city had a mall, some nice outdoor basketball courts, and, most of all, an American restaurant called Little Texas that was famous throughout our mission. I could already taste the double cheeseburger and fries when he mentioned something that stopped my heart.

He said that during the evening proselytizing hours we would be doing "street boarding" together as a zone. Street boarding is an activity commonly done in areas with a high volume of pedestrian traffic. A three-paneled board is constructed with hinges so it can stand on its own and then decorated with pictures of the Savior, temples, prophets, etc. You set up the board on a busy sidewalk and use it to attract attention and introduce people to the gospel.

There's only one catch. You don't work together as companions!

Because everyone is in the general vicinity of the board and the purpose is to contact as many people as possible, each missionary talks to people on their own. I had never done that before. I had always clung to my trainer's coattails like a toddler to his mommy's apron. Whenever anyone looked at me or asked me a question, I always pointed to my trainer and said, "I don't know anything; please talk to him!" So the thought of having to street board was terrifying.

That week passed like a blur, and before I knew it we were on a train heading up to this city for the weekend. The preparation day together was as fun as advertised. But I couldn't fully enjoy any of the amazing activities with the prospect of street boarding hanging over my head. The day flew by, and sure enough I soon found myself lugging that cursed street board through the city. We set it up along a busy walkway and were ready to get started. I still didn't know what I was going to do until our zone leader asked for volunteers to sing.

Hallelujah! That was the answer.

With the entire zone present we could spare four missionaries to sing hymns. I quickly volunteered my services and formed a quartet with three others. We started singing, and the other ten missionaries started contacting people who were passing by.

As I stood there singing I couldn't help feeling a tinge of bitterness. It was hard to just stand there and watch all the other missionaries confidently stop people, make acquaintances, and then teach them the gospel. They made it look so easy! After a half hour the three missionaries who had been singing with me traded places with three of the "contacting" missionaries. Everyone looked at me and asked if I wanted to switch, to which I replied, "Maybe in a minute." Of course that was a lie. I would keep saying "maybe in a minute" until it was time to go home.

So I stood there, singing and watching. After an hour I started to get mad. I could feel the frustration building up inside of me, and I started to have strange thoughts. It was almost like one of those "angel on your right shoulder, devil on your left shoulder" moments. The angel on my right shoulder kept saying, "C'mon, Matt, you didn't come 9,000 miles away from home just to sing. You have a strong testimony—go share it!" But then the mean devil on my left shoulder would say, "Yeah, but you're stupid, and you don't know the language." In the midst of this bizarre exchange my own brain was reeling with the thought, *Why can't I speak? I want to share the gospel so badly—if it weren't for this language barrier!*

This went on for about a half hour until finally the tension built up to the point where I felt like I was going to explode. I knew I had to do something. So out of sheer restlessness I tossed the hymn book aside, strode out to an elder who had offered to switch me places, tapped him on the shoulder, and said, "I'm ready to switch now." He smiled and graciously yielded up his territory on the pavement to me.

Seeing me join their ranks, all the other contacting missionaries started lavishing me with praise and telling me how cool I was. All the other missionaries, that is, except my trainer. He would never humiliate me in front of everyone by announcing my stupidity, but he was watching me out of the corner of his eye with a wary expression. Seeing his concerned look I knew exactly what he was thinking: *Uh, what do you think you're doing? You know you can't do this.*

The sad thing is, I knew he was right. I was obviously in way over my head, but what could I do now? Intoxicated by the praise of the other missionaries, I said the stupidest thing I've ever said in my entire life: "Hey, elders, the next guy's mine!"

Right at that moment a Romanian man appeared around the corner. The other missionaries motioned to him and said that he was all mine. My face was frozen with horror. *What had I done?* Instantly my brain started churning and presented me with two options. I could swallow my pride, admit that I couldn't speak the language, and ask one of the other elders to help me. The other option was far more appealing. This man was still about fifty feet away. If I hurried, I could sprint out and catch him away from the group. The street contact would be a disaster since I didn't know how to say anything after my one-minute memorized spiel. Without a companion to pick up where I left off, it wouldn't make any sense at all. But at least I would only look stupid to one Romanian man and not my entire zone.

I quickly settled on the second option. I ran out to meet this guy, which must have been alarming for him to have a six-foot-five stranger in a dark suit sprinting at him. As I ran toward him, I had an exhilarating thought: *Maybe he'll reject me; we get rejected all the time. Please reject me, please reject me, please reject me.* Isn't that hilarious? I must be the only missionary on earth who's prayed so fervently for someone to reject him!

A few feet away, I stopped the man and asked if he had a moment to talk. He thought about it and then after a long pause said, *"Da"* ("yes"). My heart sank. I began my memorized contact that I had done a thousand times, but mentally I skipped to the end and tried to figure out what I would say then.

I was one line away from my abrupt ending when the man interrupted me. I felt a flicker of hope; maybe this was the Lord showing mercy and sparing me brutal humiliation. I thought for sure he was going to say that he wasn't interested and excuse himself, but instead I heard him say the words, *"Am o întrebare."* ("I have a question.") I froze. I had never answered anyone's question before. Scared to death, I nodded my head and he began to speak.

I had absolutely no clue what he said. He was waiting for me to respond, and my mind was frantically racing. Suddenly, I remembered an MTC teacher saying that if we ever didn't understand what someone said, we could just say, "*Poftiți.*" Feeling a wave of gratitude, I blurted out, "*Poftiți,*" with all my little heart. It was obvious that my response registered, but then he looked at me and simply began repeating the question.

This had to be some horrible mistake! I had said *poftiți*; that was supposed to resolve any question or concern. Well, now I was in trouble. I was in such a state of panic and distress that I completely missed hearing him repeat the question. He just stood there, waiting for me to respond. At that moment the only thing I could think to say was a phrase from a vocabulary list: *Puteți să vă repetați vă rog?* ("Can you repeat yourself, please?") I used the phrase, and this man dutifully repeated his question for the third time.

It was hopeless. By this point I was so flustered that I couldn't even hear sound coming out of his mouth. I could only see his lips moving as they formed indecipherable words. It didn't help that the man was beginning to get impatient. He kept looking past me to the other missionaries who were talking to people and obviously having more meaningful conversations than ours. Finally, in a last-ditch, desperate "hail Mary," I put together the phrase, *Puteți să vă repetați vă rog?* with *poftiți* and prayed that the magical combination of the two would somehow answer his question.

Although he was getting frustrated, I could see in his eyes that he would give me one more shot. He repeated his question for a fourth time, but to my astonishment this time he said it in English. I have never felt such jubilation and relief in my entire life. We started talking in English, and I was finally able to release months' worth of pent-up frustration. I could talk! I could teach! I wasn't a mute!

I asked him what question he had been asking, and it was embarrassingly simple: "Who is this man you're talking about?" So I taught him about the Prophet Joseph Smith and the coming forth of the Book of Mormon. I had never been more in my element. We ended up talking for about twenty minutes, and at the end I asked if he'd be interested in learning more. He responded, "Absolutely," so I got his name and address and for the first time as a missionary set up an appointment. We shook hands and then he walked away.

I stood there, jotting down a few notes about the man so I could pass them along to the missionaries in that city who'd be teaching him. Then I turned to make my way back to the main group at the street board. As I looked up I noticed something strange.

Everybody was staring at me.

And I figured I knew why. I had broken a cardinal rule of foreign missions by teaching someone in English. In numerous revelations the Lord clearly outlines that people should be taught in their own tongue. I realized I'd messed up and felt a little guilty, but as I drew closer the other missionaries were staring at me like I'd killed the guy or something.

Joining the group, I decided to simply fess up. "All right," I exclaimed. "So I taught the guy in English, but he started it. I swear I tried! I tried three times to understand his question, but I just couldn't, and then he answered in English, so I just answered back and then we got into a conversation."

Everyone was looking at me like I was a raving lunatic. Finally my trainer broke the silence and said, "Elder Christiansen, what are you talking about?"

Well, now *I* was confused; what else could I be talking about? "I'm talking about me, teaching that guy in English."

Then my trainer looked at me and said, "Elder Christiansen, you were just speaking to that man in perfect Romanian."

I was stunned. Was this some type of sick practical joke?

"What are you talking about?" I demanded. "I couldn't understand his question because I'm a moron, so he started speaking in English. We were talking in English!"

Now all the other missionaries started chiming in. "No, Elder Christiansen, you were speaking Romanian. We all stopped and watched; you were speaking so well."

Well, by now I was flat-out mad. "Trust me, I'm an idiot. Watch!" At that moment, there was another man passing by, so I stopped him and started to speak.

It was like someone had turned a key in my mind. Grammar, vocabulary, accent. I was speaking fluent Romanian. My joy was too much to contain, so I started running and screaming. I couldn't believe it!

The next few days were some of the greatest of my life. I had enjoyed being a missionary before, but now I loved it more than anything else. On the four-hour train ride back to our city I offered a silent prayer of gratitude. As I prayed I remember saying to Heavenly Father, *The language was my biggest fear, my biggest obstacle, and You just removed it right out my way. Thank You so much! I can't even express how much this means to me.*

Then, in a quiet moment, I received an interesting response to my prayer.

I felt the Spirit whisper, *Matt, since your first day at the MTC I've heard and recorded every prayer in which you pled and begged for your tongue to be loosed. I have watched closely as you worked and studied and struggled. Finally you have paid the necessary price. Finally I could give you this great gift.*

I suddenly understood. Like many of the gifts of God, the gift of tongues is not bestowed without effort or sacrifice. It is extremely real, but it must be earned. I realized that for each missionary there are a certain number of hours that must be spent studying, struggling, trying. Only after this individualized quota is met will the gift be given.

Now, one caution, please realize that every missionary's experience with the gift of tongues is unique. I had a very dramatic experience with this gift because I had almost zero aptitude on my own to learn the language. In contrast, my last companion (who was considered the best Romanian speaker in the mission) didn't have an experience like mine at all. Upon arrival in the country he swiftly and steadily progressed with the language, the Lord magnifying and augmenting his own natural ability. Now that doesn't mean the gift of tongues was any less real for him. It was just different.

My guess is that these two experiences probably represent the two extremes. Your own experience with the gift of tongues will likely fall somewhere in between. But regardless of how it comes, remember to pray for the gift of tongues as if everything depends upon God, but work for it as if everything depends upon you. As I personally learned, both happen to be true.

To help you succeed in learning your mission language, I recommend the following principles:

Principle 1: It's Not If, But When

As my own story illustrates, learning a language can be a daunting endeavor. The adversary loves to use fear and doubt because these emotions destroy faith and confidence. Never let the question "What if?" enter your mind. YOU WILL LEARN THE LANGUAGE. I know I already said this, but it's worth repeating: God doesn't make mistakes. He hasn't called you to a foreign language–speaking mission to fail. Remember, it's not *if*, but *when*.

Principle 2: Don't Compare Yourself to Others

Learning a language is not a competition with the other missionaries. Comparing yourself to others inevitably leads to one of two outcomes. Either you'll think that you are better than someone, leading to pride and arrogance, or you'll think that you are worse, leading to jealousy and frustration. It's a lose/lose. I know it's hard, but please avoid falling into this trap. *You* are your only measuring stick, so do your very best and leave the rest to God. This leads to my next suggestion . . .

Principle 3: Take Pride in the Way You Speak Your Mission Language, but Never Become Prideful about the Way You Speak It

Pride is the most destructive weapon in Satan's arsenal. It destroys marriages, families, wards, and civilizations; and yes, it can destroy companionships and missions as well. As you strive to master the mission language, never do so in an attempt to get ahead or vaunt yourself above anybody else. Your motive should be a sincere love for the people and a desire to communicate clearly the precious truths of the restored gospel. Never make fun of or be critical toward another missionary about their language ability. For some missionaries the language comes quickly and naturally; for others it is extremely difficult. If you are fortunate enough to be in the first category, then devote yourself to helping and building those who are in the second. I've seen this happen. There was an elder in our mission who was not only the best missionary, he was also the best Romanian speaker. He was working one day with a younger elder who really struggled with the language and was very self-conscious about it. As they talked to people, this brilliant missionary kept messing up a very easy language principle. There were other missionaries around, and everyone kept looking at him, wondering what the heck he was doing. Finally, the younger missionary corrected him on it, explaining how to say it properly. The incredible missionary sincerely thanked him and praised him for his ability to speak. Then, when the other elder wasn't looking, he winked at the rest of the confused missionaries.

In an instant they understood. This superstar was deliberately messing up an easy principle so the young missionary could correct him and feel smart. And it worked. In that moment the self-conscious elder seemed to grow six inches taller. He had "known" something that the best language speaker in the mission did not. He quickly gained confidence and later grew to excel with the language.

Isn't that a wonderful example of humility? That a brilliant missionary would care so little about his own reputation and status and care so much about another missionary's success? I love it!

Principle 4: Don't Let Your Limited Language Skills Limit You

There's no getting around it. During the first few months of your mission your language skills will probably be limited. However, do not allow this to limit your productivity as a missionary. Find other ways to contribute and provide meaningful service. As a new missionary, I wanted so badly to pull my own weight that I memorized a simple street contact and told my trainer that I would do all of the initial contacting. I was the one who would stop people, introduce who we were and why we were there, and then turn it over to my companion to actually talk to them. He told me once that those were the greatest months of his mission, not having to stop anyone—just getting to teach. Likewise, find ways to compensate while your ability with the language develops.

Principle 5: At the Beginning, Focus on Learning Correct Grammar

I mentioned earlier that learning a language at the MTC is like drinking from a fire hydrant. You have a very limited amount of time and a seemingly endless amount of material to learn. It is overwhelming, to say the least. So here's my advice: at the beginning, focus your language study on understanding and using correct grammar.

The grammar of a language is like the foundation and framing of a house. There's no use installing carpet, hanging a window, or even putting on a roof without the foundation and framing securely in place. So what is grammar? It encompasses the following questions, among others, depending on the language:

What are verbs, and how do they conjugate?

What are subjective, and accusative pronouns?

How do I show possession? (genitive case)

How do I show indirect objects? (dative case)

What's the difference between adjectives and adverbs?

How do I form past tense, future tense, conditional tense, subjective tense?

These are the things you should be focusing on at the MTC. In order to do so you may need to refresh your understanding of English grammar. That's okay. Mastering correct grammar will lay a strong foundation for success in your mission language.

Principle 6: Do Not Settle for Mere Functionality in Your Mission Language

Surprisingly quickly you will reach a point where you can "get by" in your mission language. Many missionaries settle for this level of speaking and plateau here the rest of their mission. As representatives of Jesus Christ you owe it to God, the people, and yourself to strive for native fluency in your mission language. It's simply a fact that the better you speak, the more effective you'll be in all your labors and responsibilities. Don't get comfortable and lazy with the language. Never stop growing; never stop improving.

One of the ways to push yourself in your mission language is to diversify your vocabulary. Many missionaries are extremely comfortable when speaking about the gospel but almost nonconversant when it comes to the full range of language speaking. Attaining only this "gospel fluency" is the primary way most missionaries plateau. Once you learn and master the language's grammar, strive equally hard to broaden and increase your vocabulary. Can you speak intelligently to a mechanic, to a doctor, to a florist, to a lawyer? Each week pick a new specialty of vocabulary words to learn and incorporate into your speech. Always carry around a little vocabulary notebook and jot down new and interesting words.

Principle 7: Become a Human Parrot

Perhaps the best piece of advice I can give is obvious. Tune your ear to how the natives speak and then copy, copy, copy. Every language has its own nuances and peculiarities. For instance, in Romanian you don't say, "Stand *on* your feet"; you say, "Stand *in* your feet." When among the people, observe closely and carefully how they use words and phrases. Doing so will greatly improve your speaking and accelerate your progress.

Principle 8: Know That You're Doing Better Than You Think You Are

Finally, learning a foreign language can sometimes get frustrating because your progress seems so slow. Don't get impatient or discouraged. As you put in the work, you'll get better and better each day. Because the improvement is subtle, the adversary will tempt you to think that it's not happening. This is a lie that invites fear and destroys faith. My final words to you on the language are simple: Don't worry; you're doing better than you think you are.

Chapter 13
Those Called to "Hard Missions"

"When you have faith in Jesus Christ. . . . you are able to do miracles according to the Lord's will." —Preach My Gospel, 116

THE DAY A YOUNG MAN or woman receives their mission call is one of the most exciting and memorable of a lifetime. For many it is the culmination of a lifelong dream. That oversized envelope represents years of preparation in the past and will largely shape both the immediate and distant future. Yet there they stand in the present, with trembling hands and a goofy grin. Few things equal the anticipation, suspense, and exhilaration that occur when the green light is finally given to open the call. It's magical!

As of April 2011, there were 340 missions in the Church. None are more or less important than any other. The idea of glamorous or exotic missions should not be part of our Latter-day Saint culture. God loves His children in Indiana just as much as He loves those in India. God values the service of a missionary in Moscow, Idaho, just as much as He values that of one serving in Moscow, Russia. When it comes time to receive the call, a prospective missionary must exercise faith that they will be sent to the mission where they are needed and where they will have experiences that are needful. As expressed in the chorus of an old Jewish folksong, "We have come to the land to build her, and to be built by her."

I have a pet peeve regarding mission calls that needs venting. Somehow, certain areas of the world have been branded as easy missions, while others have been labeled hard. The supposedly "easy missions" are found in South America, Africa, the Philippines, the islands of the South Pacific, and, of course, any mission in Utah. The so-called hard missions encompass western Europe, Asia, and certain regions of the United States.

There are serious flaws with defining any mission as hard or easy. Do our scriptures not declare: "Is any thing too hard for the Lord?" (Genesis

18:14). Yet we who assert that mission calls are divinely inspired sometimes seem intent on limiting what God can accomplish through His appointed servants. Equally misleading is the idea that some missions will be easy. Elder Holland reminds us that missionary work was never intended to be easy and that salvation and exaltation are not obtained cheaply (see "Missionary Work and the Atonement," 15).

No matter where a missionary is called to serve, much effort, dedication, diligence, obedience, sacrifice, prayer, faith, and work will be required. Simply put, "hard" and "easy" missions should be categorized with Santa Claus, the tooth fairy, and healthy donuts: they don't exist.

So why the big deal?

From the moment they receive their mission call, a young man or woman begins to form feelings and opinions about the mission to which they've been called. This occurs without ever setting foot in their future destination and is largely shaped by the opinions and perceptions of others. While most of the time this "opinion shaping" period has a positive effect on a future missionary, occasionally the effect is negative—especially when a person is called to a "hard" mission.

When we stereotype a mission or a language as being "hard," we create a negative stigma that is not easily overcome. This stigma places unnecessary burdens and anxiety on the newly called missionary. Enthusiasm is dampened, optimism fades, and the two greatest qualities of a new missionary are jaded. No missionary should ever enter the MTC with any "baggage" other than their suitcases.

Let me offer an example of what I'm talking about. My wife had always been open to the possibility of serving a mission, so when the opportunity came, she submitted her papers. Having heard stories of missionaries baptizing hundreds of people, she secretly harbored the desire to be called to a South American mission. Imagine her shock instead when she was called to Rome, Italy. For a few days she was crushed. Why had she been called to serve in the capital of Catholicism? She wanted to baptize people and have great success. Was that even possible now?

Quickly the disappointment of her earlier hopes began to pass. She would just have to exercise more faith. She promptly set about studying and preparing with renewed zeal and again began to feel optimistic about her mission. Yet daily this optimism was challenged by numerous encounters with friends, ward members, even strangers around town. Upon hearing the destination of her call, they would invariably give a version of the following speech: "Italy, huh? What a beautiful country. The history and architecture will be fascinating, the food delicious. You're going to have an amazing cultural experience. . . . Just don't expect to baptize anyone!" Hearing this day after day slowly chipped away at my wife's determination and resolve. Maybe her initial reaction had been right.

While working at the MTC, I taught in the same area as the Italian missionaries and frequently had the chance to spend time with them. Over and over I learned that my wife's premission experience was not unique. Every single missionary called to Italy had dealt with the exact same thing.

So here's my question to you. If we're telling these young people they won't baptize, why in the world are they going? Are we sending them on some type of glorified LDS study abroad program? Moreover, does God's power to provide a way and work miracles mysteriously cease at the gates of western Europe? Have all the elect been harvested?

Having served in the Romania Bucharest Mission, I've often thought how ironic the very notion of "hard" missions actually is. I was born at the height of the Cold War when the chasm between the United States and the USSR was unbridgeable. It was West versus East, democracy versus tyranny, capitalism versus communism, us versus them. If someone would've informed my parents on the day I was born in 1981 that their infant son would grow up to serve a mission in a Soviet bloc country, it would have seemed utterly impossible. Back in the early 1980s no one could foresee that the end of the decade would bring the collapse of the Soviet Union and the end of the Cold War.

No one, that is, except the prophet of the Lord.

By then President Spencer W. Kimball had already verbalized the opinion that the Spirit of the Lord was brooding over the nations of the earth. As an authorized seer he declared that the time was soon at hand when the light of the gospel would pierce through the Iron Curtain that had fallen over a large part of the world (see "When the World Will Be Converted," *Ensign*, Oct. 1974). You see, my mission wasn't a "hard" mission. It was a miraculous one.

Three decades later our modern-day prophet has again felt the Spirit of the Lord brooding over the nations of the earth. The restored gospel must go forth to all the world in preparation for the triumphal return of our Savior Jesus Christ. To this end, President Thomas S. Monson recently urged members of the Church to pray for those areas of the world in which we are unable to openly share the gospel message. He then promised that as we demonstrate faith, miracles will unfold in bringing this about ("Welcome to Conference," *Ensign*, Nov. 2008, 6).

This request from our beloved prophet is extremely significant. It now remains for us as members of the Church to exercise faith and intensify prayers to see it come to fruition. Just as my father could never have imagined that his son would one day be called to serve in Romania, I can't help but wonder what mission call awaits my seven-year-old boy. If President Monson's vision is to come to pass, we must all ditch the "hard missions" mentality.

We of all people should not be guilty of this error. We who have the Book of Mormon should know better. If I'm not mistaken, there's a story in the Book of Mormon about a group of young men who embarked on the ultimate "hard" mission. I guarantee that when Ammon and his brothers informed friends and family in Zarahemla of their upcoming mission to the Lamanites, no one responded in the following manner: "Oh, the Lamanites! I've heard they're a wonderful people with a beautiful language and delicious cuisine. Their history is absolutely fascinating. You are going to have the most incredible cultural experience. . . . Just don't expect to baptize anyone!"

Instead, take a moment to imagine how Ammon's friends and family members *did* react. I'm guessing it went something like this: "You're going to teach *who*? I must have misunderstood you 'cause I thought I heard you say the Lamanites. What!? Are you out of your mind? You know they hate us—they even teach their rotten kids to hate us. The second you cross into their territory they're going to take you, torture you, and then kill you. *You'll die!* How can you think you could ever teach them? Don't go!"

Yet we know what happened. The sons of Mosiah had received their errand from the Lord and could not be deterred by the perceptions and opinions of others. They simply put their trust in God and took a massive leap of faith. Over the course of their missions, they faced challenges, discouragement, and opposition. But in the end, they became powerful instruments in the hands of the Lord, bringing thousands to a knowledge of the truth. President Monson's recent request leads me to believe that the fulfillment of his prophetic vision will require a new generation of Ammons—young men and women who courageously put their faith and trust in God and by so doing see mighty miracles unfold in His service. It calls to mind the words of President Kimball when he declared, "We have paused on some plateaus long enough" ("Let Us Move Forward and Upward," *Ensign*, May 1979). In summary, I believe that first among a missionary's Bill of Rights is the right to enter the MTC with an optimistic, excited, and untainted view of their future mission. Is Japanese going to be a difficult language to learn? Of course. But what good does it do to incessantly point this out to an already apprehensive young man? Instead, can't we build up the faith of the prospective Japanese missionary by offering encouraging words? If God can part the Red Sea or help Nephi build a boat, I'm pretty sure he can help a nineteen-year-old missionary learn Japanese.

Is the city of Amsterdam a sinful place? From what I've heard it certainly is. But so was ancient Ninevah, and Jonah helped its inhabitants repent. Can't we focus on that with the missionary called to serve in the Netherlands?

Is it going to be difficult for the missionary called to Rome to baptize in the shadow of the Vatican? Probably. But I'll bet there's still an "Amulek" or two waiting for their "Alma" to come find them.

The way a young man or woman perceives the mission to which they've been called *will* have an impact on the type of missionary they become. In this chapter I've invited all missionaries—no matter where they've been called—to approach their missions with excitement, optimism, and faith. Let us understand that there are no "hard" or "easy" missions, only wonderful missions that provide the opportunity to labor with the Lord and see His mighty hand revealed.

Chapter 14
Sisters

*"We have a mission in the world: each man, **each woman** . . . ought . . . to be qualified to preach the truth, to bear testimony of the truth."* —President Joseph F. Smith, in *Preach My Gospel*, 12 (emphasis added).

WHY LET THE BOYS HAVE all the fun? That's the slogan for the young women who attend my mission prep class. Serving a full-time mission is, in my opinion, the most life-enriching, soul-stretching, perspective-changing experience of a young adult's life. During the brief window of full-time service, a missionary will grow more spiritually, emotionally, and even intellectually than in all their previous years combined. Christlike attributes will be refined and developed. New talents will emerge. Valuable social skills will be gained and sharpened, and a depth of character will be forever forged.

With this in mind, it is unsurprising to see more and more of our amazing sisters preparing for and choosing to serve full-time missions. They know a good thing when they see it, and they want in on the action.

This trend of more sister missionaries is an enormous blessing to the missions of the world. I am not discriminating against my own gender when I say that sister missionaries bring attributes, talents, and experience to a mission that the elders simply don't have. Teaching at the MTC for nearly three years, I noticed a significant difference in the level of preparation between the elders and the sisters. Some of the elders didn't really know why they were there and needed time to acquire the right motivation. Now, 99.9 percent of the time these young men figured things out and became great missionaries, but this process took time and delayed their ability to fully dive into the work. In contrast, I don't remember a single sister missionary who wasn't ready from day one to get going. They knew why they were there, and their level of desire was through the roof.

My respect for sister missionaries is well founded. In fact, one of the coolest miracles of my mission occurred because two incredible sister missionaries ignored my advice. They were teaching a young couple, and as their district leader I received updates on how things were progressing. Each time I'd follow up, the report was always the same: the wife was sweet and lovely and ready to be baptized, but the husband was an immature, obnoxious jerk. Though the wife wanted to be baptized, she refused to do so without her husband. The sisters tried everything they could think of to reach this man, but nothing seemed to work. Frustrated by his unreceptive and complacent attitude, they asked if my companion and I would accompany them on their next visit to see if he might respond differently to us.

Well, differently he did respond. On the night of the appointment, we went over to their home and met this couple for the first time. The sisters began the lesson and tried their best to invite the Spirit, but it was useless. The husband constantly interrupted, went off on random tangents, and basically sabotaged everything they tried to do. I knew drastic measures were needed, so I took over and established a new rule that I was the only one in the room permitted to speak. This guy wasn't happy about it, but after some convincing, he finally agreed.

I then introduced the Book of Mormon and taught why it was so important. I opened to the passage in 3 Nephi 27:20 where the Savior commands all men everywhere to repent and be baptized. As I read this passage the Spirit entered powerfully into the room, and the husband became visibly uncomfortable. I paused for a moment to allow the influence of the Spirit to intensify then looked him straight in the eye and asked if he was willing to obey this commandment of the Savior.

I'll never forget his response. He sprang to his feet, took a step toward me as if he would charge, and then pointed his finger and hissed, "Never, Elder Christiansen! I'll never get baptized!"

Then he stormed out of the room and out of the house, slamming both doors behind him. His wife broke down in tears, and the sisters hurried over to console her.

Walking home to our apartments, we discussed what had happened, and the sisters asked my opinion on what they should do with this couple. I told them bluntly that the husband was spiritually dead and that if the wife really insisted on getting baptized together then it would never happen. I suggested they keep visiting her every now and then to keep the flame of testimony alive but added that this couple should no longer be considered serious investigators.

They were baptized two weeks later. *Both* of them.

So what happened? Those sister missionaries, whom I instructed to give up on these investigators, returned the very next night and set them both up for baptism. It's irrefutable: while elders get the fancy leadership positions, sisters are the unsung heroes of the mission.

As you can see, I am biased on this particular topic. Yes, I understand that a full-time mission is completely optional for our young sisters. And yes, I realize that there are millions of wonderful, accomplished, spiritual women in the Church who have not served missions. However, if a young woman came to me for advice and expressed even the smallest desire to serve, I would tell her to guard that desire with her life and prepare as if it will happen. (I might also tell her to pretend she's a nun until her twenty-first birthday, but that's a secret I'd rather not share.)

Why am I so pro-sister missionaries? My opinion was largely shaped by my mission president and his wife. President and Sister Jarvis were the ideal couple that every missionary wanted to emulate in the future. While President Jarvis was universally loved and respected by both missionaries and members alike, Sister Jarvis was every bit his equal. She spoke at every zone conference, always giving memorable and powerful talks. She organized special projects that greatly blessed the infant Church in Romania. But even more impressive was the way she personally ministered to the members and people of Romania. Rarely could she be found back at the mission home twiddling her thumbs; instead, she always seemed to be out blessing lives with her service and care.

We may have admired President Jarvis, but we *adored* his wife. In fact, it's funny to note that most of the missionaries had secret—but wholesome—crushes on her. I say *funny* because Sister Jarvis was well into her sixties. My love for this incredible woman only deepened when I was assigned to work more closely with her and her husband during the latter portion of my mission.

During that part of my mission I logged thousands of miles on the road with President and Sister Jarvis. These long drives provided rare access into their relationship. One day we were driving through the countryside when Sister Jarvis spotted a peasant woman working on a craft outside her home. Her curiosity was piqued, and she asked if we could stop the van to check it out. President Jarvis objected, insisting that we keep to our tight schedule, but Sister Jarvis continued to plead and beg.

Somewhat irritated, President responded that if we stopped at every quirky or bizarre sight in Romania we would never get anywhere. Dejectedly,

Sister Jarvis relented, and the van grew quiet. I knew what was coming and silently began counting down from ten. Sure enough, at "one," President Jarvis's voice broke the heavy silence: "Elder Christiansen, turn the van around."

Sister Jarvis's face erupted into a broad smile, and she clapped her hands in excitement. She playfully rubbed her husband's head expressing her appreciation. President Jarvis's eyes sparkled, the result of making his wife happy. My companion and I just laughed and shook our heads; we had seen the same scene play out a hundred times. Sister Jarvis always got her way.

I turned the van around, and Sister Jarvis got out to meet this woman. We stayed behind with President and watched as she approached and introduced herself. For a few minutes this poor peasant woman seemed very confused and suspicious of the strange foreigner. Her face was marked by a dark scowl, and she clearly felt intruded upon.

Inside the car, President was watching and giving his assessment of the situation: "I don't think this woman knows what to make of Sister Jarvis. Maybe you should call out to her and tell her to come back to the van so we can be on our way."

Then, in an instant, everything changed. This peasant woman's face lit into a smile, and she started speaking excitedly to Sister Jarvis. She proudly held up the craft she was working on and demonstrated the technique she was using. Before long they were like two old friends reunited on that beautiful stretch of obscure Romanian highway. I glanced over at President Jarvis, and his whole countenance beamed as he observed his remarkable wife in action.

"Look at her, Elders," he said. "Speaking Romanian, making new peasant friends, charming everyone she meets. . . . That is quite the woman."

While we were smiling and laughing, President suddenly grew serious and said to us, "Elders, do you want to find your own Sister Jarvis?"

Both my companion and I sprang to attention. We were down to our final months and would soon be home, dating with marriage in mind. In unison we expressed that marrying a girl like Sister Jarvis would be our ultimate dream. He smiled and then gave the following counsel: "When you go home and begin dating, take a very serious look at the returned sister missionaries."

My companion and I were both a little surprised; we weren't expecting that at all.

He continued, "These girls who serve missions learn how to work, how to sacrifice, how to serve others. They learn how to set goals and achieve; they find a clear identity about who they are and what they can become. Sister Jarvis's mission to France helped develop and magnify all the wonderful talents and attributes that she possesses today. Every day of my married life has been blessed because Sister Jarvis is a returned missionary."

Right at that moment Sister Jarvis burst into the van—completely unaware that we had just been talking about her—ending President's impromptu advice on marriage. She immediately began telling us about her adventure, providing endless details about her new peasant friend's life. My mission president smiled at me and my companion, and we were off.

There are a multitude of blessings available to sisters who decide to serve a mission. Let me focus on just two and then give three cautions specifically for sisters.

The Blessings

1. Doctrinal Depth/Spiritual Maturity. In terms of doctrinal understanding, women need not be one millimeter behind the men. Teaching the gospel for eighteen months lays an impressive doctrinal foundation for the rest of your life. This increased understanding of the gospel will prepare you for many responsibilities and assignments within the Church. You will be more qualified in your future callings in Relief Society, Young Women, Primary, etc. But even greater, your mission will qualify you to teach the most important investigators of your life: your children.

I have seen this in my own home as my wife has done the bulk of the teaching of our kids. One day I sat down with my three-year-old son, and we started looking at the Book of Mormon reader for kids. He wanted me to tell him about Captain Moroni, so I showed him the pictures and paraphrased the story. Trying to simplify it to a child's level I said, "Then Captain Moroni made a really cool flag out of his coat so all the people could see it."

Immediately little Roman interrupted me and said, "Daddy, Captain Moroni didn't make a flag: he made the title of liberty!"

I couldn't believe it! He was only three years old. I didn't know that when I was thirteen. Impressed, I asked him how he knew that. I bet you can guess his response: "Mommy taught me."

At that moment I said a silent prayer of gratitude that I married a girl who was so centered on the gospel of Jesus Christ.

As I mentioned before, women may equal and even excel men in their understanding of the gospel. Here again let me present exhibit A—my lovely wife, Bethany. In nearly eight years of marriage I have never seen her miss a day of personal scripture study. My record during that same span is not so unblemished. Her daily example of faithfulness and diligence in studying the gospel makes me want to do better. I see her studying each day, and the little voice inside my head says, *Umm, so are you going to get around to doing that or what?*

Not only is her consistency noteworthy, but also the quality of what she learns and her willingness to apply it. Oftentimes she'll be excited about some insight she has found in the scriptures, share it with me, and later on I'll use it in a lesson and claim it as my own. When people ask how I came up with the idea, I smile and think to myself, *I married a dang smart woman.* In the words of the Savior, she truly "hunger[s] and thirst[s] after righteousness" (3 Ne 12:6).

So I proudly admit it. My wife and I *are not* equal in our spirituality and doctrinal understanding—she far outpaces me, largely due to the influence of her missionary service.

2. The Law of Attraction. Some young women worry that a stigma surrounds returned sister missionaries. They fear that serving a mission might somehow make them less appealing or "dateable" when they get home. Allow me to officially close the casket on that stigma and bury it at the bottom of the Dead Sea.

The idea that serving a mission could serve as a strike against you is insane. In fact, according to the "Eternal Law of Attraction" outlined in D&C 88:40, nothing helps your future dating prospects like serving a mission. It reads: "For intelligence cleaveth unto intelligence; wisdom receiveth wisdom; truth embraceth truth; virtue loveth virtue; light cleaveth unto light; mercy hath compassion on mercy and claimeth her own; justice continueth its course and claimeth its own."

So what is the Eternal Law of Attraction?

You will attract what you are.

According to this law, if you want to marry someone who has a strong testimony, you'd better strengthen your own testimony. If you want to marry someone who is morally clean, then that's what you need to be. If you want to marry someone who loves the Savior and puts the gospel first in their lives, do so yourself.

Thus, serving a mission will make you more attractive to a higher caliber young man. Rarely do you see sister missionaries come home and marry total dirt bags; they just don't attract that type of guy. So use your mission to develop the qualities and attributes that you would value most in an eternal companion. Then trust that the Eternal Law of Attraction will take care of itself.

Those are a couple extremely significant blessings associated with full-time missionary service; now let's turn our attention to some serious cautions.

The Cautions

1. Use time wisely. Go back to the beginning of chapter 11 and reread everything I wrote about the incomparable value of mission time. Now chop six precious months off that total and read it again. My first caution to sisters is this: *Make every day count.* Eighteen months minus the weeks spent at the MTC leaves barely enough time to accomplish all that you must do. Now, before you reach for a paper bag and start hyperventilating, let's calm down for a second. I'm not saying you need to spend your mission frantically running around like the sale-crazed women on Black Friday. I think you're mature enough to realize that fretting and worrying about time is a surefire way to waste it.

So what am I trying to say?

The best sister missionaries I knew all displayed a healthy urgency about their overall purpose and time management. It was obvious that they tried to maximize each day spent in the Lord's service. In your quest to become this type of missionary, I suggest you *set attainable goals and structure your efforts around those goals.* Missionaries who effectively set goals are far more successful than those who don't. Inspired goals provide focus and direction to your work. Think of goals as key landmarks that indicate you are traveling toward your desired destination. To find more information on effective goal setting, read *Preach My Gospel* for some excellent insights and guidelines (see p. 146).

In addition to goal setting, the ability to *prioritize* is critical in making every day count. Prioritizing your time should be one of the central purposes of your daily and weekly planning meetings. During these planning meetings you could adopt the following motto: "The most important thing is to make the most important thing the most important thing." As you plan, let all your proposed activities be guided by the question *What are the most important things we can do today/this week to help people come unto Christ and strengthen this ward or branch?* If you keep that question in mind and plan accordingly, you will never regret the way you used a single second of your mission.

2. Don't let a strength become a weakness. The second caution is something most sisters will deal with throughout their mission. The Lord commands each of His servants to serve with all their "heart, might, mind and strength" (D&C 4:2). No missionary can ever stand approved while holding back part of what they have to offer. This total investment, however, creates a serious hazard for our sisters. Women are by nature the experts of the heart. They are more emotionally sensitive than men and possess a greater ability to feel and show genuine Christlike love. Undoubtedly, this incredible capacity to love makes sister missionaries so successful in their labors. The Savior uses these divine gifts to stir souls that have long been stagnant and to soften hearts that have long been hardened.

Yet this emotional depth and sensitivity can also be a curse. The adversary despises the Lord's servants and works tirelessly to render them ineffective. When it comes to sister missionaries I believe his hatred is even stronger because of your miraculous ability to love. Satan will seek to exploit this strength and make it a weakness. He knows your emotional sensitivity leaves you vulnerable to doubt, discouragement, and even depression. Little by little he'll try to drain you of faith and desire. He will take the normal ups and downs of a mission and amplify them to shatter your confidence and sense of worth. In sum, he would love to send you on an eighteen-month emotional rollercoaster and ruin what should be one of the sweetest and most spiritual experiences of your life.

So there's the caution; now let me tell you how to insulate yourself from Satan's pernicious attacks. Before entering the mission field, you have to steel yourself for rejection. Yes, we all love the on-fire, "I'm going to baptize everyone I meet," new-missionary spirit. It's what makes the MTC the greatest place on earth. But the reality remains that missionary work entails a healthy dose of opposition, disappointment, and rejection. As is the case with life, all of these things are part of the mission plan. Tasting the bitter will help you savor the sweet, and failure makes success even more satisfying. That person who says yes to your message will mean so much more because a hundred before him said no. So invest your heart, mind, and might, *but* prepare for the full spectrum of missionary experiences—the good with the bad.

Here are some additional thoughts as you begin the "steeling" process.

As a missionary, you can't internalize or personalize rejection. Remember, you are not representing yourself. You're not saying to people, "Hi I'm Sister _____, and I'm here sharing a message about me." A full-time missionary is set apart as a personal representative of the Lord Jesus Christ and His true Church. Never forget that. I think we can safely assume the Savior experienced rejection every single day of His ministry. In some instances, the rejection turned to open hostility, hatred, and violence. So why did He keep trying? Why didn't He get discouraged or depressed?

I believe it's because He knew how important His life's mission and message really were. The conviction of His calling gave Him the courage and ability to keep going despite rejection and failure. He never gave up; He never lost faith. And many listened, believed, and were saved.

So what are you going to do when you go through a period where no one seems to care about your message? Or when the investigator family you love so much asks you to discontinue your visits? Or when you learn that someone you baptized has fallen away? Or when you experience personality conflicts with one of your companions? In each of these potentially devastating situations only a reliance upon Christ will anchor your emotions, preventing them from drifting out to an open, turbulent sea. For truly He declared, "Come unto me, all ye that labour and are heavy laden, and I will give you rest. Take my yoke upon you, and learn of me; for I am meek and lowly in heart: and ye shall find rest unto your souls. For my yoke is easy, and my burden is light" (Matthew 11:28–30).

In any moment of difficulty you must remember the Savior, His life, and His love. You must trust in the *infinite* and *intimate* power of His Atonement to mend your broken heart, heal your wounded soul, and restore hope and happiness to your countenance. While you are focused on the Savior and His Atonement, the Spirit will direct your mind to a related doctrine that is fundamental to the plan of salvation: moral agency.

Without the Atonement of Christ, there could be no moral agency. Agency requires different choices, and without the Atonement, our choices would be limited to death and hell. Satan's distortion of our Heavenly Father's plan was to force, manipulate, control, and coerce. In contrast, Father wanted to teach, testify, warn, and invite—but never through compulsory means. The progression and divine destiny of His children hinged upon freely offered obedience. Understanding the importance and purpose of agency will greatly enhance your ability to cope with rejection.

Agency oftentimes can be a frustrating thing. It's frustrating for parents, it's frustrating for priesthood leaders, and it's certainly frustrating for missionaries. As a missionary you know your message is true, you know it will make people happy, and you know that God lives and rules in the heavens. Wouldn't it just be easier if people *had* to listen to you? *Had* to obey the commandments? *Had* to join the Church? Wouldn't it just be easier if that whole agency thing would go away?

In moments such as this we either trust that Heavenly Father possesses infinite wisdom and knows what He's doing or give in to doubt and despair. I recommend choosing the former. Never forget that God was willing to lose a third of His children to preserve the gift of agency. And this agency cost the blood and life of His Only Begotten Son. Clearly this demonstrates how paramount a doctrine agency really is.

So what does this all have to do with you?

Nearly all of the opposition you will face as a missionary is the inescapable byproduct of moral agency. No matter how much you love, no matter how much you serve, no matter how much you pray and fast, there will be people who stumble along the path toward conversion and ultimately reject the message you are called to bear. Most of the choices they make are beyond your control. And anything that's beyond your control should not be allowed to control you.

Lastly, when dealing with failure and rejection, do not blame yourself or second-guess the things you have done. Dwelling on the past only wastes the present and clouds the bright future. Of course it is appropriate and wise to learn from the past through healthy processes of evaluation, but never do so in a negative or critical manner.

3. Lock your heart (just for sisters). Fact: Boys act differently around girls. There's no way around it. You serving a mission will change the dynamic of every district you belong to. If you are not vigilant in maintaining appropriate relationships with members of the opposite gender, you could end up being a hindrance rather than a help to the work of the Lord. My final caution is to be professional during your period of full-time missionary service.

The relationships you forge as a missionary are some of the most priceless and cherished of a lifetime. Because these relationships are spiritual in nature they will transcend the superficial and reach the very soul. As a sister missionary you will be unified with the elders in many powerful spiritual experiences. Equally powerful thoughts and feelings often accompany these experiences, and therein lies the danger. It is easy to confuse a spiritual connection with a romantic connection.

Romantic thoughts and feelings are like seeds that should not be planted in the mind and heart during your mission. If by chance a romantic seed happens to appear in your hand, go hide it away at the bottom of your luggage and never search for it again until you return home. It might also be wise to do a personal assessment of how that seed got in your hand in the first place. Perhaps your eye needs to be taken off that elder and refocused on the glory of God. The following guidelines will help you maintain appropriate elder/sister relationships as you serve:

Don't be flirty at all. If there were a flirty on/off switch, now would be the time to find it and shut it down. This starts with what you wear and includes the things you say, the way you say them, and a dizzying array of other subtle little gestures. To aid you in your antiflirt efforts, I propose an even more stringent standard: *Don't even be friendly.* Now I know you're reading this thinking, *Man, this guy is like the relationship Nazi!* But hear me out for a second. In my mind I draw a clear distinction between *friendliness* and *kindness*. In my life I try to be kind to everyone I meet: I smile, I'm polite, I'm considerate, I'm positive. To me these are all elements of kindness.

Friendliness, however, is something entirely different. Take for example the way I greet a friend; it's very different than the way I greet my mailman. I talk to my friends differently and about different things. I have inside jokes with each of my friends and things that only we share together. As you can see, the very nature of friendship is close and casual, and that's what makes friendship between a sister and an elder off limits. If somehow your relationship with an elder has become too close and casual, then you have crossed the line. Be friends with your companions and fellow sister missionaries, but keep the elders as acquaintances whom you treat with kindness and respect.

Keep time spent with the elders to a minimum. Don't allow your district to become what we negatively dubbed "a country club district." A country club district is one where the missionaries find every excuse to hang out with each other instead of doing actual missionary work. These districts are hotbeds for inappropriate elder/sister relationships because of the inordinate amount of time spent together.

Sisters, I don't know how many ways I can say this, but you shouldn't have time to waste idling away with the elders. Nothing would have made me respect or appreciate my sister missionaries more than them not having time for us. Now, I can't and wouldn't presume to list all the times it's appropriate to be with the elders and all the times it's not. I'm certainly not suggesting you treat them like strangers and skip district meeting as a precautionary measure. What I am saying is that a mission isn't a college apartment complex. You should never just be hanging out. Don't allow the nature of your relationship to change from professional to social. Don't lose control of your heart. Your purpose is to bless the lives of the people by bringing them to Christ. Stay focused. Stay on task.

Avoid special connections or unusual spiritual experiences with the elders. Sisters, you do not need to talk about most problems with the elders, especially problems of a personal nature. There are cases in the mission field where sisters become emotionally reliant on others. Not only does divulging these issues to elders change the nature of your relationship, it also drains the time and strength of companions and mission leaders. Now don't misunderstand, I'm not saying you can't have a bad day every now and then or that you have to be completely void of feelings like some human cyborg. But when you are having difficulties, the best answer is almost always to lose yourself in the work and focus on the lives and needs of others. Remember the simple but profound advice of President Hinckley's father: forget yourself and go to work ("Sweet is the work; Gordon B. Hinckley, 15th President of the Church," *New Era*, May 1995, 8)!

Likewise, I might warn against having special spiritual experiences with elders. Unless it's an emergency, I'd recommend turning to older priesthood holders for blessings of comfort or healing. Blessings of this nature bond individuals together in a way that could spark romantic feelings between them. Much better to rely on your mission president for occasional blessings of comfort and local priesthood leaders for needed blessings of healing. Remember, you should be having spiritual experiences *with the people*, not with the elders.

Make sure you dress appropriately. And yes, while we're being frank with each other, I would like to address one last issue that I mentioned before only in passing. After you get your call and begin the process of assembling your mission wardrobe, be extra careful about the outfits that you buy. Try to find the most old-fashioned, conservative woman in your ward and ask her to give your mission wardrobe a thorough inspection. Better yet, take her shopping with you to get on-the-spot vetoes/approval. I mean it! If she thinks a shirt is too tight or has a neckline that's a little too low or a button placed just a teensy bit too far down, don't buy it. If she thinks a skirt is too formfitting or not long enough, put it back on the rack.

You might complain that doing so will make your wardrobe plain and unfashionable (which is a gentle way of saying ugly, hideous, Aunt Berthalike), but consider what's at stake. You would never want to be a stumbling block to some elder who is trying to serve the Lord. You would never want people to focus on what you're wearing rather than what you're saying. With that said, I truly believe you can still look both nice *and* appropriate.

The prophets have said that every worthy and able young man should serve a full-time mission. For young women a mission is entirely optional (but if you're reading this book then chances are it's a strong possibility). In the end a full-time mission might not be right for you, and that's fine. You can still be a powerful, accomplished woman in the Church. But if the opportunity arises and the Spirit compels you to go, then rich blessings await: By way of review . . .

Your knowledge of the scriptures will increase, your understanding of the plan of salvation will deepen, your capacity to love and serve others will expand, and your ability to teach within the home will grow. You'll be better prepared to make the most important decisions of your life, including the selection of an eternal companion, and you'll bless the lives of hundreds, if not thousands, of people in the process.

Like I said, *Why let the boys have all the fun?*

Chapter 15
Seniors

"There is neither man or woman in this Church who is not on a mission. That mission will last as long as they live. —President Brigham Young, in *Preach My Gospel*, 12

THE KINGDOM OF GOD NEEDS more manpower. Early in His ministry Christ lamented, "The harvest truly is great, but the labourers are few: pray ye therefore the Lord of the harvest, that he would send forth labourers into his harvest" (Luke 10:2).

The metaphor of a harvest is quite striking. I picture trees sagging with perfectly ripe fruit or gardens full of vegetables ready to be picked. Then I imagine the senseless waste of good fruit spoiling on the branch or vegetables rotting on the vine because no one was there to garner them in. It's haunting to think that God has souls ready to harvest—people who are prepared and would accept the gospel—but not enough missionaries to find them and bring them the truth.

All right, we may as well pause to acknowledge the elephant in the room. You've looked at the "About the Author" page and seen my picture, and now you're probably thinking, *Who does this young pup think he is, talking about senior missions when he has never served one and is half our age?* It's true. I readily admit that this topic is in no way my specialty and that this chapter would be better written by numerous other people besides me. However, I have put an immense amount of thought behind what I've written and promise you will learn something of benefit.

We've all heard it expressed that a mission is like a two-year tithe on the nearly twenty years of life God has given to young men and women. If this is the case, then think of a senior mission as a tithe on the decades of blessings you have subsequently received. A wonderful family, a successful career, health and strength of mind and body—all of these have come directly from a loving, kind, and merciful Father in Heaven. Now, if you are able, it is time to offer your tithe.

As I was thinking about senior missions, I had a flash of insight that I believe came from the Spirit. There are basically two age periods where Heavenly Father encourages His children to go on missions: between the ages of nineteen and twenty-five and sixty-five and seventy-five. On the surface, these age groupings couldn't be any more different, but look a little closer and an interesting commonality emerges. Both are periods of life when individuals are sorely tempted to be focused on self.

A nineteen-year-old kid can get a job, make some money, move into an apartment, buy a car, spend time with his girlfriend, and maybe take a college class or two on the side. In other words, he can live a carefree, pleasurable, self-centered life.

The justification is simple enough: He thinks he's earned it. He just graduated from high school and survived the tumultuous teenage years. Why shouldn't he take some time for himself? Doesn't he deserve a break?

But what does God, in His infinite wisdom, do? He sends that same young man to Mongolia, where for two years he will spend every second of every day serving others, thinking about others, and giving his life to others. When he returns home he is an entirely different person. He has developed greater spiritual strength and maturity and is ready for the serious responsibilities of life.

A sixty-five-year-old retired couple can upgrade homes, buy that luxury car they could never afford, and get new furniture. They can travel, devote more time to hobbies, or simply relax and enjoy a new leisurely pace of life.

The justification is simple enough: They think they've earned it. They just spent decades providing for and raising a family. They have filled callings in the Church, some of which were very time intensive. Everything they've done up to this point has been sacrificing for others. Don't they finally deserve some time for themselves?

But what does God, in His infinite wisdom, do? He sends promptings and impressions that ultimately cannot be ignored. This couple is wanted and needed in His work. They yield to the will of the Lord and trade their life of comfort and ease for one of full-time missionary service.

Why does God do this? Is He some type of fun police who can't stand His children enjoying some time off? Is He categorically against a little R&R? Actually it's just the opposite. Heavenly Father knows that true joy and fulfillment can only be found in the service of others; thus, the Savior's paradoxical but true statement "He that loseth his life for my sake shall find it" (Matthew 10:39).

Sleeping in, reading the newspaper, enjoying a nice brunch, heading to the golf course, taking an afternoon nap, going to your favorite restaurant for an early dinner, watching a program or two on television, and then off to bed—that schedule would be the envy of the world. To some degree it is every working man's dream. There's just one problem: it won't make you happy. There is nothing on that schedule that will bring anything more than a fleeting moment of joy or satisfaction. It's not necessarily bad—it's just not good.

Let's return now to that senior couple who has left behind the utopian life of every retiree's dreams.

As they begin to serve, their focus shifts to the needs of those around them. They become immersed in the work and are filled with love and concern for the people. God rewards their sacrifice with success, joy, and fulfillment. Together they draw nearer to the Savior, which in turn brings them closer to each other. When they come home, their level of testimony and enthusiasm is through the roof. They are more focused on building the kingdom of God and better prepared for the judgment that ultimately awaits.

I realize that there are very legitimate reasons for a retired couple not to serve a full-time mission. Unique family situations, health challenges, and a variety of other factors may prohibit them from doing so. However, some of the obstacles preventing seniors from serving might benefit from closer inspection. Let's evaluate what a few of these might be.

Some retired couples rule out a full-time mission because they consider themselves unfit or inadequate for the work. They wonder how much good they could actually do and assume it is probably better just to stay home. To any who feel this way, I suggest that you've spent so much time focusing on what you *don't* have to offer that you've become blind to all that you *do* have to offer. Consider the following evaluation, which is probably a fair representation of most senior couples:

Your weaknesses:

You're not the spring chicken you used to be.

Learning a language seems as promising as learning kung fu.

The rigorous schedule of a full-time mission seems daunting.

You struggle with fear of the unknown or fear of leaving your comfort zone.

Your strengths:

You've amassed a lifetime of experience in the Church.
You possess wisdom that only comes with age.
You've gained stability and depth of character.
You've honed unique talents and skills over the course of many years.

Hopefully this evaluation opens your eyes to how desperately needed you truly are. It's amazing to realize that all of your weaknesses are the strengths of the young elders and sisters. Thus your talents and attributes serve as a perfect complement to those of your younger counterparts. Trust me, every mission has plenty of vigorous, bold, 9:00 a.m. to 9:00 p.m. proselytizers. What every mission needs, however, is some well-placed couples who possess wisdom and life experience. These couples provide stability and perspective as they mentor, support, and labor beside the younger missionaries. It is also worth noting that senior couples are able to adapt their daily schedule to fit their unique situation and abilities. So don't worry about being the missionary you once were. Get excited about being the missionary you are now!

Perhaps the most common reason seniors don't go is the fear and difficulty of leaving family behind. Believe me, I understand this one. My parents have eight little grandkids who all live close by. We eat Sunday dinner together, spend every holiday with each other, and otherwise find any excuse possible to gather as an extended family. I see how attached my parents are to their grandkids and know that leaving for a full-time mission will be one of the hardest things they ever do (especially for Grandma). But as I've spoken with several returned senior couples about this, I've found something surprising: *While they served as full-time missionaries they actually felt closer to their families.*

They couldn't really explain it; they just had learned from experience that the Lord has a miraculous ability to compensate when we sacrifice for His kingdom. It also helps that the world has gotten considerably smaller in the last ten years. The snail-mail world of decades past has been replaced with cell phones, texting, e-mail, instant messaging, Twitter, Skype, Facebook, and a host of other instantaneous ways to communicate and stay in touch. It sounds strange, but if you want to develop a closer relationship with your family, leave them behind for a little bit.

Another major concern holding back many seniors is the financial aspect of serving a full-time mission. It's true that the recent economic downturn has affected the finances of many retired persons. Pensions have dwindled, 401ks have shrunk, and the need to be frugal with your nest egg has become critically important. Although it's true that every retired couple's situation is different, don't let finances rule out the possibility of a mission until you have thoroughly crunched the numbers and evaluated every possible option.

I wonder if some couples simply say, "We can't afford it!" without really doing their homework about the costs. In your financial evaluation, I invite you to turn to the Lord and express your righteous desires to Him. Remember, He is a God of miracles and can make the necessary arrangements for you to serve. Also, might I note that many returned senior couples have told me *mission life was actually cheaper than home life*. Obviously this depends on the mission to which you're called, but consider it another element of the Lord's law of compensation. When you sacrifice for the gospel's sake, He rewards you in miraculous ways.

In conclusion, I might express how much I loved the senior couples who served alongside us in Romania. I watched in awe and admiration as they journeyed from their homes 9,000 miles away to build up the Church in that obscure corner of the vineyard. They were anchors to fledgling branches, mentors to inexperienced priesthood leaders, and a source of strength to members and missionaries alike. On numerous occasions I heard our mission president express appreciation for their work, calling the contribution they made "invaluable." As we delve further into these last days the Lord will need more laborers to proclaim His gospel and gather in the harvest. To any retired couple I would echo the invitation of the Lord: "If ye have desires to serve God ye are called to the work" (D&C 4:3).

Chapter 16
Members

"We will attain our exaltation in the Celestial Kingdom only on the condition that we share with our Father's other children the blessings of the Gospel of Jesus Christ . . ." —President George Albert Smith, in *Preach My Gospel*, 12

WE ALL KNOW THE PHRASE "every member a missionary," coined by President David O. McKay. The Lord Himself said in revelation that "it becometh every man who hath been warned to warn his neighbor" (D&C 88:81). Preparatory to the Savior's Second Coming the earth's inhabitants must receive the opportunity to hear the gospel, yet there is simply no logistical way the full-time missionary force can meet this demand, even with increasing numbers of sister and senior missionaries. But if millions of members were to take seriously the duty assumed as part of their baptismal and temple covenants, millions—even billions—could be reached.

The obligation to share the gospel is inescapable. Unfortunately, an inaccurate stigma exists regarding member missionary work, which I fear prevents many from fulfilling this responsibility. When we hear the phrase "member missionary work," our minds instantly conjure up images similar to the following: trekking over to an inactive or nonmember neighbor's home to invite them to church; making a list of all your acquaintances, prayerfully selecting a name or family from the list, and creating a plan to share the gospel with them; or giving away a Book of Mormon or pass-along card to a stranger on an airplane, bus, or subway.

Don't get me wrong—all of these are incredible ways to share the gospel. There's just one problem: each of these actions can be very intimidating. Doing any or all would certainly earn someone a PhD in member missionary work. But what about the members who are looking for something a little more introductory? The members who want to take Member Missionary Work 101, not Advanced Quantum Mechanics Member Missionary Work 850?

To stick with the college analogy, I believe it would be helpful to start customizing the member missionary work curriculum to individual needs and capabilities. This doesn't seem to happen often enough in our wards and branches. When the topic of member missionary work comes up, we (including myself) usually give powerful talks admonishing others to "buck up" and have more faith. Yet instead of producing faith, these sermons usually only produce guilt. The result is a body of members who are not only afraid to do missionary work but are also laden with guilt because of it. With fear and guilt paving the way, inaction and failure will inevitably follow.

In order to be successful, member missionary work cannot be pigeonholed into one of a limited number of activities. Yes, missionary work will always require faith, courage, and trust in the Lord. Yes, getting out of our comfort zone will be part of the equation. But there are so many ways to pitch in a hand to this great work.

With that in mind, might I offer seven nonthreatening, 101-level suggestions that could accelerate missionary work throughout the world in miraculous ways:

1. Live the Gospel More Fully

Elder James E. Faust said, "You cannot convert people beyond your own conversion" (in *Preach My Gospel*, 182). If you are stagnant in your testimony or going through the motions in your worship, the time has come to relight the fire inside. The way to do so is clear but will require effort, discipline, and sacrifice. Recommit yourself to daily scripture study and make it a rule to read until the Spirit enlightens your mind and touches your heart. Never let a day go by where you don't sincerely communicate with your Father in Heaven in prayer. Find yourself in the temple more regularly, and increase the quality of your visits. Make an effort to identify and then disentangle yourself from worldly snares that have latched onto your life.

When you recommit to living the basic tenets of the gospel more fully an amazing thing happens: it shows in your countenance. You are happier, kinder, more selfless, more composed, more fun, and more likable. Living the gospel makes you a walking advertisement for the Church. When your family members, friends, neighbors, coworkers, and acquaintances see the gospel bear fruit in your life, they'll either approach you about the gospel or be more receptive when the Spirit prompts you to approach them.

2. Get Out / Reach Out

The least threatening and most powerful form of missionary work is service. As a member of the Church, look for opportunities to perform anonymous acts of service for nonmembers and less actives in your neighborhood. There are thousands of possibilities here. You could leave treats, rake leaves, shovel snowy driveways, mow lawns, or weed gardens. Be perceptive to needs. Plan monthly to find ways to serve these choice people around you. Doing so will set a great example for your children and bring your family closer together. The service you provide may also motivate other ward members to follow your lead in reaching out to those around you.

3. Make a More Concerted Effort to Get to Know All Your Neighbors, Especially Those Who Are Less Active or Nonmembers

Too often nonmembers and less-active members become ciphers in the neighborhoods. We become friends with members of the ward but neglect everyone else. This can lead to situations where nonmember or less active neighbors feel alienated, excluded, uninvolved, and even unwelcome. Now I realize that in some cases a family will ask not to be contacted by the Church. But I've never heard of a less-active member or nonmember demanding their neighbors to stop being neighborly. In fact, a family who has asked not to be contacted needs good neighbors even more. You are the only lifeline they have, and they don't even know it!

If you have the desire and are willing to extend yourself a little bit, opportunities will arise for you to break the ice and develop a relationship with these good people. We often pass up these opportunities because "we're in a hurry" or "we're just too busy" or because we think "they probably just want to be left alone." You don't have to talk about anything churchy; in fact, it's probably wise not to. If they're outside working on something in the driveway, go have a look and ask them what they're doing or if they need a hand. When you see them shooting hoops, grab your kids and go play with them. Over time they will come to see that your friendship is genuine. When or if they want to talk about the Church, they'll know that they have true friends willing to help them along the way.

4. If You Don't Recognize Someone at Church, Go out of Your Way to Introduce Yourself and Make Them Feel Welcome

No one should ever feel alone, unnoticed, or neglected at any church meeting. Having members who reach out to newcomers is a vital ingredient in missionary work. This simple act alone would increase convert baptisms and strengthen our efforts at retention. Keep in mind that there are stake presidents, bishops, Relief Society presidents, elders quorum presidents, Young Men/Women leaders, Primary presidents, etc., who, during any given week may have felt impressed to visit a less-active member or nonmember and invite them to church. These leaders are bravely putting themselves out there, and they need us to back them up by doing our part as well.

One of my favorite member missionary experiences was of this variety. It was a typical Sunday morning as I walked into opening exercises for priesthood. Immediately I noticed an unfamiliar man sitting all by himself in the middle of the room. He was wearing a very outdated sweater and smelled heavily of cigarette smoke. It was obvious he was uncomfortable and even more obvious that everybody else was too. Like I said, there wasn't a person sitting within three rows of him. As I took my usual spot in the back I remember thinking, *Man, that's not right. Someone should go sit by that guy.*

Then I realized how foolish my thinking was and replaced the word *someone* with the word *I*. I stood up, made my way to the middle, approached the man, and asked if I could sit down next to him. I'll never forget the look of relief that washed over his face when he knew he wouldn't have to sit there all alone. We started chatting, and the story he had to tell was amazing:

He had been active as a youth but during his teenage years had fallen away. He found work in the natural gas mines and had acquired some of the bad habits of his environment. The night before, the stake president had dropped by his home unannounced and uninvited and visited with him and his wife for over an hour. At the end of his visit, the stake president challenged this man to come to church the next day.

"So here I am," he said to me. "It's the first time I've been to church in over fifteen years." Then he said something that I'll never forget: "I was actually thinking about ducking out after this, until you came and started talking to me."

Unbelievable. It was the simplest act of missionary work I had ever done—sitting by someone and talking to them—but it was also one of the most important.

To make a long story short, this man and his wife became active again. I was able to see him ordained to the priesthood and was honored to have him assigned to me as my home teaching companion. A year later he and his sweet wife were sealed in the temple.

Do you see why this is important? A new face at church should be positively bombarded with attention, love, and fellowship. Elder Russell M. Nelson even challenged each member to seek out and greet at least one person they didn't know before at church ("Be Thou and Example of the Believers," *Ensign*, Nov. 2010, 48). That is the spirit of member missionary work.

Just a final observation here: I realize that some wards are better than others at being warm and welcoming but that, as a whole, every ward or branch in the Church probably has room to improve. However, I refuse to believe that we fail in our fellowshipping duty because we're a cold, cliquey, or indifferent people. It couldn't be more opposite! Instead, I believe the main reason we don't go out of our way to welcome new faces is that we are too busy and preoccupied—*especially at church*. There are classes to get ready, children to drop off at Primary, home teaching appointments to make, PPIs to set up, tithing to pay, and so on.

All of these things are good, but none is more important than our duty to minister to those who may need our love and attention. Think of the Savior and what He would do. I'm convinced that if He were a member of your ward, He'd take a moment or two after sacrament meeting to seek out and personally greet an unfamiliar face. He would show such sincere interest and love that the person would immediately feel welcome and wanted. Though our love will never approach the love that Christ possesses, we should try with all our might to be His eyes, voice, and hands to our Heavenly Father's children here on earth.

5. Strengthen Those Who May Be Wavering

On the scene of an accident, the first thing a paramedic determines is whether the victim has a pulse. If they have a pulse, the situation is far less critical, and the outcome is much more likely to be positive. There are people right now in your ward or branch who are on the brink of inactivity in the Church. Yet they are there! Faint as it may be, they have a spiritual pulse. Please remember that their souls are precious to God and that a decision to leave the Church will not only affect them, but hundreds and thousands of their future posterity.

We all know that the bishop, Relief Society president, high priest group leader and elders quorum president have special stewardships to watch out for the spiritual welfare of ward members. Nonetheless, *every* member should likewise consider himself a shepherd and guardian of his brothers and sisters. If members will pray for the ability to discern who needs their encouragement, their friendship, and their love, God will lead them to His struggling children.

Oftentimes this discernment will manifest itself in small and simple ways. For instance, if someone in your ward or branch misses church two weeks in a row, stop by for a visit or give them a call to make sure they're all right. I wonder if people who are struggling spiritually might experiment and miss a couple of weeks just to see if anyone will even notice or care if they stop coming. A phone call or a visit expressing sincere concern will quickly answer this question and could make a tremendous difference to them.

Now, in doing this we don't need to be the attendance Gestapo, demanding to know where they were and why they didn't come. The simple question "Hey is everything okay?" followed by "We've missed you at church—it's not the same without you!" will most likely jolt them to their spiritual senses, giving them motivation to return. As you look outward to the spiritual welfare of those around you, God will help you strengthen those who are wavering.

6. Invite Other Families to FHE

Family home evening is one of the greatest secret weapons of member missionary work. The social aspect of FHE provides a nonthreatening climate in which to get together, yet the spiritual side provides opportunities to share testimony. It's the perfect combination. Regularly (every few months) invite a nonmember or inactive family over for FHE. Focus the lesson on beliefs that you have in common in order to maintain the inclusive and comfortable atmosphere. This is a simple way to add a spiritual dimension to your relationship, opening doors to share the gospel.

7. At Some Point You've Got to Take the Leap of Faith

In case you hadn't noticed, I've deliberately numbered these suggestions from easiest to hardest. I may as well just come right out and admit it—this last suggestion is a little threatening and may take you far outside of your comfort zone. There's no escaping the reality that at some point in member missionary work you're going to have to put yourself out there, boldly testify of the truth, and invite them to find it out for themselves. You're going to have to take the leap of faith.

Recently I met a man who is absolutely on fire in the gospel. Everything about his countenance radiates a love for the Lord and the Church. In my mind I was guessing that he was a bishop or stake president, but as we became acquainted he surprised me by saying that he had been inactive for nearly twenty years and had only lately come back to church. Curious,

I asked to hear his story and was captivated by what he had to share. With his permission, I include the following excerpt from a talk he recently gave in stake conference:

> For me, even direct service to my family by ward members was not enough to simply warm me back into the Church. Setting a good example is not enough; at some point you actually have to risk the friendship or comfortable relationship to bring salvation to that neighbor or colleague.
>
> This happened several times during my long period of inactivity. A business colleague bore his personal testimony several years ago in which he promised me a richer life in Christ if I would live the gospel. He told me he had never wondered about or doubted the truthfulness of the Church and had enjoyed peace, comfort and joy his entire life as a result.
>
> Another business partner challenged me on three separate occasions to get a testimony of the gospel. He told me plainly that it was critical for my eternal salvation and that nothing in life would mean more to me than activity in Christ's true Church. Ten years later, I can still see his face and hear his voice as he bore that witness to me. His words were impossible to discount. I had observed this man and had a tremendous amount of respect for him. I watched as he conducted his business fairly and treated both member and nonmember employees with dignity and love. At the time, I was not ready, but his testimony and challenge is one of the reasons I am here tonight.
>
> Dear brothers and sisters, why should you do missionary work? Because my salvation and my family's salvation hangs in the balance. It all depends on whether or not you are willing to go outside of your comfort zone and challenge and bear testimony and invite a 'rebel' like me back to church. I had received a witness at one point of my life but was ignoring that witness. Please do it for me and people like me who are stuck, who simply can't do it on their own.
>
> Because of people like you who were willing to take a leap of faith, my children and beautiful wife have an active

priesthood leader in our home. Thank you for accepting me back into the Church. Thank you for making the Atonement real in my life. Thank you for preparing the way for my family to be sealed in the temple. Thank you for the Spirit and testimony that literally burns inside of me.

Doesn't that testimony just give you goose bumps? To think that someone who was spiritually dead has been revived and brought back to life—it's a miracle! I know that somewhere in your neighborhood or at your work or among your acquaintances is a man just like this who, beneath a shell of excuses and stubbornness, is waiting to burst free and enjoy the fruits of the gospel in all their fullness.

So there is Member Missionary Work 101. I realize it takes a little extra effort, prayer, and faith, but the potential impact is incalculable. If every member would do those seven simple things, there's no telling how many additional souls could be brought into the Church each year.

We'll never know until we try.

SECTION FOUR
Leftovers

Chapter 17
On the Brink

"When you have hope, you work through trials and difficulties with the confidence and assurance that all things will work together for your good. Hope helps you conquer discouragement." —Preach My Gospel, 117

WHEN I THINK OF THE book of Helaman, two things come to mind: the pride cycle and Gadianton robbers. It's no wonder this book can be frustrating to read. Yet in the midst of these pages filled with wickedness and corruption, we find one of the greatest examples in all the Book of Mormon: the prophet Nephi.

If you aren't familiar with the story of Nephi, grab your Book of Mormon, read Helaman chapters 5 through 11, and enjoy. His Lamanite mission described in chapter 5 is amazing, but I'm going to pick up the story at chapter 7.

After serving an unsuccessful mission to the north, Nephi returns to his home in Zarahemla and finds the city entirely given over to wickedness. Secret combinations have infiltrated and overrun the government, the people have forgotten God's past deliverance, and the entire civilization is on the verge of collapse. Nephi is so overwhelmed by the spiritual decay that "his heart [is] swollen with sorrow within his breast" (Helaman 7:6), and he gets up on his roof to pray. His home is located next to a major thoroughfare, and a crowd of curious onlookers soon gathers down below (see Helaman 7:1–12).

Opening his eyes, Nephi sees the multitude of people and immediately seizes the opportunity to preach to them. "Why have ye gathered yourselves together?" he cries. "That I may tell you of your iniquities?" (Helaman 7:13). He asks why they are choosing misery and death through their misuse of agency. He asks how they could have forgotten the Lord when He has delivered them time and time again. Nephi then warns that the judgments of God hang over them if they do not repent and prophesies that their chief judge has at that very moment been murdered upon the throne (see Helaman 7:13–29; 8:11–28).

Of course this causes a stir among the people, and they organize a party to go check things out. They indeed find the chief judge murdered, but the Gadiantons quickly devise a scheme to pin the crime on Nephi himself. They arrest him for the murder, saying it was part of an elaborate plot to fool them into believing he was a true prophet. Nephi condemns their gross wickedness and instructs them to find the slain judge's brother and question him about the crime. They do so, and the brother quickly confesses exactly as Nephi has foretold. The corrupt leaders then make a lame attempt to discredit Nephi by claiming he gets his powers from the devil, but most of the people concede that Nephi must be a true prophet (see Helaman 9:1–40).

What follows is beyond comprehension: Everyone just leaves him!

Some say he's good, some say he's bad, but in the end they really couldn't care less. Not one person goes up to Nephi after this whole episode and asks if he'll teach them the gospel. Not one person humbly approaches and asks for help to repent. They simply leave him standing there all alone. The apathy is heart-wrenching.

Stunned by the turn of events, Nephi starts the journey back to his home. Of his emotional state, the scriptures say, "He was . . . pondering—being much cast down because of the wickedness of the people of the Nephites, their secret works of darkness, and their murderings, and their plunderings, and all manner of iniquities" (Helaman 10:3).

Let's pause here for a second to analyze what's happening. The phrase "much cast down" conjures up the image of a steep cliff or ledge. Emotionally, Nephi has been brought to the brink and is about to tumble over. As I picture this verse in my mind, I see Nephi walking slowly, aimlessly home. His shoulders are slumping. His whole being is weighed down by the failures he's experienced and the burdens that he carries. I really see him approaching the point where he can go no further, the point where he says to God, "I can't do this anymore; it just hurts too much."

As a full-time missionary you will experience your own "brink moments"—moments of failure, rejection, and sorrow that will weigh down your mind, crush your spirit, and break your heart. In the midst of such times, the thought of carrying on in the work may seem as daunting and pointless as trying to stop the flow of a mighty river with your pinky finger.

This discussion would be depressing if we were to stop here, but thankfully our story has just begun. Watch closely what happens to Nephi in his moment on the brink and what will happen to you during your brink moments.

> And it came to pass as he was thus pondering in his heart, behold, a voice came unto him saying:
>
> Blessed art thou, Nephi, for those things which thou hast done; for I have beheld how thou hast with unwearyingness declared the word, which I have given unto thee, unto this people. And thou hast not feared them, and hast not sought thine own life, but hast sought my will, and to keep my commandments.
>
> And now, because thou hast done this with such unwearyingness, behold, I will bless thee forever; and I will make thee mighty in word and in deed, in faith and in works; yea, even that all things shall be done unto thee according to thy word, for thou shalt not ask that which is contrary to my will. (Helaman 10:3–5)

Isn't that incredible? I promise that if you will pattern your labors after this heroic prophet, laboring unwearyingly with faith rather than fear, always according to God's will and commandments, then in your moments on the brink you will feel His voice speaking peace and comfort to your soul. Furthermore, these moments of divine encouragement will rejuvenate you in your efforts. As proof of this renewing power, just watch what happens to Nephi. The Lord continues, "And now behold, I command you, that ye shall go and declare unto this people, that thus saith the Lord God, who is the Almighty: Except ye repent ye shall be smitten, even unto destruction" (Helaman 10:11).

Notice how God simply reextends the exact same calling that Nephi has been filling for years. He doesn't say, "Look, I know you're really burned out and frustrated with this whole prophet thing, so let's give you a change of scenery and get you doing something else. Maybe the nursery leader or ward chorister." Nope, God throws him right back into the fire of his previous calling.

How does Nephi respond? "Now it came to pass that when the Lord had spoken these words unto Nephi, he did stop and did not go unto his own house, but did return unto the multitudes who were scattered about upon the face of the land, and began to declare unto them the word of the Lord which had been spoken unto him, concerning their destruction if they did not repent" (Helaman 10:12).

Do you remember how we pictured Nephi *before* the voice of the Lord came to him? He was on the brink, much cast down, with the weight of the world pressing heavily upon on his shoulders. Now picture Nephi. I see him in a dead sprint running back to find those people, so excited for the opportunity to share the gospel. What a miraculous turn of events! I especially love the phrase "He did stop and did not go unto his own house." Nephi didn't even go back to his house to grab a sandwich. He was so excited to fulfill his calling that he did a U-turn right there and headed back to find the multitude.

Consider for a moment the impact this experience must have made on Nephi's life. Not only did he receive much-needed comfort and rejuvenation, but he also gained a depth of spiritual maturity and love for God that would bless the rest of his life. In fact, study Helaman 11 and you'll see a marked change in Nephi. He is powerful and confident, unshakable and firm.

People sometimes wonder why a mission accelerates the spiritual maturation of young men and women so rapidly and visibly. How many times have you heard the phrase "He's like a whole new person" used to describe a recently returned missionary? There's no magical secret; it's simply the cumulative effect of dozens of these "on the brink" experiences that brings about such a miraculous change.

I had an "on the brink" moment that is very sacred to me. One evening we were street contacting and stopped a young father walking with his little boy. I introduced who we were and then taught how our family relationships do not need to end with death but can continue into the next life. I asked if we could come to his home and share more of our message, and he responded, "*Nu mă interesează.*" ("I'm not interested.")

This was a common response, but for some reason this time it just felt so unsatisfying.

Instead of saying good-bye and walking away like usual, I knew I had to testify again. "Sir," I began, "I really don't think you understand how important this message truly is. We can show you how to be with your family forever."

He listened, thought about it for a second, and then said, "*Dar, nu îmi pasă.*" ("But I don't care.")

His response cut me deeply. How could he not care about what I was saying? I was telling him the most important thing he would ever hear in his life!

Normally at this point I would move on. I had taught, testified, and invited; I had shown persistence and determination. But for some reason I still couldn't give up. So I started again: "I really don't mean to bother you, but I just have to say again that the message we bear comes directly from God and will bless you and your family in this life and throughout eternity. Please give us the opportunity to share it with you." I was now testifying with every ounce of my heart, hoping and pleading that this man would realize the treasure we were offering him.

Unmoved, he looked at me and my companion and said flatly, *"Mă, lasă-m în pace!"* ("Dude, just leave me alone!")

We shook hands, said good-bye, and parted ways. I remember just standing there, watching him get farther and farther away with his cute little boy until they turned a corner and vanished out of sight. I had been in Romania for over a year. By this point I clearly understood that rejection was part of the deal. But for some reason this one hurt so deeply and differently. It was truly as if a piece of my heart had been ripped from my body.

As we slowly started on I couldn't help directing my thoughts toward my Heavenly Father. My silent prayer went something like this: *Heavenly Father, I just don't know if I can keep doing this. It hurts so much to share something that you love, something so eternally important, and have people not even care. I've been rejected a thousand times, but this pain is worse than anything I've ever experienced before. Why?*

I listened for a moment and then felt the Spirit communicate a message in return:

Matt, now you finally know how I feel. I have given you this experience as a glimpse into the pain and sorrow I suffer when my children reject me and turn away from my commandments.

What a profound lesson. This indescribably powerful emotion I was feeling was not just godly sorrow—*it was God's sorrow.* I suddenly thought of God's love, how He cares about each of His children in a divinely infinite way; and then I realized that His sorrow must be equally infinite. Thinking my lesson was over, I began to tell God that I finally understood—when the shocker came:

And Matt, this is how I have felt when YOU have turned away from me and my commandments.

I couldn't believe it. It was like someone had hit me in the gut and the air was knocked out of me. In an instant my years as a teenager flashed before me, and I recognized many of the characteristics of the man I had just stopped . . . in myself. Too often I had been so entangled with the things of the world that the gospel just "didn't interest me." Too often I had apathetically stated, "I don't care." And ashamedly, I even saw times when I had rebelliously turned away from God, yelling at Him to just "leave me alone."

Prior to my mission, I only thought disobedience was bad because it was self-destructive and hurt the individual. It had never occurred to me how deeply my choices had impacted my Father in Heaven. Sure, I knew that He noticed and that He cared, but never could I have imagined just how *much* He cares!

With every ounce of my soul I offered the following prayer to God: *Father, I'm sorry I was such an idiot in the past. Please know how badly I want to change. I never want to hurt You like that again.*

Then in an instant, I felt the sweetest peace and joy envelop my body; it was like being wrapped in an electric blanket of warmth and comfort and love. In fifteen minutes I had aged spiritually fifteen years. That one experience alone would have validated my entire two years of service. I wouldn't trade what I learned that day for anything in the world. This and numerous other experiences are why I was "not the same person" when I returned home.

Missionary service brings the highest of the highs and the lowest of the lows. In the midst of those lows always remember that you represent "he [who] descended below all things, in that he comprehended all things" (D&C 88:6). When you feel overwhelmed, confused, and frustrated, when you find yourself "on the brink," ready to be cast down to the depths of despair and sorrow, trust in the power of Him whom you serve. "I will not leave you comfortless," He promised. "I will come to you" (John 14:18).

Chapter 18
Leftovers

"The Lord will reward and richly bless you as you humbly and prayerfully serve Him. More happiness awaits you than you have ever experienced as you labor among His children." —The First Presidency, in *Preach My Gospel*, v

FINALLY, I LEAVE YOU WITH some thoughts that didn't fit into any of the other chapters. Just because these ideas are collected under the title "leftovers," however, doesn't mean they aren't important. In fact, if you were my son or daughter, these are the last pieces of advice I might be giving you while driving to the MTC to drop you off.

Build the Church.

One of the main goals for your mission is to leave every ward or branch stronger than you found it. As you search for people to teach, look for families and individuals who will add strength to the ward and can make an immediate, positive contribution. Most wards and branches outside of Utah need more dependable people to help share the burden of leading the Church. Missionaries everywhere should seek to find the next bishop or branch president, the next Relief Society or Primary president, the next rock-solid family that will bless the ward.

Some missionaries mistakenly think they need to baptize lots of people to be successful. If the people you baptize are flimsy in their testimony or unstable in character, then these baptisms have weakened, not strengthened, the Church. The success of your mission will be far greater if you baptize one quality family that remains active throughout their lives and serves faithfully in various capacities than if you baptize a hundred people who eventually fall away. The Lord clearly instructed His missionaries whom they should seek out. He said: "And ye are called to bring to pass *the gathering of mine elect*; for mine elect hear my voice and harden not their hearts" (D&C 29:7, emphasis added). Pray to find the elect, and the Lord will lead you to them or them to you.

If you're not having fun as a missionary, you're doing it wrong.

Now please don't misunderstand—I'm not talking about "amusement park" fun or "lazer tag" fun, or "running through the sprinklers" fun or "food fight at Chuck-A-Rama" fun. I'm talking about a new and better type of fun that you may not have fully yet experienced.

This new type of fun combines adventure, camaraderie, excitement, novelty, joy, and the deepest fulfillment you can possibly imagine. I can't stress this strongly enough—if you are unhappy as a missionary or dread doing the work, then you are doing it wrong. By wrong, I mean you've lost focus of the right motivation; you are thinking too much about yourself and too little about the Savior and His infinite love. The solution might be working harder, working smarter, or working more creatively. More often, the solution is simply realizing that a mission is a once-in-a-lifetime opportunity that cannot be squandered. Whatever the problem, figure out what you need to do to infuse life and joy back into your daily service and make the necessary adjustments.

Whenever I think about the joy of missionary service I always think of my trainer. I'll never forget how excited he was to leave the apartment each morning. He was like a little kid on Christmas morning waiting to go downstairs to see his pile of presents. Another of our most successful missionaries once stood up at zone conference and said, "I've been in Romania for over a year now, and I've had a Kool-Aid smile on my face ever since I got here." That may have been the single greatest line I ever heard on my mission. Classic!

Talk to more people.

Elder Ballard visited our mission and gave the most practical but inspired counsel I've ever heard. He taught that missionary work is effectively a numbers game. The more people you talk to, the more people you teach; the more people you teach, the more people you will bring into the Church. It's that simple. He then gave us the challenge to double the amount of people we were contacting. Our mission took this challenge seriously, and in subsequent months our number of convert baptisms skyrocketed. The Lord said in revelation, "Speak freely to all; yea, preach, exhort, declare the truth, even with a loud voice, with a sound of rejoicing, crying—Hosanna, hosanna, blessed be the name of the Lord God!" (D&C 19:37). Later on He cautioned against the opposite scenario: "But with some I am not well pleased, for they will not open their mouths, but they hide the talent which I have given unto them, because of the fear of man. Wo unto such, for mine anger is kindled against them. And it shall come to pass, if they are not more faithful unto me, it shall be taken away, even that which they have" (D&C 60:2–3).

The injunction to "open your mouth" is one of the most oft repeated by the Lord to his elders. Absolutely nothing can happen in missionary work until you have the courage to speak up. Track how many people you contact each day and set goals with your companion to improve. Go out of your way to talk to people in unorthodox places like the grocery store, post office, doctor's office, etc. In so doing you will experience greater success, fulfillment, and joy in the Lord's service.

Write in your journal every single day.

Force yourself to do it; make it a nonnegotiable habit. You will kick yourself if you don't.

There are many reasons why you should be faithful in your missionary journal writing. Never again in your life will you be having the type of spiritual experiences you enjoy while serving the Lord. These experiences must be recorded if you don't want to lose them. When you write, be specific about the things you are doing. The more specific an entry is, the more meaning it will hold. For example, don't just write, "Went tracting." Instead, focus on a few individuals or contacts that stood out to you and write about them.

Missionary work also produces rare and unique insights into the gospel and about life in general. Each of these insights is a pearl of great price that should be properly valued and dutifully written down. A great example of this is the book *In the Eye of the Storm* by Elder John H. Groberg. In this book Elder Groberg recounts an experience and then writes the lesson(s) he learned from that experience. This would be a great pattern for you to follow.

Many of these experiences and insights will also be included in your e-mails or letters home. It would be wise to ask your parents to preserve them as an additional source for your personal mission history. The record you keep of your mission will not only bless you but will be priceless to future family members. Commit now to do it; you'll regret it if you don't.

Compile reliable contact information.

Your journal is also a great place to record the contact information of converts, members, investigators, and fellow missionaries. Gathering this information will allow your influence as a missionary to continue long after you've returned home. I'll never forget one of my favorite Romanian members offhandedly saying, "You missionaries go back home to America and after six months completely forget about us here in Romania." It was obvious she felt forgotten and neglected by the missionaries who had brought her the gospel. An occasional letter, e-mail, phone call, or Christmas card would have meant everything to this good woman.

It's hard to believe now, but the two years of your mission will come and go in the blink of an eye. Even though your mission will end, your love and concern for the people you served will not. Years later the thought will pop into your head, *I wonder how _____ is doing?* and you will kick yourself if you have no way of finding out.

Collect the contact information of everyone with whom you build a close relationship. This includes fellow missionaries and also investigators who didn't get baptized. You never know when a letter or e-mail might touch someone's soul and spark a desire to resume meeting with the missionaries. Be sure to write this information legibly and to keep it neat and organized. You may also want to write a little bio of each person so years later you can remember who they are.

The missionary Ammon told King Lamoni he was desirous to remain with the Lamanites as long as he lived. This attitude of total commitment demonstrated sincere love for the people and engendered trust between him and the king. Likewise you can "remain" with the people you serve as long as you live. By compiling reliable contact information and maintaining an active interest in their lives, your missionary influence will never end.

Love the people.

Like most guys, I look up to my dad and admire him more than any other man. Before I left for my mission, I scheduled some time to sit down with him and ask his advice on how to be a good missionary. I figured we'd have a long father/son chat, but instead his counsel lasted only about ten seconds. "Love the people!" he said.

I asked what exactly he meant by that, to which he looked at me, smiled, and said, "Love the people!"

At the time I felt a little cheated, thinking it couldn't be that simple. But as I served in Romania, I came to realize how profound and inspired his words really were. Without trying to be critical, I couldn't help noticing that some elders seemed to be playing a type of "Missionary Hokey Pokey" with one foot in their mission and one foot still back at home. It bothered me to hear these missionaries criticize, complain, and compare things in Romania to how they were "at home." I never could understand this because after only a short time I considered Romania to be "home."

An experience Elder Groberg records in his book *In the Eye of the Storm* illustrates perfectly what I'm talking about. At the beginning of his Tongan mission, Elder Groberg was assigned to labor on a small, distant, primitive island, and he stayed there for an entire year. After this year had passed, the young elder was called back to the main island to receive a new assignment. Returning to civilization, he was overwhelmed by the cars, buildings, electricity, and other modern amenities. Because he was from the States, his mission president arranged for him to stay in the mission home for the days leading up to the actual transfer.

Elder Groberg describes his day in the mission home as one of the most miserable and lonely of his life. He found the soft beds extremely uncomfortable, the food strange, and the language (English) unfamiliar. His mission president sensed something was wrong and inquired what the matter was. Hesitantly, Elder Groberg tried to explain how he would be much more comfortable if he could just stay with the Tongan missionaries who were sleeping in huts outside. While a little concerned, the mission president granted the request, and Elder Groberg was able to rejoin his native companion, Feki, outside.

Of this experience Elder Groberg writes: "I found out years later that this little act of moving in with the labor [Tongan] missionaries, which I did because I was more comfortable, is one of the things that solidified my acceptance among the members on the main island of Tongatapu. When they saw I truly preferred to eat Tongan food and sleep on the floor and be with Tongan people, rather than staying in the big house with fancy food and the soft beds, they felt my love for them came from my heart and that I did what I did because I wanted to, not because I had to. They said: 'He understands us. He can feel the way we do'" (*Eye of the Storm*, 150).

Thirteen years from now, my little boy, Roman, will probably ask my advice on how to be a good missionary. I'll look at him, smile, and say three words: "Love the people!"

Live in the land of miracles.

My mission president, George K. Jarvis, is one of my greatest heroes. I had the incredible privilege of serving as his last assistant and watched as he painstakingly worked on his final zone conference address. This would be his concluding message to the mission he loved, and he labored for weeks to get it just right.

The title of his talk was "Living in the Land of Miracles." He began with the observation that some missionaries seemed to constantly experience miracles while others did so rarely, if ever. He then taught what made the difference: "If you want to live in the land of miracles, *you have to get outside of your comfort zone.*"

During your mission you should never be comfortable. When you get comfortable you begin to rely on yourself, allowing pride and apathy to creep into your life. Faith becomes less and less important, and you slowly adopt a status quo that is far beneath your potential. Remember the timeless admonition of President Spencer W. Kimball: "We have paused on some plateaus long enough." As a missionary, always stretch higher, strive harder, reach deeper, grow stronger.

Throughout this book I've repeatedly held up the sons of Mosiah as the ultimate missionary heroes. Here again they exemplify this principle perfectly. After their run-in with the angel, they could have just repented and been good guys from that point on.

That would have been comfortable. But instead they went out and labored to repair the damage they had done among the Nephites.

After that they could have been satisfied with their efforts and settled back into normal life.

That would have been comfortable. But instead they saw the Lamanites dwindling in unbelief and sought to bring them to the truth.

Basically, the sons of Mosiah were comfortable being uncomfortable. And because of this they became permanent citizens in the land of miracles.

You can do the same. Get comfortable being uncomfortable, and you will quickly see that we live in a day of miracles. For "God will show unto you, with power and great glory at the last day, that they are true, and if they are true has the day of miracles ceased? . . . Behold I say unto you, Nay" (Moroni 7:35, 37).

About the Author

MATTHEW CHRISTIANSEN WAS BORN AND raised in the bubble of Utah County, only leaving for two years to serve as a missionary in eastern Europe. There, Matt enjoyed endless adventures and experiences, including a friendship with the gypsy king of the world. Returning home, he caught the eye and won the heart of a fellow MTC instructor named Bethany. They married, and together they are the parents of three beautiful children. During the day Matt can be found pontificating upon the solemnities of eternity with the youth of the Church in seminary. During the evenings he can be found jumping on the trampoline with his three little friends. And yes, he currently serves as a ward missionary.